Routledge Revivals

History and Society

R. H. Tawney believed that the subject of economic history raises questions which touch the fundamental concerns of all thinking people. By setting economic development firmly within the framework of cultural and political life, he provided an alternative to the recent fragmentation of economic history into a number of increasingly technical specialisms.

First published as a collection in 1978, these ten essays, spanning the length of Professor Tawney's career remain as controversial and potent as ever, and the original introduction by J. M. Winter provides the first full evaluation of R. H. Tawney's approach to economic history. Among the essays included in this volume are the indispensible studies of 'The Rise of the Gentry' and 'Harrington's Interpretation of His Age', as well as 'The Abolition of Economic Controls, 1918-1921'. Other selections, such as Tawney's celebrated inaugural lecture as Professor of Economic History at the London School of Economics in 1933, 'The Study of Economic History', offer a representative sample of the range and sweep of Tawney's historical imagination. Taken together, these essays demonstrate the validity of Tawney's conviction that economic historians must confront not only the creation of wealth, but also the moral questions surrounding its distribution.

History and Society

Essays by R. H. Tawney

Edited and with an Introduction by
J. M. Winter

Routledge
Taylor & Francis Group
ROUTLEDGE REVIVALS

First published in 1978
by Routledge & Kegan Paul Ltd

This edition first published in 2011 by Routledge
2 Park Square, Milton Park, Abingdon, Oxon, OX14 4RN

Simultaneously published in the USA and Canada
by Routledge
711 Third Avenue, New York, NY 10017

Routledge is an imprint of the Taylor & Francis Group, an informa business

A Library of Congress record exists under ISBN: 0710089538

ISBN 13: 978-0-415-69188-8 (hbk)
ISBN 13: 978-0-203-15395-6 (ebk)
ISBN 13: 978-0-415-69244-1 (pbk)

History and Society

Essays by R. H. Tawney

Edited and with an Introduction by

J. M. Winter

Routledge & Kegan Paul
LONDON, HENLEY AND BOSTON

First published in 1978
by Routledge & Kegan Paul Ltd
39 Store Street,
London WC1E 7DD,
Broadway House,
Newtown Road,
Henley-on-Thames,
Oxon RG9 1EN and
9 Park Street,
Boston, Mass. 02108, USA
Set in 11 pt. Plantin by
Computacomp (UK) Ltd, Fort William, Scotland
and printed in Great Britain by
Lowe & Brydone Printers Ltd
Thetford, Norfolk

British Library Cataloguing in Publication Data

Tawney, Richard Henry

History and society.
1. Economic history – Collected works
I. Title II. Winter, Jay Murray
330.9'181'2 HC21 78–40519

ISBN 0 7100 8953 8

Contents

Introduction: Tawney the Historian

Study the historian before you begin to study the facts.
(E. H. Carr, *What is History*, 1961)

R. H. Tawney's career as an economic historian spanned the formative phase of the development of the discipline in Britain. When he published his first book in 1912, the subject was still in its infancy. In 1958, when his last book appeared, it was firmly established and thriving, and had, in the *Economic History Review*, which he had helped to found, one of the most highly respected academic forums in the world. Even after his death in 1962, the shadow of his work continued to fall over whole areas of research. Some historians lament the fact. Others celebrate it. But few doubt Tawney's fundamental contribution to the development of historical study in Britain. It is surprising, therefore, that there has been as yet no full evaluation of the evolution and significance of his work. Such an appraisal can tell us much as well about how perceptions of the nature of economic history have changed in this century. Tawney believed and represented the idea that his subject had a bearing on the lives of people outside the university. As the discipline has become more professional and more sophisticated, its ability to command the attention of educated people not initiated into its mysteries has waned. Tawney's work has had an audience because it reflects the ambitiousness of a generation unafraid to place the history of economic activity within a totality of social relations. In a particularly skilful way, he set economic development firmly within the framework of cultural and political life. His writing has provided, therefore, an alternative to the recent fragmentation of economic history into a number of discrete and increasingly technical specialisms. Herein lies one of the reasons why his work has appealed to marxists and non-marxists alike, and why his work is still controversial.

Tawney did not believe that his views on enclosure, Puritanism, or the political role of the gentry would stand indefinitely, untroubled by the interventions of later scholars. Since his books have appeared, new evidence has been quarried and new techniques devised to assay it. But much of the necessary revision has taken place largely in terms of the questions Tawney himself has posed. What matters in an evaluation of his work, in the end, is not the validity of a particular interpretation, but the quality of his historical imagination, and his ability to fire the imagination of later historians, even when they dissented from his views.

There is an influential school of thought which maintains that detachment from the world is the only safe path to historical wisdom. Tawney's whole career was devoted to disproving this assertion of monasticism. Consequently, the only way we can understand his historical writing is to place it in the context of his social, political, and religious concerns.

In this respect, it may be useful to consider a division between two aspects of Tawney's history in order fully to appreciate the development of his work. The first phase encompasses his analysis of the *Agrarian Problem in the Sixteenth Century*, published in 1912, the introduction to Thomas Wilson's *Discourse upon Usury* (of 1569), and *Religion and the Rise of Capitalism*, which appeared in 1925 and 1926 respectively. In these writings, Tawney approached economic history as the study of the resistance of groups and individuals to the imposition on them of capitalist modes of thought and behaviour. In their responses to the clash between traditional views on social justice and newer notions of economic expediency, Englishmen in the sixteenth and seventeenth centuries had left, Tawney believed, an important legacy of ideas which the economic historian was well placed to explore.

The second phase of Tawney's work can be dated from the 1930s. In the sombre years of the world economic crisis and the advance of fascism in Europe, Tawney's research no longer focused on ethical problems of past economic activity. At this time and in later years he turned, instead, to the study of the economic roots of political dominance, political collapse, and revolution.

This is not to say that his Christian beliefs waned or that he retired to a more comfortable agnosticism about the relevance of religious principles to social behaviour. Rather Tawney responded indirectly to the crisis of European society in the period prior to and during the Second World War by adopting new emphases in and approaches to the study of economic history. The economic collapse of the period 1929–34 and the political upheavals and threat of war it brought in its aftermath gave a particularly contemporary ring to historical discussions of the relationship between economic change and political stability. It is in this turbulent period and during the 1939–45 war that Tawney wrote his celebrated and controversial articles on 'The rise of the gentry', and 'Harrington's interpretation of his age', as well as an unpublished history of the American labour movement. This phase of his work also extends to his last study, an account of the career of Lionel Cranfield as merchant and statesman in the early seventeenth century. What all these writings share is a primary interest in the social-structural determinants of political activity.

Although he never confronted systematically or directly Marx's historical ideas, Tawney never considered himself a marxist, in his history or in his politics. But during the 1930s and 1940s he developed an interpretation of the relationship between landholding and political conflict in sixteenth- and seventeenth-century England compatible with some marxist views on the subject. By placing the question of the social distribution of property at the centre of historical debate on the origins of the English Civil War, Tawney helped to transform the historiography of the period by injecting perhaps unintentionally a marxist component into it. In succeeding years, this aspect of his work has inspired a younger generation of historians to test his social interpretation of the political upheavals of the 1640s and 1650s.

Briefly, the social concerns of Edwardian England provided the impulse for the first phase of his historical writing. The social and political crisis of the interwar years and of the Second World War, in contrast, was the setting in which the second and later aspects of his work must be set.

I

Tawney's decision to write economic history was motivated largely by his early experiences in teaching the subject to working men. His education at Rugby and Balliol had given him enough of a facility in language to write humorous epigrams in Greek,[1] and fine Miltonic prose, but he had little formal training in those areas which mattered most to his students. He lectured in economics at Glasgow University from 1906 to 1908, but left to lead the Workers' Educational Association's (WEA) pioneer tutorial classes at Longton and Rochdale. The first of these classes was formed in response to a request by local people who had flocked to occasional extension lectures on such subjects as the Puritan Revolution, sponsored by the Longton Borough Council and paid for by the local education authority. This public response convinced the secretary of the local extension centre, E. S. Cartwright, who was also clerk of the borough council, that there was a proven need to establish tutorial classes in the Potteries.[2] A similar case had been made by the Rochdale Educational Guild, which appealed to the town's co-operative tradition to win support for workers' education.

What these people wanted to study was economics in historical perspective, and Tawney was brought in to meet this demand. The first classes were held in early 1908 on the subject of the industrial history of England in the sixteenth and seventeenth centuries. The extent to which Tawney saw the subject in terms of the contemporary interests of his students is shown in the phrasing of the first essay question he set for them. He asked them, 'If you were going to devote six months to the study of economics, what branch should you select, and why; and how should you set about it?' Once the students had replied, Tawney proceeded to direct their attention to the historical development of various economic problems and attitudes. To E. S. Cartwright's first essay, Tawney appended these comments:[3]

> Our problem at the present day is to put economic activity in proper relation to the other elements of human life. But if we forget the economic motive altogether and overlook the material conditions on which the production of wealth depends, we become mere sentimentalists and dreamers.

These material conditions were, Tawney thought, historically determined, and a good dose of history was, therefore, an essential part of any education.

The success of the classes in Rochdale and Longton played an important part in establishing a permanent sponsorship of these and other tutorial classes. In August 1907, the WEA sponsored a conference in Oxford. The subject was the possibility that Oxford would go some of the way to meet 'the growing desire on the part of workpeople for Higher Education ...'.[4] Seven university members and seven working-class leaders nominated by the WEA formed a committee which met five times between Christmas 1907 and October 1908, and which produced a report on Oxford and working-class education. This document, which has become something of a classic in the history of adult education, called for the development and extension of the tutorial class experiment in which Tawney and his students were engaged. The plan was for students in these classes to follow a two-year course which would prepare them to continue their education at Oxford. In fact, of the hundreds of students who passed through WEA classes before 1914, only two reached Oxford. But other 'graduates' spread the gospel of workers' education by opening new tutorial classes and by becoming teachers and organisers of them.[5]

The recommendation of *Oxford and Working-class Education* which had the most direct bearing on Tawney's historical work was the one following: 'That in view of the lack of textbooks suitable for the use of these classes, the Standing Committee ... be asked to make arrangements for the provision and publication of such text-books.'[6]

The standing committee took the name of the Oxford University Tutorial Classes Committee, and by the end of 1908, it formally took over responsibility from local authorities for Tawney's classes. He was to be paid £200 per year plus £40 for each class that he would lead.[7] While he was expected initially to take five classes, the committee decided on 24 April 1909 that 'Mr. Tawney should take four classes and, as an equivalent to the fifth class should be commissioned to prepare a book on the Industrial History of the late 15th and early 16th centuries'. Tawney was asked as well to consult A. L. Smith of Balliol and L. L. Price of Oriel College 'on the subject of a book on the 18th and early 19th centuries'.[8] This second book did not materialise. But the first did in the altered form of the *Agrarian Problem*.

Tawney spent the next three years working on the book. At the same time, he travelled between Rochdale, Longton, Littleborough, Wrexham, in all of which he had tutorial classes, and Manchester, where he lived after his marriage in 1908 to Jeanette Beveridge. She was the sister of William (later Lord) Beveridge, who had been his friend at Balliol at the turn of the century. The wedding ceremony was a WEA affair. The organisation's President, William Temple, later Archbishop of Canterbury, assisted Canon S. A. Barnett of Toynbee Hall in the service. The organisation's treasurer was best man, and Albert Mansbridge, general secretary and guiding force of the WEA, was in attendance.[9] In the following years, the Tawneys settled in Manchester, which was an ideal base for his teaching.

In 1909, Tawney was appointed the first 'All Souls' Teacher' of the Oxford University Tutorial Classes Committee.[10] This post was made possible by the support of the Warden of All Souls', Sir William Anson, who had been Parliamentary Secretary at the Board of Education between 1902 and 1905. Anson was instrumental in silencing donnish objections to the very idea of the intrusion of working men into the university.[11] As Warden he provided Tawney with help in another way. He made available to him the rich college archives and manorial records upon which Tawney drew effectively in the *Agrarian Problem*.

The Oxford Tutorial Committee instructed Tawney to keep them informed about the progress of his 'textbook' for the WEA classes. His writing was a complement to rather than a substitute for his teaching, which placed a considerable travel burden. In 1910 he reported a bit of trouble in keeping attendance up in Wrexham, and commented, 'Probably the Lancashire people spoil one for any more feeble stock.'[12]

Such difficulties did not stand in the way of progress on the *Agrarian Problem*, which was completed in April 1911. The tutorial committee then 'proposed that Messrs. Longman, Green & Co. should be invited to publish R. H. Tawney's book.'[13] This they agreed to do the following year. The extent to which Tawney saw his first major work as a product of the tutorial classes is seen in the fact that not Tawney but Mansbridge signed the publication contract on behalf of the Oxford University Tutorial Classes Committee, to which all royalties would go.[14]

In the year between completion of the manuscript and its publication, Tawney sent copies to a number of historians, some of whom helped him make last-minute revisions. Paul Vinogradoff, Corpus Professor of Jurisprudence at Oxford, sent his comments on legal aspects of land tenure. George Unwin, Professor of Economic History at the University of Manchester, whose influence on Tawney will be discussed below, sent his advice and words of encouragement. Unwin wrote[15]

> I must express the joy I feel that you have got so excellent a piece of work so nearly done. The great thing is to get it out fairly soon and not to keep it back because you realise (as one always does) in revising that another year would enable you to rearrange it in better order.

Tawney took Unwin's advice, and on 1 March 1913, the tutorial committee formally expressed 'its appreciation of R. H. Tawney's book'.[16] Sales during 1913 produced for the tutorial committee the sum of £10. 16*s*. 3*d*., which suggests that about 300 copies were sold.[17] Perhaps more important than the income was the scholarly recognition the tutorial class movement received through Tawney's historical writing. As W. J. Ashley, perhaps the doyen of British economic historians, put it in his review of the *Agrarian Problem*, 'If in any degree the book can be called the outcome of the Workers' Educational Association, then for the scholar, at any rate, the WEA is beginning to be justified by its fruits.'[18]

While the *Agrarian Problem* was being produced by Longman, Tawney had been asked to begin a second project for the WEA. This time a book of documents was needed to use in tutorial class work. It emerged in 1914 as *English Economic History: Select Documents*, edited by A. E. Bland, P. A. Brown, and R. H. Tawney, WEA tutors all.

By the time the book was published, however, Tawney had left three of his tutorial classes on a three-year leave of absence 'in order that he may devote himself to research work into the causes of poverty'[19] as Director of the Ratan Tata Foundation at the London School of

Economics (LSE). Although this work obliged him to spend most of 1913 and 1914 in London, Tawney did not sever his ties with Lancashire completely.

One of the reasons was the profound influence which George Unwin exerted over Tawney's work as an economic historian. Unwin and Tawney came from completely different backgrounds. Unwin never wavered in his loyalty to his native Cheshire.[20] His father was a railway clerk and passed on to his son an affection for Stockport; a place with attractions which have often tended to escape the gaze of outsiders. Tawney's father was a Sanskrit scholar and Principal of Presidency College, Calcutta. Tawney himself was born in Calcutta, but grew up in the south of England. Unwin's schooling took place formally at the Edgeley Wesleyan Day School until the age of thirteen; afterwards, informally, in intervals from his work in a Stockport hat-making firm. Tawney's path was the well-trodden one from Rugby to Balliol. Unwin won a scholarship to University College, Cardiff, and then in 1893, at the age of twenty-three, went to Lincoln College, Oxford, as a classical scholar. Unwin was born a Wesleyan but became a firm Unitarian. Tawney was a high Anglican throughout his adult life. It would have been difficult to predict that in George Unwin, Tawney would come to find an inspirational teacher and friend.[21]

Unwin was ten years older than Tawney, and by the time the latter began to collect material for the *Agrarian Problem*, Unwin had already published two major studies in sixteenth- and seventeenth-century economic history.[22] Together with Ashley and Cunningham, he was one of the few economic historians committed to bringing the fruits of German scholarship to bear on the development of research in this country. Unwin did so partly as a result of an Oriel College travelling scholarship which enabled him to go to Berlin in 1897 and to attend the lectures of Adolph Wagner and Gustave Schmoller on economic history.[23] While rejecting the nationalistic views of Schmoller, Unwin nevertheless warmly acknowledged the influence of the great German historian on his own writing.[24] In Tawney's words, Unwin had become, after his visit to Berlin, 'fired with the idea of founding a school of economic history like that of Schmoller in England'.[25] In the years before the First World War, Unwin devoted himself to this aim, and the *Agrarian Problem* must be seen in part as a reflection of Unwin's approach to economic history.

In 1908 Tawney completed the term of his first university appointment, as assistant lecturer in economics at Glasgow University. Just as he left Scotland for Lancashire, Unwin went to Edinburgh as lecturer in economic history. Two years later, he returned to his native territory to take up the first chair in the subject at the University of

Manchester.[26] His lectures and informal seminars in the following years provided Tawney with an opportunity to discuss the *Agrarian Problem* in its final stages and to profit from the work of Unwin and his students.

What particularly attracted Tawney to Unwin was his view of economic history as a branch of moral philosophy.[27] Unwin waged a battle throughout his work against what he took to be the exaggeration of the role of the state in social development which marked contemporary historical and political thought. It was his intention to free economic history from its subservience to political history so as to give proper recognition to the part played by voluntary associations in historical affairs. In this form, Unwin's views appealed to Tawney. We know that at this time Tawney was suspicious of theories of socialism, such as that of the Webbs, which accorded to the state the prime role in the transition to socialism.[28] But Unwin had a distaste for the political world as a den of thieves, a distaste which Tawney did not share. To Unwin 'political history was largely pathological' since the state was merely 'bald-headed gentlemen in offices, with strong class prejudices, an inclination to magnify their own authority, and a comprehensive ignorance of the lives of nine-tenths of those over whom it is exercised'.[29] To Tawney, in contrast, the state was an instrument, a mechanism, which could prevent injustices as well as perpetuate them. Tawney's first work in economic history was thus an attempt to chart a course somewhere between the theoretical views of the Webbs and those of Unwin by an examination of the history of land and labour in sixteenth- and seventeenth-century England.

Unwin's major contribution to economic history was, in Tawney's view, that he 'altered [its] perspective ..., freed it from much conventional lumber, and gave it a new objective and centre of interest. He found it strongly biassed towards politics. He left it with a bias towards sociology'.[30] That 'bias' is apparent in Tawney's treatment of the response of villagers to enclosure in the sixteenth century, a central theme of the *Agrarian Problem*. It is also clear that in Unwin's writings, Tawney had found a model appropriate to the first phase of his work. In 1926, at an Anglo-American Conference of Historians, Tawney sketched out a strategy for the development of economic history which bears the full imprint of Unwin's ideas. Tawney was writing the moving introductory memoir to Unwin's collected papers at the time of this conference, and undoubtedly spoke for them both when he urged[31]

> that, in the past, economic historians had made three mistakes: they had tended to treat economic history within the framework of political history, employing a ground plan of periods, etc., which

> were often inapplicable; they had been insufficiently analytical and too purely narrational; and in England, at least, they had treated the subject on purely national lines, which were too narrow. In future the teaching and writing of the subject ... must be (1) more sociological, making more use of the comparative method and ceasing to confine itself to simple narrative; (2) more analytical, philosophical, and argumentative, on the analogy of legal history; (3) more international, students studying the economic history of Western Europe in its main phases.

Much of Tawney's early work, including the *Agrarian Problem*, can be understood fully only when placed in the context of these beliefs.

In writing his first book, Tawney benefited not only from Unwin's work, but also from a deluge of publications on English agrarian history from all parts of Europe. As Vinogradoff noted in his book *Villeinage in England*, written while he was professor at the University of Moscow, Russian historians in particular were concerned with English manorial history as a source of contemporary social policy in their country. Russia's late economic development required them to help answer questions which elsewhere were merely academic, such as[32]

> how far legislation can and should act upon the social development of the agrarian world. Are economic agencies to settle for themselves who has to till the land and who shall own it? Or can we learn from Western history what is to be particularly avoided and what is to be aimed at?

The same interests guided the research of one of Vinogradoff's students, Alexander Savine, whose work on sixteenth-century enclosure and customary tenure[33] provided the evidence for many of Tawney's own judgments in the *Agrarian Problem*.

Imperial Germany's land problem occasioned the writing of several influential studies of English economic history. In addition to Steffen's massive study of sixteenth-century price movements,[34] Tawney also drew on Pauli's discussion of the debate over problems of landed society in the reign of Henry VIII,[35] on Schanz's survey of English foreign trade in the fifteenth and sixteenth centuries,[36] as well as on two books written in German on more recent aspects of English agrarian history, Hasbach's *History of the English Agricultural Labourer*,[37] and Levy's *Large and Small Holdings*,[38] both of which had appeared in English just before the *Agrarian Problem* was completed.

This wealth of European comment on English history is in part a continuation of Marx's emphasis on this country's pioneering role in economic development. It took the precipitate decline of Britain's military and economic strength to put an end to the Anglocentrism of some European historians. Paralleled as it was by Elie Halévy's early publication on English history,[39] these writings testify to the major role non-British scholars played in the development of historical studies of this country in the period prior to the First World War.

Among English writers, Ashley provided the general framework for Tawney's work on the sixteenth century,[40] although the latter did not accept Ashley's view of the complete insecurity of tenure of customary tenants in the Tudor period.[41] Tawney refused as well to accept the diametrically opposite conclusion of I. S. Leadam that such tenants were perfectly secure in law and in practice.[42] And although Leadam's work has provided ammunition for the most severe attack on the *Agrarian Problem*, and on Tawney as an historian,[43] he did not disregard the valuable contributions which Leadam made to agrarian history in his studies of the Inquisition of Depopulation of 1517.[44]

Many Victorian historians tended to find in agrarian history instructive illustrations of general political principles. After the 'Great Depression' of the 1870s and 1880s, there was an outpouring of scholarly studies inspired by the debate over how to revive British agriculture. Several learned discussions followed the passage of the Liberals' Small Holdings Act of 1892. This measure empowered local authorities to purchase land and to make it available to labourers as freeholders. The 1892 Act turned out to be, on the whole, a failure, as was recognised in its amendment in 1908. But even the subsequent creation of 12,729 statutory tenancies under the amended Act failed to deflate the ideological campaign for land reform, for which the Liberal governments of Campbell-Bannerman and Asquith claimed to stand.

Historians, as usual, joined in the fray. Lord Ernle, agent-in-chief of the estates of the Duke of Bedford, published *English Farming Past and Present* in 1912. The later chapters of this book form part of his retort to Liberal land policy.[45] A more radical view of the land question was expressed by J. L. and Barbara Hammond, whose *Village Labourer 1760–1832*, appeared in the same year. Similarly outraged by the eighteenth-century enclosure movement was Gilbert Slater, who produced a book 'at the suggestion of Graham Wallas and at the request of J. A. Spender' in which he concluded that 'the principle of the collective ownership of the soil must be established or re-established'.[46] Less overtly political was the work of A. H. Johnson, who used land-tax assessments in his Ford Lectures of 1909 to show that the period prior to the late eighteenth century was the most difficult for smallholders. Additional information appeared two years later when E. C. K. Gonner brought out his thorough study of *Common Land and Enclosure*.[47]

The ground had been well prepared, therefore, for the study of the social implications of changes in agriculture in sixteenth-century England which Tawney produced. But it was his single achievement to use this study to explore 'those dimly conceived presuppositions as to social expediency which influence the actions not only of statesmen, but of humble individuals and classes, and influence, perhaps, most decisively those who are least conscious of any theoretical bias'.[48] Economic history, in his hands, was a tool to uncover the responses to economic change of ordinary men whose voices are rarely recorded in political chronicles. 'Their silence is the taciturnity of men,' wrote Tawney, 'not the speechlessness of dumb beasts.'[49] What moved many of them to action was not the quickening pace of economic activity itself, but that such development seemed to take place at the expense of the majority of the village community and their 'customary level of prosperity'.[50] Enclosure in moderation and by agreement had gone on for decades before the 1540s, Tawney argued, without disturbing the fabric of rural life. But the increasing substitution of pasture for arable farming, as an outcome of the growth of the textile industry in the sixteenth century, produced an outcry because it ignored the fact that 'Commons and common rights, so far from being merely a luxury or convenience, were really an integral and indispensable part of the system of agriculture, a linch pin, the removal of which brought the whole structure of village society tumbling down'.[51] What was at stake in the debate over enclosure was the ability of smallholders to preserve the 'considerable control over the management of their own economic affairs'[52] that they had enjoyed in the open-field system. Their appeal was to customary rights which they believed stood against 'the acquisition by individuals for themselves of such rights as they could obtain by economic power, or by the accumulation of capital'.[53]

It is in this sense that Tawney meant to characterise the custom of the manor as a form of 'collective bargain'[54] recognised by the lord and his customary tenants. These smallholders were, in his view, 'trade unionists to a man'.[55] They subscribed to the 'corporate management of common interests' and abided by a 'system of common rules' which regulated, by reference to the needs of the village as a whole, the uses to which land could be put.[56] The 'increasing predominance of the large farm' made inevitable, therefore, 'a collision of interests' between those who stuck by the traditional view of landholding as defended by custom and those who treated it as 'an income-yielding investment'.[57] By 'turning agriculture into a business', Tawney claimed, 'the capitalist farmer had succeeded in breaking down the personal relations of landlord and tenant ... a tie which was almost sacramental'.[58] Since pasture farming required a smaller labour force than did arable, it was inevitable that some customary tenants and those who lived at the will of the lord would be displaced. To Tawney, this disruption of rural society was but one example 'of the depreciation of particular kinds of human labour in comparison with capital, of the kind to which the modern world has become accustomed in the case of machinery—become accustomed and become callous'.[59] In the eighteenth century, Tawney claimed, enclosure had not occasioned the stiff resistance of early times. Tawney believed that this was partly because Tudor villages were relatively prosperous and their inhabitants were not starving as many of their descendants would be.[60] But more importantly, the Tudor opponents of enclosure acted vigorously, he argued, because they shared 'a living body of assumptions as to the right conduct of human affairs, which feels that more than material interests are menaced, and which braces itself anxiously against the shock'.[61] The enclosers were the revolutionaries, men who acted against that 'public opinion' on the land and in the cities which

> still clings to the conception that there is a standard of fairness in economic dealings which exists independently of the impersonal movements of the market, which honest men can discover, if they please, and which it is a matter of conscience for public authorities to enforce.[62]

Thus what had made the agrarian problem more than an economic or legal matter was the fact that in sixteenth-century England, 'Economic issues are not yet separated from questions of personal and political morality'.[63] The economic historian, Tawney maintained, had no choice, therefore, but to treat agrarian life as a totality, and to appreciate the force of ethical beliefs which contemporaries applied to every aspect of social behaviour. This collectivist mentality, offended by the high costs of agricultural change as it was by later industrial developments, is the real subject of Tawney's book.

Tudor statesmen were not unsympathetic to these appeals to conscience in evaluating the benefits of economic policy. But the effect of government action was, in Tawney's words, to retard, 'though it could not check altogether, economic changes. It imposed a brake which somewhat eased the shock of sudden movements'.[64] The theme of the limits of state power, which is dealt with in one context in the *Agrarian Problem*, was examined in greater detail in Tawney's second major contribution to economic history in the years before the outbreak of the First World War. This research was published in two parts in the *Vierteljahrschrift für Sozial- und Wirtschaftsgeschichte*, in 1913 and 1914, under the title 'The assessment of wages in England by Justices of the Peace'.[65] This article was probably written while Tawney directed the Ratan Tata Foundation at LSE.

In these articles, Tawney comprehensively refuted conservatives' claims about the supposedly revolutionary character of twentieth-century state intervention in wage regulation. The opposition's wrath was directed at the Liberal government's Trade Boards Act of 1909, which set up agencies to fix wages in poorly organised trades, and at the Minimum Wage Act of 1912, which set a floor to miners' wages after the successful coal strike of 1912. What Tawney did was to show that the period of the withdrawal of the state from active regulation of economic life in the eighteenth and nineteenth centuries was a temporary phase. The clear implication of his case was that free enterprise would come to be seen, in time, as a caesura between two longer and more stable periods of collectivism. Here again, Tawney took on the role, as an economic historian, of stripping a relatively modern system of property relations of its claims to a dignified antiquity.

Hewins and Cunningham, both Conservatives and economic historians, had argued that the provisions of the 1563 Statute of Artificers affecting wages were largely inoperative, and that after 1640 the assessment of wages by local authorities had come to an end. Tawney uncovered enough evidence to establish that the statute was not a dead letter. On the contrary, it had given birth to a system of third-party intervention in wage negotiations which lasted throughout the succeeding century.[66] Of course, the ways wages were assessed varied considerably. Justices of the Peace frequently asked for the advice of juries in making wage awards, and juries were likely to contain men in whose interest it was to keep wages down. But its persistent application was, Tawney believed, undeniable and could be understood only as 'part of a general system of Government intervention in economic matters, which was on the whole endorsed by the public opinion of the age ...'.[67]

The 1563 statute aimed to remedy the plight of small producers and landholders under what Tawney took to be conditions of severe labour shortage. Tawney pointed out that labourers had preserved their scarcity value by working at home and refusing wages or by colonising new land and thereby moving away from employers who needed their services. The freedom of action, or inaction, of labourers thus worked against the interest of small producers and property holders who formed the majority of the population. The needs of the bulk of the productive nation were best served, therefore, by the establishment of a *maximum* wage on the land, where most of the labour force lived. Only in regions where the textile industry had developed most fully was a *minimum* wage set. Labourers in this, the most advanced sector of capitalist industry, were the most debased, Tawney argued, but their peers elsewhere had tried to squeeze out of the community more than what was deemed their fair share. The labourer who hoarded his labour was like the miller who hoarded grain. Both did so at the expense of other small property owners, who applied, with the help of the state, the same principles of moral economy that opponents of enclosure or usury had applied in their related disputes.[68] The fact that some workers tried to assert an antisocial individualism, which was restrained by the law, was evidence enough for Tawney that wage labourers in Tudor England were neither 'the helpless victims of economic oppression'[69] nor above the commonly accepted moral code governing economic behaviour in their society.

Tawney's historical work came to an abrupt halt shortly after the appearance of the second part of his article on wage assessment in the sixteenth century. After dispelling some doubts as to the merits of the British case, he volunteered for the Army in November 1914. He saw action in the ranks with the Manchester Regiment, and was one of the many who bore the burden of General Haig's insane policy of frontal assault on the Somme in July 1916. Severely wounded, he was fortunate to survive the first day of the battle. He was sent back to England to recuperate and recovered his strength and his bearings at the home of the Bishop of Oxford, Charles Gore.[70] In the next few years Tawney drew together the threads of his old life. He was active in church reform, contributed to the work of the reconstruction committees of 1917 and 1918, stood as a candidate in 1918 for the Labour Party, and returned to tutorial class teaching at Longton and more general duties as WEA 'resident tutor' in North Staffordshire.[71] In 1919, he served on the Sankey Commission on the Coal Industry as a representative of the Miners' Federation of Great Britain. He supported the nationalisation of the mines, which nevertheless the Lloyd George government rejected. At the same time, Tawney began to return to his historical work, in part through the support of Balliol, to which he was elected a Fellow in 1918, and in part through his securing the following year a permanent post as lecturer in economic history at the London School of Economics. In the next five years, he contributed significantly to the teaching of Tudor economic history in the University of London, in conjunction with Eileen Power, who jointly edited with him the widely-used textbook on *Tudor Economic Documents*, published in 1924.

Tawney's writings in the next five years prepared the way for what is perhaps his most widely-read book, *Religion and the Rise of Capitalism*, published in 1926. In many ways the book was as much a response to contemporary affairs as the *Agrarian Problem* had been. By the early 1920s, partly through his friendship with William Temple, by then Bishop of Manchester, Tawney had become one of the most influential spokesmen of Anglican socialism.[72] In the last year of the war Tawney had served on a Church of England Committee of Enquiry into Christianity and Industrial Problems. He wrote most of the document this group produced. Therein one can find a crystallisation of the spirit of radical social criticism which had come to dominate the church in the years prior to and during the war. As Henley Henson, Dean of Durham and a Conservative critic of this tendency within the church remarked, this committee's 'dominating spirit was evidently supplied by Messrs Lansbury and Tawney and their episcopal shadows, Gore, Talbot, Kempthorne, and Woods'.[73]

In the following year, Tawney joined Temple in the preparation of an interdenominational conference on the churches' attitude to social problems. In 1921, Tawney was appointed to the sub-commission charged with consideration of the questions related to industry and property. In April 1924 an assembly of 3,000 met in Birmingham as the Conference on Christian Politics, Economics and Citizenship (COPEC).[74]

Temple's personality and ideas marked this venture from the start. His statement of purpose shows the direction that their theological and Tawney's historical thought had taken. Temple wrote[75]

> The Basis of this Conference is the conviction that the Christian faith, rightly interpreted and consistently followed, gives the vision of the power essential for solving the problems of to-day, that the social ethics of Christianity have been greatly neglected by the Church with disastrous consequences to the individual and to society, and that it is of the first importance that these should be given a clearer and more persistent emphasis.

When the ninth report of COPEC on Industry and Property was discussed and adopted, few could have missed the signs of Tawney's authorship.[76] Many of the phrases were already known to those who had read Tawney's indictment of the 'acquisitive society', which appeared first in the *Hibbert Journal* in 1919,[77] shortly afterwards as a Fabian Society pamphlet, and finally as a short and pungent book, *The Acquisitive Society*, in 1921.

Tawney was shrewd enough to choose to direct his efforts towards making Christians into socialists, rather than to try to turn socialists into Christians. His continuing involvement in the radical wing of the Church of England is the context in which his celebrated exploration of Christian social thought after the Reformation must be set. There is no evidence at all that Tawney came to this research through a reading of

Max Weber's essays on the 'Protestant ethic', published in 1904–5.[78] Tawney did confide to his pre-war Commonplace Book the disarmingly simple question, 'I wonder if Puritanism produced any special attitude towards economic matters.'[79] But in 1912 Tawney seems to have been blissfully unaware of Weber's views on the subject. A full exposition of Weber in English was at hand at the time. In 1910, P. T. Forsyth published two articles which simply reported Weber's work which, he noted, 'broke new ground and produced a remarkable impression in Germany both among economists and theologians'.[80] In addition, an English translation of Ernst Troeltsch's lecture on 'Protestantism and the modern spirit' had appeared in 1912. Most of the salient points of the work of Weber, Sombart, and their critics were discussed therein.[81]

But only after fifteen years had passed since Weber's essays appeared, and when the refashioning of the church's social message seemed possible, did Tawney devote himself to a careful reading of authorities on Christian social thought.[82] When he did so, he turned to Ashley, just as he had done in the preparation of the *Agrarian Problem*. In his discussion of usury and other matters, Tawney followed Ashley's early interpretation.[83]

Tawney was asked to deliver the first series of Scott Holland Lectures in 1922, on an aspect of 'the religion of the Incarnation in its bearing on the social and economic life of man'. These lectures, delivered at King's College, London, ultimately became *Religion and the Rise of Capitalism*. Various drafts and sections of the book appeared in the *Hibbert Journal* in 1922[84] and in the American *Journal of Political Economy* in 1923.[85] Surprisingly, Tawney had some trouble in finding a publisher for the book, because of publishers' singularly wrong-headed assumption that 'it would make little appeal to the general public'. A dozen translations and even a 'pirated edition in Fascist Italy'[86] testify to the enduring appeal of its message. But, despite the delay, the book was published in 1926, dedicated to Bishop Gore. Thanks to Harold Laski's friends on the *New Republic*, the book's final chapter was serialised in that radical American journal. The first article appeared, incidentally, the day after Tawney had signed the contract for the publication of the first issue of the *Economic History Review*, in the middle of the General Strike of 1926.[87]

The long introduction Tawney wrote for his 1925 edition of Thomas Wilson's *Discourse upon Usury* of 1569 established the line of interpretation underlying *Religion and the Rise of Capitalism*. The two works overlap at many points, but Tawney incorporated into his edition of Wilson's *Discourse* a detailed account of the growth of finance and commerce in the sixteenth century which was in itself a significant contribution to economic history.

The author of the *Discourse upon Usury* had been Ambassador to the Netherlands, Secretary of State, and a Master in the Court of Requests. At an advanced age he had been made Dean of Durham in what Tawney referred to as 'one of the agreeable abuses of the Tudor church'.[88] Wilson brought to his *Discourse* the fruits of his wide experience of diplomacy and trade, which, as a state official and civil lawyer, it had been his business to possess. What Tawney found most intriguing about him was 'the economic outlook, the preoccupation with morality' of such a man of affairs. A concern with Christian principles as applied to all aspects of social life had led him to write his *Discourse* as an attack on the 'individualism' which he believed was a threat to the fabric of his society.[89] He worked within the traditions of More and Latimer[90]

> whose social philosophy was based ultimately on religion, and who saw in the economic enterprise of an age which enclosed land and speculated on the exchanges, not the crudities of a young and brilliant civilization, but the collapse of public morality in a welter of disorderly appetites.

Just as in the *Agrarian Problem* Tawney's purpose was to emphasise the 'collision between these clamorous economic appetites' whetted by the prospects of an unprecedented expansion of trade and industry and 'a long established body of religious and political doctrines'. This conflict 'produced the struggle of ideas and interests portrayed in Wilson's book'.[91] And as in his earlier writing, Tawney was clearly on the side of those like Wilson who believed that[92]

> economic relations, in particular those of borrower and lender, are one department of moral conduct, that they are to be judged by a rule of right, not merely by considerations of economic expediency, and that the standards to be applied to them, while they ought to be enforced by the State, are derived ultimately from the teaching of the Church.

To introduce the reader to the business world in which Wilson lived, Tawney began by surveying the ubiquitous role of credit in the lives of both peasants and small masters and those of impecunious gentlemen. Such lending was unremarkable and familiar to all contemporary observers. But by the sixteenth century the primary recipients of credit, Tawney argued, were no longer small property owners. 'Loans to enable rich capitalists or landowners to finance profitable undertakings, which had been the exception, were becoming the rule.'[93] The social implications of this change were as ominous, in his view, as were those associated with enclosure. They meant the 'transference of the control of industry from the individual producer to the commercial capitalist' and the consequent loss of independence of the craftsman whose employer not only 'provided raw materials, marketed the goods, but advanced the working capital' as well.[94] In other words, a sophisticated credit system tended to deprive the majority of the productive nation of control over the means of production. To Wilson this was a moral as much as an economic problem.

Equally ominous to him was the growth of an international money market. That opportunities existed for profit 'out of movements in the relative values of different currencies'[95] may seem familiar enough to us. But[96]

> To writers like Wilson, who were concerned with credit as a problem of economic ethics, the practitioner on the international money market seemed to epitomise every characteristic which had made the usurer a moral abomination. ... To take advantage of deviations from the mint par of exchange, still more to cause them, was an act of fraud the more heinous because it corrupted the very life-blood of legitimate trade.

Foreign exchange transactions, Tawney pointed out, presented traditional thinkers like Wilson 'with an *experimentum crucis*' of their beliefs. Their response, like that of Tudor statesmen, was clear. It was the forceful and repeated reassertion of the relevance of Christian ethics to business affairs in general and to questionable currency transactions such as 'dry exchange' in particular.[97] In Wilson's *Discourse*, the Preacher manages to convert the Common Lawyer and the Merchant to his sober Christian business morality, which made no distinction between the responsibility of men to the community in their personal or in their commercial lives. This dramatic reconciliation, Tawney admitted, was the reflection of a set of beliefs soon to be eclipsed. He had little doubt that by 1600 'the day of Wilson's preacher and civilian was nearly over'. But, though their position was ultimately lost, 'They did not surrender without a struggle'[98] during which a case had been made which Tawney wished to bring to the attention of his own generation.

It should come as no surprise, then, that among the drafts of sections of *Religion and the Rise of Capitalism* to be found in Tawney's papers is a COPEC working paper on a proposed Christian Investment Society.[99] Indeed, Tawney was completely open about the concerns which he brought to the book. 'It is evident today', he wrote in 1923, 'that the line of division between the spheres of religion and secular business ... is shifting.' There were still those who were shocked if churchmen tried to analyse social and political affairs in terms of their beliefs as Christians. The Prime Minister, Lloyd George, had taken just such a line in a speech at Portmadoc in June 1921 wherein he chastised the Anglican bishops who had dared to criticise his government's policies on Ireland and on the lockout of miners in Britain.[100] But that such a collision had taken place at all was one bit of evidence among many which convinced Tawney that 'the treaty of partition has lapsed and the boundaries' between religion and social affairs 'are once more in motion'. Men throughout the world, Tawney noted, were engaged in an effort[101]

> to restate the practical implications of the social ethics of the Christian faith, and to restate them in a form sufficiently comprehensive to provide a standard to judge the collective actions and institutions of mankind, in the sphere both of international politics and social organization.

Consequently, 'issues which were thought to have been buried by the discretion of centuries have shown in our own day that they were not dead, but sleeping'.[102]

Their revival, in Tawney's view, required a fresh look at the circumstances which surrounded the relegation to the purely personal sphere of Christian standards of economic and social behaviour. As Tawney had shown in his introduction to the *Discourse upon Usury*, many Christians in the sixteenth century had found utterly repugnant any break with what were deemed to have been the traditional social ethics of the medieval church. How then did it happen? This question is at the heart of *Religion and the Rise of Capitalism*.

The first answer Tawney offered was that the authority of the Church of England to pronounce on economic affairs could not have survived unscathed the assault on the powers of the church of Archbishop Laud and his followers. The abuse of office by Laud and his followers not only undermined their own position. It had worked as well, he believed, to discredit 'the whole conception of religion which regarded it as involving the central control of economic self-interest'.[103] Both the political power of the church and state control over its activities had had profound dangers in the seventeenth as indeed they had in the twentieth century. 'In identifying the maintenance of public morality with the spasmodic activities of an incompetent Government', Tawney noted, 'the Church had built its house upon the sand. It did not require prophetic gifts to foresee that the fall of the City would be followed by the destruction of the Temple.'[104]

The second cause of the waning influence of the church on the way businessmen conducted their affairs was the imprecision of the lead it offered. Traditional protest used categories of judgment derived from the experience of a simpler stage of economic development. By reiterating eternal truths rather than reformulating older ethical statements in specific terms related to a more complex economic environment, Christian moralists had set the seal on their own fate. They were treated as irrelevant, Tawney suggested, because their doctrine 'was never made concrete enough to supply detailed rules of social and economic conduct' sufficiently realistic and flexible to accommodate economic developments of which the Schoolmen had never dreamt.[105] 'The social teaching of the Church had ceased to count', Tawney argued, 'because the Church itself had ceased to think. ... It was neglected because it had become negligible.'[106] Between the assertion of the absolute authority of ancient precepts and the denial that those precepts applied in any way to economic affairs lay a yawning gap. But no Christian position emerged to bridge it by translating the language of Thomas Wilson's preacher into terms that his successors' congregations could understand and heed. Indifferentism, therefore, triumphed by default.

The third source of the restriction of the Anglican conscience to questions of individual behaviour lay, Tawney argued, in developments within Protestant thought itself. He showed that the legacy of Calvinism was complex and contradictory, because it managed to place at the centre of religious discussions of economic activity ambiguities which permitted diametrically opposed conclusions to be drawn from what appeared to be the same premises. On the one hand, Calvin adopted a much more urbane approach than did Luther to questions of business affairs. Consequently the Genevan theologian produced 'the first systematic body of religious teaching which can be said to recognize and applaud the economic virtues'.[107] But on the other hand, Calvin was a strict disciplinarian who was in no way an advocate of economic licence. Tawney claimed that he and his followers 'welcomed the world of business to its fold with an eagerness unknown before', but they 'did so in the spirit of a conqueror organizing a new province, not of a suppliant arranging a compromise with a still powerful foe'.[108]

The same oscillation can be found in Puritan writings. While warning of the 'numberless disguises assumed by the sin which striketh fast between buying and selling', the Puritans and other Protestant sectarians had given 'a whole-hearted *imprimatur* to the life of business enterprise', which was turned by 'some of Calvin's later followers' into 'a frank idealization of the life of the trader, as the service of God and the training-ground of the soul'.[109] By adapting for their own purposes the idea of the 'calling' so that it described and glorified 'the conscientious discharge of the duties of business',[110]

> Puritanism in its later phases added a halo of ethical sanctification to the appeal to economic expediency, and offered a moral creed, in which the duties of religion and the calls of business ended their long estrangement in an unanticipated reconciliation.

Tawney's argument here is that Calvinism had within it 'contradictions which live in vigorous incompatibility together',[111] but that the resolution of these conflicts was never in doubt once Calvin had departed from judging economic activity in terms of 'Christian tradition' to evaluate it in terms of 'commercial common sense, which he is sanguine enough to hope will be Christian'.[112] Sooner or later, in every case—in Geneva, Edinburgh, Amsterdam, or New Salem—'the social theory of Calvinism went through the same process of development. It had begun by being the very soul of authoritarian regimentation. It ended by being the vehicle of an almost utilitarian individualism'.[113] The speed of the change depended on the political and economic environment of Protestant communities. But in the long run the result in all cases was the same: the fundamental diminution of the standing of the Protestant churches as arbiters of economic behaviour. And, Tawney concluded, if the church was silent, who was left to speak about economic justice as of more importance than economic growth?

Had any reader managed to miss the contemporary references in the book, he would have been set right by its review in the *Times Literary Supplement*. The reviewer placed the book squarely in the context of the efforts of those who stressed 'the need of respiritualizing our civilization, especially in economic life ...'. He thought that Tawney had proved his case that Christian doctrine had an appreciation of the frailties of human nature and of the need for constraining economic appetites which 'so far from being obsolete ... is most modern'. But the writer of the review, who may have been J. H. Chapham, felt that Tawney had not shown the relevance of earlier writings to the most pressing contemporary problem, which was not the accumulation, but rather the diffusion, of wealth. On this point Christian doctrine was unclear, and 'So the Devil shuffles the cards again for a game with Archbishops' Committees and other earnest Christians'.[114]

An appreciation of the religious concerns which inform *Religion and the Rise of Capitalism* makes it difficult to accept the fusion of Tawney's work with that of Max Weber on the spirit of capitalism. It is time to disentangle the mythical entity commonly known as the 'Tawney-Weber thesis'.[115] The grounds for divorce are incompatibility of approach, method, and conclusions.

Tawney's literary elegance helped mask the tension between his writings on this problem and those of Weber. Tawney was characteristically generous in acknowledging his debt to certain of Weber's interpretations, such as that related to the secular function of the idea of the 'calling'. His criticisms of Weber's work were indirect, muted, and, he admitted, unoriginal, 'unless, indeed to be less anxious to refute an author than to understand him is in itself to be original'.[116] In addition, Tawney's heavily ironic style obscured some of his fundamental disagreements with Weber. Consider this passage which opens the final chapter of *Religion and the Rise of Capitalism*:[117]

> Societies, like individuals, have their moral crises and their spiritual revolutions. The student can observe the results which these cataclysms produce, but he can hardly without presumption attempt to appraise them, for it is at the fire which they kindled that his own small taper has been lit.

No doubt could have existed, though, about Tawney's evaluation of the consequences of the emergence of religious indifferentism. His history was judgmental throughout, despite his own ambiguous disclaimers, and can in no way be accommodated within the framework of Weberian 'value-free' analysis, which few scholars, including Weber, have managed to sustain.

Weber was emphatic in his denunciation of the kind of history that Tawney wrote. The German sociologist's works were not written for those who saw in history a guide to contemporary political action or ethical judgment. His advice to such people was blunt:[118]

> He who yearns for seeing should go to the cinema, though it will be offered to him copiously today in literary form in the present field of investigation also. Nothing is farther from the intent of these thoroughly serious studies than such an attitude. And, I might add, whoever wants a sermon should go to a conventicle. The question of the relative value of the cultures which are compared here will not receive a single word. It is true that the path of human destiny cannot but appal him who surveys a section of it. But he will do well to keep his small personal commentaries to himself, as one does at the sight of the sea or of majestic mountains, unless he knows himself to be called and gifted to give them expression in artistic or prophetic form.

In contrast, Tawney made no attempt to hide the Christian standard against which, in *Religion and the Rise of Capitalism*, he measured the 'relative value' of capitalist culture. With premises so different, the content and character of their historical analyses naturally diverged.

Weber's purpose in his discussion of the spirit of capitalism was to explore the role played indirectly by religious ideas in the formation of what he took to be the characteristic personality of the modern capitalist entrepreneur and worker. The methodical and ascetic attitude of such men to work and its rewards was, Weber argued, profoundly untraditional and had to be created and nurtured in order that capitalism in its modern form could emerge. In this process certain Protestant beliefs were of particular importance, in that they served as the source of an 'ethically coloured maxim for the conduct of life'. This 'ethos' or 'spirit', produced unwittingly by the Reformation Fathers, was what separated the traditional capitalism of China, India, and medieval Europe from modern capitalism. Earlier capitalism lacked what the teachings of Calvinism provided, that is, a 'social ethic' able to dissolve the 'inner obstacles which the adaptation of men to the conditions of an ordered bourgeois-capitalistic ēconomy has encountered everywhere'.[119] Indeed, this 'spirit of capitalism' was so powerful that even when the religious convictions from which it sprang had faded, it still managed to survive in a form which pervaded the all-encompassing, systematic, rational, routinised structure of economic and social activity which was modern industrial capitalism.

The points of contact between Weber's interests and those of Tawney are clear. Like Weber, Tawney held that 'The fundamental question to be asked, after all, is not what kind of rules a faith enjoins, but what kind of character it values and cultivates'.[120] Both believed that the 'character to which [Puritanism] specifically appealed was one pre-eminently fitted to take advantage of economic developments'.[121] They agreed as well that there was in Calvinism a corrosive force which undermined traditional doctrines of social morality in ways which would have shocked the early Reformers.[122] And they shared the view that in Protestant teaching there was an important emphasis in religious terms on the 'inner isolation of the individual' which reinforced a more general individualism of social and economic behaviour.[123]

But what differentiates their work is the uses to which they put their interpretations of Protestantism. Weber's essay was but one part of a comprehensive study of the sociology of religion, in which great emphasis was laid on ideological obstacles to the development of capitalism in the non-European world.[124] It also reflects his overriding concern with the development of what he termed the rational bureaucratic character of European society. In both of these facets of his work he charted the progressive, relentless, and irreversible demystification of the world. Hence the deep pessimism underlying his description of the process whereby the social teachings of the Protestant churches helped create an 'iron cage' which constrained and ordered the behaviour of men whose religious beliefs had withered long ago.[125]

Weber's ideal-typical analysis of this process helped give to his interpretation a logical consistency and rigour which Tawney recognised and admired. But Weber's method produced a distillate of the spirit of capitalism which Tawney believed to be inaccurate and, in so far as it was a static concept, profoundly misleading. In an early draft of *Religion and the Rise of Capitalism*, Tawney wrote:[126]

> A celebrated theory has suggested that Puritanism was the parent of individualism. But in reality, Puritanism was not one single social philosophy. Dominated by quite different interests, it contained social elements whose social outlook was widely different. The battle between collective discipline and individualism had, in fact, to be fought out within it.

This statement encapsulates neatly the purpose of Tawney's book, which was similar to that of the *Agrarian Problem* and other early writings. Here again Tawney the historian is primarily interested in the resistance of men to the erosion of what he saw as traditional standards of social behaviour. The Church of England had made its peace with the world of nascent industrial capitalism, of this there could be no doubt. But it did so not without a struggle, and—of equal importance to Tawney—not for ever. His subject was the clash within religious opinion which preceded the abnegation of the social responsibilities of the Anglican church. The victors were those who held that economic and social relations were primarily matters of marginal concern to religion. But their victory, Tawney believed, was a transitory one, and in the twentieth century the same struggle was being fought out again.

'In our own day', he wrote in an early draft on Puritanism, 'Protestant writers have denounced the attempt to state the social ethics of Christianity as an abandonment of the principles of the Reformation.'[127] Nothing could have been further from the truth, as both Tawney and Weber demonstrated conclusively. But Weber's writings had helped to foster a belief in the bleak permanence of the spirit of capitalism which Tawney laboured to refute throughout his work. *Religion and the Rise of Capitalism* was written, therefore, to help counter the view that social indifferentism in religious thought and individualism in economic thought were unchangeable principles. Weber's analysis did not allow for change or transformation of the mental world of contemporary capitalism. Whereas his purpose was to describe the demystification of the world, Tawney's was to help in the demystification of capitalism, by stripping it of some of its more powerful ideological supports.

II

Within a few years of the publication of *Religion and the Rise of*

Capitalism, the world economic crisis of the early 1930s and the political convulsions it occasioned brought about a change in Tawney's approach to economic history. It is important, however, not to overemphasise the discontinuity of his interests in this period. As is clear from the inaugural lecture he delivered at the London School of Economics in October 1932, Tawney never abandoned his belief that the economic historian must study the cultural environment in which economic systems are born, thrive, decay, and die.[128] But in a period which was marked both by the decline of liberal capitalism and by the menacing rise of fascist power, Tawney began to work on a series of studies in which the problem of economic morality received less attention than the problem of the social formations on which political power rests.

His belief that economic history should become more comparative is reflected particularly well in this second phase of his historical work. His acute responses to contemporary American society, described below, were matched in this period by his perceptive discussion of the state of Chinese society in the early 1930s, written after an eight-month mission to China as an educational adviser to the League of Nations.[129] The author of the *Agrarian Problem* was well placed to grasp the nature of the land problem in China and the sources of the failure of the Kuomintang to deal effectively with it. In a book entitled *Land and Labour in China*, Tawney drew on his knowledge of pre-industrial agriculture to highlight for a European audience the parallels between Chinese and Western developments. As in sixteenth-century England, the central features of Chinese landed society in the 1930s, Tawney held, were the scarcity of wage labour and the wide distribution of smallholdings.[130] In both countries, as indeed 'in all countries where farming is in the hands of small producers', Tawney argued, 'the fundamental problem is not that of wages, but of credit'.[131] Furthermore, while recognising the dangers of equating the Chinese system of land tenure with that of Europe in the past, nevertheless he believed that the attitudes of Chinese peasants to land were not dissimilar to those of European villagers of the not too distant past:[132]

> In China, as in Europe during long periods of its history, the ideal commonly accepted, though too rarely attained, has been, not progress, but stability. The primary concern has been, not to secure the maximum return for the minimum effort, but to distribute limited and unexpanding resources among the largest possible number of human beings.

And as in Europe this attitude has been decisive in the formation of 'Custom, which means in effect the law of the locality', and which 'has created rights as secure, and obligations as binding, as those which in the West have been established by legislation'.[133]

So far we are still in the first phase of Tawney's work as an historian. But in the last part of this book, Tawney moved away from the subject of the material interests and mentality of the Chinese peasant and turned to a consideration of the political conditions of China's economic backwardness. Again, he argued by analogy, to refute contentions, such as those voiced by the Webbs on an earlier visit to China, that her economic problems were the result of racial inferiority.[134] On the contrary, Tawney wrote,[135]

> The effects of war, defective communications, scarcity of capital, political insecurity and heavy taxation, which retarded economic development on the continent of Europe during the first half of the last century, have in China paralyzed it. They have been aggravated by almost continuous internal disorder, the absence of any government whose writ ran without question throughout the country as a whole, the poverty of the agricultural population, a social environment set in the mould of the past and intractable to change, currency and exchange difficulties, the control by foreign interests of key positions in finance, transport and commerce, and the fact that China's limited mineral resources are to a considerable extent exploited by foreign firms, which ship part of the product abroad to become the basis of manufacturing industries in countries other than China. ... Dr Sun Yat-sen's description of China as a colony is, from an economic point of view, not inappropriate.

Since China's poverty was in part an outcome of Western imperialism, the struggle for political unification and for economic development had to be waged together or both would fail separately. 'Economic progress is paralyzed', Tawney wrote, 'by political anarchy, and will continue, till order exists, to be fitful and intermittent. The first problem, therefore, is to create an efficient system of government.'[136] But even an effective local and national administration would founder, unless agrarian reform were to become its first priority. The reason was that 'Political organization rests on economic foundations; when the latter crumbles, it crumbles with them'.[137] As long as the land question remained unresolved, Tawney surmised, Chinese communism could not be defeated;[138] a perspicacious prediction as it turned out.

After his visit to China, Tawney developed in his research the concern for political questions which informs his later historical work. By the 1930s, he had had considerable experience of the politics of the Labour Party and had formulated many important party statements as well as most of its educational policy. But in earlier years he had treated political conflict as of secondary importance in the process of social change. By 1933, the Japanese invasion of Manchuria and the Nazi seizure of power had convinced even the most idealistic observers of contemporary affairs of what Leninists call the primacy of the political. Consequently, after his return to Europe, on the eve of one of the darkest phases of European history, the problem of the relationship between political and economic power became central in Tawney's research. One of the results was the appearance of two essays reprinted here, 'The rise of the gentry' and 'Harrington's interpretation of his age'.

Before he completed these seminal articles, he developed his interest in aspects of seventeenth-century English social structure in two ways. The first was in the analysis undertaken jointly with his wife Jeanette of the occupational structure of Gloucestershire in the early seventeenth century. From a muster roll of 1608 Tawney drew statistical confirmation of his contention, first expressed in his 1913 article on assessment of wages, that the most important features of English rural society before 1640 were the scarcity of wage labour and the wide diffusion of property.[139]

The second occasion for his discussion of this new phase of his work was the invitation to deliver the Ford Lectures in Oxford in Hilary Term 1936. Unfortunately, Tawney never published these lectures, the texts of which have not survived intact. But it is likely that he used in them material from the Cranfield Papers which he incorporated in his final book, *Business and Politics under James I*. Tawney also probably used this forum to explore the divergence of the fortunes of aristocratic and gentry landowners which, he believed, had undermined the political power of the Stuart monarchy.[140]

The full formulation of the thesis that in the two generations prior to the English Civil War 'The centre of social gravity has shifted; political power is shifting with it'[141] came after the outbreak of the Second World War. It is difficult to appreciate the place this much-debated theme occupied in Tawney's work without reference to the period of political turmoil and armed conflict in which it was conceived. Tawney's commitment to egalitarian principles and to their embodiment in the international labour movement made it inevitable that he would react with horror to the Nazi seizure of power and its aftermath of repression and ultimately of war. But unlike some of his contemporaries, Tawney did not throw up his hands in disgust at the ineptitude of social democracy and join the Communist Party. While devastatingly critical of the Labour Party's policy, he none the less retained his old political loyalties. However, we can see his subtle response to contemporary events in the extent to which his history is marked by a form of economic determinism that is not as prominent in his earlier or later writings.

The test of any political theory is the adequacy with which it describes the contemporary world. By the late 1930s, the antagonisms tearing European society apart seemed to many to make sense in terms of a marxist outlook. In these circumstances, it would have been surprising had Tawney carried on unchanged his earlier discussions of the morality of business transactions. At this time what mattered more was an historical investigation of social forces which cause redistributions of political power. While Tawney never subscribed to the view that the English Civil War was a 'bourgeois revolution' for the commendable reason that the bourgeoisie was on both sides, nevertheless he came to conclusions on the nature of the Civil War which are not far removed from some explicitly marxist interpretations. As usual he preferred an eclectic approach in which marxism was one historical tool among many. This attitude is apparent in his later discussion of Maurice Dobb's work (see below, pp. 202–14).

In his Raleigh Lecture to the British Academy in 1941, Tawney discussed the work of James Harrington in terms of the assumptions which he himself adopted in his article on 'The rise of the gentry'. In both essays Tawney advanced an explanation of political change in seventeenth-century England which is marked by a high degree of determinism. What Tawney referred to as the 'dominant *motif*' of Harrington's *Oceana* is apparent in his own interpretation of the period:[142]

> It is that the revolution of his day had been determined by changes in social organization which passed unnoticed till too late, that the old regime had been destroyed neither by the errors of the ruler on whom the Tower of Siloam fell, not by the intransigence of the Parliament, but by impersonal forces too strong for both; and that political stability was not to be expected till political institutions were brought into accordance with economic realities.

The economic historian as moral philosopher had been replaced by the economic historian as political prophet.

We can see this emphasis on the structural limits of political action also in the last product of the research Tawney began in the 1930s, the study of *Business and Politics under James I*, the title of which alone suggests the second facet of Tawney's work. This book focuses on the role played by Lionel Cranfield as merchant and minister in the early seventeenth century, but it is in no sense a biography. In the first chapters of the book Cranfield does not appear at all, and even later he occupies a minor part in an elaborate structure of business rapacity and political intrigue which ultimately destroyed him. His personal life is neglected. His creation as Earl of Middlesex and his second marriage are relegated to inconspicuous footnotes.[143] His ideas are not assessed for the simple reason that they were 'conventional to the point of platitude outside ... his own administrative field'.[144]

What marks this study is not a concern with the moral problems of Cranfield's business or public life, but rather an interest in the constraints on the actions of men, however well-meaning, by the machinery of social and economic power.[145] By the late 1950s, the extension of state power on the foundations laid during the Second World War and by the Labour governments of 1945–51 had highlighted the problem of bureaucracy as a determinant of social affairs. But this is only a minor change in the line of approach adopted by Tawney in the 1930s, according to which political events cannot be understood in terms of purely personal conflicts or ideas. It may be of some interest to record that Tawney completed the study of Cranfield only after he had given up a commitment to write the life of the administrator *par excellence* of twentieth-century Britain, Sidney Webb. Only fragments of Tawney's work remain, but in them we can see that he intended to write the life in terms of the institutions he built and which determined the limits beyond which his ideas could not reach.[146]

This emphasis on structural explanations, which broadly characterised the second phase of Tawney's historical writing, is clear as well in two essays which he wrote in the first instance at the invitation of the British government. The first was an essay on the dismantling of the British war economy and its disastrous consequences in the aftermath of the First World War.

In February 1941, Sir George Crystal of the Cabinet Office invited Tawney to undertake a study of a number of aspects of reconstruction policy during the First World War.[147] The work was to be done for Arthur Greenwood's Reconstruction Committee and was to concentrate on six matters:

(1) the technological and economic problems of industrial transfer;
(2) the effect of financial policy on the rate of industrial transfer;
(3) the interaction between demobilisation and the rehabilitation of the economic system;
(4) the relaxation of economic controls;
(5) the scope and nature of emergency relief measures;
(6) the disposal of surplus stores.

It was hoped that a comparison of French, German, American, and British experience on these questions 'will provide a safe guide in solving the problems of economic demobilization at the end of the present war'.[148] After some confusion about whether Tawney could have access to confidential papers (he could not), he agreed to use the secondary literature at least at the start.[149] In August 1941, he produced a paper on a variant of item 4, the abolition of economic controls, which is published here in full for the first time. None of the other papers was written, because of the pressure of other official work which will be discussed below.

Two years later, the editor of the *Economic History Review*, M. M. Postan, tried to get official permission for publication in that journal of a reduced version of Tawney's paper. He argued that its appearance in the *Review* would not endanger any vital secrets. 'I should like to point out that this is a strictly and even severely academic publication', Postan wrote. 'The readers of the Review are a very esoteric crowd, mostly professors in economics and economic history.'[150] The official who handled the request, A. Baster, agreed to it. He told his superiors that 'I can confirm that the review has a limited circulation, as I once wrote an article for it but I never met anybody who had read it'.[151]

In 1942, While Tawney was adviser on 'social and politico-economic affairs' to Lord Halifax, British Ambassador in Washington, he wrote a short history of the American labour movement.[152] This document was considered by the Foreign Office to be too controversial to be published during the war.[153] Tawney never pressed the matter, and the memorandum was not one of the items that Tawney himself wanted reprinted in a collection of his historical writings.[154] He simply may have forgotten about the memorandum when he returned to his academic and political responsibilities in wartime Britain.

The memorandum on the American labour movement, which is to be published separately, is a remarkable document. It shows us Tawney's historical powers at their best. It stands today, thirty-six years after it was written, as one of the most succinct and penetrating analyses of the politics and industrial activity of labour in the United States. In addition, it bears all the marks of the new structural emphasis in Tawney's historical thought after the 1930s.

The circumstances surrounding the preparation of this history, though, are of more than merely historiographical interest. Tawney wrote it to help British diplomats to cope with problems presented by the deep divide between the older and conservative American Federation of Labour (AFL), and the upstart and more militant Congress of Industrial Organisations (CIO). With the British war effort reliant in part on American industrial production even before the Japanese attack on Pearl Harbour, the diplomacy of labour became a subject of undeniable importance. And after the Nazi invasion of Russia in June 1941, the need to forge links between the labour movements of the anti-fascist powers was accepted by men of all political persuasions.

Just prior to the 1941 Trades Union Congress (TUC) in Edinburgh, the General Council proposed the formation of an Anglo-Soviet trade union committee, along the lines of a similar body established to link British and French labour before the débâcle of May 1940. Gone were the memories of the demise of an earlier Anglo-Russian committee, which had perished after the General Council of the TUC turned down £250,000 of Russian assistance during the General Strike. In 1941, the Russians were prepared to let bygones be bygones, and agreed to join the group, as long as its title be changed from Anglo-Soviet to Anglo-Russian, as befitted the circumstances of the Great Patriotic War.[155]

After a visit to Russia in October 1941 by Sir Walter Citrine, the General Secretary of the TUC, and five members of the General Council, a Russian delegation came to England early in 1942. During these consultations, Citrine agreed to approach leaders of the American labour movement to persuade them to join what would be an Anglo-American-Russian trade union committee. To this end, Citrine wrote to William Green, President of the AFL, and offered to go to America to discuss the matter. Green agreed, and Citrine arrived in New York on 3 May 1942.

Citrine's mission was an unmitigated failure, and during it he managed to antagonise people along the whole continuum of American labour. This episode would have been merely a comic interlude in American-British relations, were it not for the fact that he had complicated delicate negotiations, initiated indirectly by President Roosevelt, for at least a wartime armistice in the hostilities between the AFL and the CIO. By even mentioning a Russian connection, Citrine offended the conservative AFL. By refusing to meet openly with the CIO before completing discussions with the AFL, he outraged the younger organisation, whose members were engaged in war work vital to both Britain and her allies. And all these diplomatic blunders were made in the run up to the American congressional election of 1942.[156]

It is not surprising that Citrine was a major headache for the British Embassy in the spring of 1942. He did not consult them about his plans, nor did he seek their advice about the wider political implications of his mission. Citrine's hostility to the Embassy staff—and to Tawney—probably reflected his innate belief that working-class leaders did not need their 'social superiors' to tell them what to do. Whatever its source, Citrine's avoidance of diplomatic channels and controls created major problems for Embassy officials, who turned to Tawney for assistance. The immediate result was that, together, Lord Halifax and Tawney worked out a strategy to limit the damage that Citrine would do.[157] Halifax decided to follow Tawney's advice directly on this matter, and to commission him to prepare a number of papers on aspects of American labour, so that the Embassy could act intelligently and quickly on similar occasions in the future. Preparation of these papers kept Tawney busy until the day he left Washington in mid-September 1942, a year to the day after his arrival.[158] The longest and the last to be submitted was the history of the American labour movement.

Tawney understood the new configuration of power in American labour in a way that never dawned on the General Secretary of the TUC. In three other memoranda which Tawney wrote in his last month in Washington in 1942, he reiterated his argument that changes in the structure of American industry had made an explosion of trade union membership inevitable. The legislation of the early years of FDR's administration had removed the legal obstacles to unionisation, and as a result there had been a change both in degree and in kind in the organisation of American labour. All observers of American affairs who did not take account of that fact, Tawney argued, would be bound to misread the new situation. The CIO could not be dismissed as a temporary phenomenon in the world of labour; it was there to stay.[159]

To introduce the Foreign Office to the then current state of the labour movement and to provide an historical perspective for their future deliberations on related issues were Tawney's aims in drafting his long memorandum on American labour. This document is different from many of his earlier historical writings in several ways. First, it was written for an audience primarily interested in the policy implications of his interpretation rather than in its historical validity. As a result, it has few of the stylistic flourishes which are the hallmarks of Tawney's more academic writings. Gone are the Biblical allusions and classical irony of *Religion and the Rise of Capitalism*. No one need have read Milton or Dante to see what Tawney meant to say. Second, since he was writing for British diplomats, Tawney adopted a more explicitly comparative approach than in any of his other writings, with the exception of the essay on China. 'The American labour movement' is comparative social history at its best, on an altogether higher plane than the uninspired survey of the British labour movement which he had published in 1925 for American audiences.[160]

As a work of history, the major achievement of the 1942 memorandum is that it places developments in the labour movement firmly within the context of the growth of American industry and industrial society. His account of the emergence of the CIO is one case in point. Another is his discussion of the difference between the politics of British and American trade unions. The social and political outlook of American unions differed from that of their employers, Tawney held, because industrial capitalism came to the United States 'not as a *parvenu*, but as a pioneer'.[161] In Britain, the growth of factory production clashed with deep-seated traditions of industrial solidarity. But in America, there was no need to disrupt an earlier way of life and work, since 'In most industrial regions west of the Alleghenies, the town did not precede the factory; the factory made the town. To the mobile and individualistic population which poured into both, industrial capitalism was not one type of civilization, but civilization itself'.[162] Consequently, the political character and ideology of American trade unionism contrasts sharply with that of European trade unionism. Tawney's memorandum is, therefore, one of the most lucid expressions of the thesis that the weakness of American socialism must be sought in the social structure of American industrial capitalism.

III

It is appropriate to begin a brief consideration of the legacy of Tawney's work in terms of his writing on the American labour movement. This essay demonstrates particularly well Tawney's belief in the absurdity of any strict distinction between social history and economic history. To treat these subjects as 'independent entities, poised each in majestic isolation on its private peak'[163] is to ensure, Tawney argued, a truncated, if not desiccated, treatment of past social life. Tawney's inaugural lecture at the London School of Economics (see below, pp. 47–65), which bears the marks of both phases of his work, points to an ecumenical approach, the cultivation of which was the aim of all his scholarly work. His writing still serves as an example of *histoire intégrale*, in the same way that that of Marc Bloch and Lucien Febvre, whom Tawney knew and respected, does in France.

The distinction between what may be characterised roughly as the moralist and structuralist phases of Tawney's history is useful in describing another aspect of his influence. After 1956, a number of scholars who had broken with the Communist Party in Britain began to develop an interest in a kind of cultural history which was rooted in marxist approaches, but which aimed primarily, as Tawney had done in the *Agrarian Problem*, to portray what has been called the 'moral economy' of agricultural and industrial labourers.[164] This phrase is due to E. P. Thompson, whose work has helped to encourage the further cultivation of fields which Tawney explored years ago, such as the role of custom and law in landed society,[165] and the persistence in industrial societies of a tenacious and deeply-felt craft consciousness shared by large groups of working men.[166] That the recovery of the many facets of working-class culture is a central part of European historical writing today is in part because of Tawney's work and example, and that of a group of his contemporaries, among whom G. D. H. Cole, H. L. Beales, the Webbs, and the Hammonds are the most prominent. The extent to which Tawney saw his work as part of a wider campaign to broaden the areas in which economic historians labour can be seen in the obituary of J. L. Hammond which he wrote for the British Academy (see below, pp. 229–54).

More directly within the discipline of economic history in Britain, however, there is evidence that the Tawney tradition is in decline. On the one hand, no one contests the value of his work in launching the Economic History Society and its *Review*. Equally appreciated is his work encouraging local history and agrarian history (see below, pp. 198–201; 215–20). Furthermore, his students at the LSE and elsewhere are to be found in universities and institutions of adult education all over the world.

But on the other hand, his critics have been numerous as well. Undoubtedly, they have provided necessary correctives to some of his interpretations. H. R. Trevor-Roper and J. P. Cooper have brought out well some of the problems involved in the counting of manors and in aspects of the work of Tawney and Lawrence Stone on the fortunes of gentry and aristocratic families.[167] The Regius Professor at Oxford has also raised doubts about some of Tawney's views on the relationship between Calvinism and capitalism in early modern Europe.[168] In a more intemperate outburst, J. H. Hexter has carried on the campaign against any attempt to link religious beliefs and economic activity in seventeenth-century England. Although his immediate target was Christopher Hill, a fervent supporter of the Tawney tradition, the founder's ghost was his adversary as well.[169] Eric Kerridge and G. R. Elton have brought to our attention weaknesses in the *Agrarian Problem*[170] but the ferocity of their criticisms testifies to the lingering appeal of Tawney's message.

There are few historians who would not be proud to have been the occasion of the learned controversies which have developed around Tawney's work. Furthermore his opponents would command more respect if instead of complaining about the intrusion of his values in his writing on history, they simply admitted that they did not share them. To adopt a magisterial tone is not to prove that any historian is beyond the claims of his particular social situation. Still, Tawney's reputation has suffered recently because he took the now unfashionable line of admitting that his non-professional life and beliefs had a direct bearing on the way he conducted his work as an historian. What is seen today by some as the vice of committed scholarship may well be recognised in future as the virtue that it is.

Tawney's influence has waned, though, not merely because he refused to cut off his history from his politics and both from his religion, but also because of the particular nature of his beliefs. His Christian values have been expressed rarely by younger economic historians. One must look to the work of the late Richard Titmuss or the former Bishop of Stepney, Trevor Huddleston, to find men who do not share the cynicism of many contemporary scholars. Indeed, a consensus of scepticism, at times bordering on despair, about the possibility of social progress in a declining economy separates many contemporary historians in Britain from those of Tawney's generation, who wrote history as a political act reflecting their faith in the future. There is little left of the pioneering appeal of the WEA, for example, which did much to generate enthusiasm for economic history in its early years.

Furthermore, Tawney was more patriotic than many British historians today, though less insular than most. His particular brand of Englishness may appear to some to be a relic of a bygone age. Of course styles in the writing of history always change. Perhaps we should not be surprised or concerned if scholars have looked elsewhere for models of professional decorum.

Most importantly, though, Tawney's work has been eclipsed recently because in a sense he stood outside the most significant development in economic history since the Second World War: the application to the subject of the concepts and methods of economic theory. The fruits of this work have been most abundant in studies of the one period on which Tawney wrote virtually nothing, that is, the Industrial Revolution. As we have seen, Tawney's work centred first on the ethics of wealth distribution and then on the relationship between political and economic power. Later economic historians, many of them trained at LSE by Tawney's friend T. S. Ashton, have tended to explore the economics of wealth creation, a subject on which Tawney was conspicuously silent.[171] Only in his surveys of American or Chinese problems did he confront the question of the causes and determinants of industrialisation, and in those cases he did so entirely from the secondary literature.

Perhaps Tawney thought his temperament ill-suited to enter empathetically the world of nascent industrial capitalism in Britain. Perhaps the role of the Tawney family in contributing to capital accumulation in country banks had something to do with it.[172] But whatever the reason, it is easy to understand why a generation disturbed by the terrible human price paid by countries desperately trying to industrialise in this century should seek out the work of those historians, like Alexander Gerschenkron, who have helped them to understand economic backwardness in historical perspective.[173]

Nevertheless, Tawney's importance as an historian is unquestioned. Like most pioneers, he provided a starting-point, which is after all a place from which to move on. But as long as historians insist that men's ideas matter in an examination of past economic life, and that the subject of economic history raises questions which touch the fundamental concerns of thinking people, working men and scholars alike, we can be confident of the survival of the Tawney tradition.

Notes

All works published in London unless otherwise noted.

1 British Library of Political and Economic Science. Beveridge Papers. II.a. 106, Tawney to W. Beveridge, August 1902 and 10 July 1903.

2 L. T. West, 'The Tawney legend re-examined', *Studies in Adult Education*, IV (1972), pp. 105 ff. D. J. Booth, 'Albert Mansbridge's formative years: a re-appraisal', *Journal of Education, Administration and History*, VI (1974), pp. 10–17.

3 Rewley House, Oxford. E. S. Cartwright Papers, essay by Cartwright, 17 February 1908, comments in Tawney's hand.

4 *Oxford and Working-class Education* (Oxford, 1908), p. vii.

5 Rewley House, Oxford. Oxford University Tutorial Classes Committee Minutes (hereafter cited as OUTCCM), 6 October 1913. The two were Albert Emery, a potter, who was admitted to Balliol, and Maud A. Griffiths, an elementary school teacher, admitted to St Hilda's Hall. John Elkin, a miner, was not placed in an Oxford college despite repeated attempts to do so.

6 *Oxford and Working-class Education*, p. 87.

7 OUTCCM, 14 November 1908.

8 OUTCCM, 24 April 1909.

9 'The caravan', *Highway*, I (1909), p. 162.

10 OUTCCM, 6 August 1909.

11 B. Simon, *Education and the Labour Movement 1870–1920* (1965), p. 306.

12 OUTCCM, 29 January 1910.

13 OUTCCM, 17 April 1911.

14 OUTCCM, 2 March 1912.

15 British Library of Political and Economic Science. Tawney Papers, Box on the Agrarian Problem, Unwin to Tawney, undated.

16 OUTCCM, 1 March 1913.

17 OUTCCM, 23 May 1914.

18 W. J. Ashley, review in *Economic Journal*, XXIII (1913), pp. 85–9.

19 OUTCCM, 2 August 1912.

20 R. H. Tawney (ed.), *Studies in Economic History: the Collected Papers of George Unwin* (1927), pp. xi–xv.

21 Tawney (ed.), *George Unwin*, passim.

22 *Industrial Organisation in the Sixteenth and Seventeenth Centuries* (1904); *The Gilds and Companies of London* (1908).

23 G. W. Daniels, *George Unwin: a Memorial Lecture* (Manchester, 1926), p. 2.

24 Unwin, *Industrial Organisation*, p. iii.

25 Tawney (ed.), *George Unwin*, p. xxii, n. i.

26 N. B. Harte (ed.), *The Study of Economic History* (1971), p. xxvi.

27 Tawney (ed.), *George Unwin*, p. xviii.

28 J. M. Winter, *Socialism and the Challenge of War* (1974), ch. 3.

29 Tawney (ed.), *George Unwin*, pp. xxxv, lxix.

30 Tawney (ed.), *George Unwin*, p. lxii.
31 'The Anglo-American conference of historians', *Bulletin of the Institute of Historical Research*, IV (1926), p. 110.
32 P. Vinogradoff, *Villeinage in England* (Oxford, 1892), p. vi.
33 A. Savine, 'English customary tenure in the Tudor period', *Quarterly Journal of Economics*, XIX (1904), pp. 36–80.
34 G. F. Steffen, *Studien zur Geschichte der Englischen Lohnarbeiter* (3 vols, Stuttgart, 1901–5).
35 R. Pauli, *Drei volkswirtschaftliche Denkschriften aus der Zeit Heinrich VIII von England* (Göttingen, 1878).
36 G. von Schanz, *Englische Handelspolitik gegen Ende der Mittelalter* (Leipzig, 1881).
37 ... which appeared in Germany in 1894, and in 1908 in its English translation.
38 ... which appeared in Germany in 1904, and in 1911 in its English translation.
39 The first volume of his history of the English people in the nineteenth century appeared in French in 1913.
40 See Ashley, *An Introduction to English Economic History and Theory* (4th ed., 2 vols, 1906), i, pt II, ch. 12.
41 R. H. Tawney, *The Agrarian Problem in the Sixteenth Century* (paperback ed. 1967), pp. 290–1 (hereafter cited as *AP*).
42 I. S. Leadam, 'The Inquisition of 1517. Inclosures and evictions. Edited from the Lansdowne Manuscripts I.', *Transactions of the Royal Historical Society*, n.s., VI (1892), pp. 167–314.
43 E. Kerridge, *Agrarian Problems in the Sixteenth Century and After* (1969).
44 *AP*, pp. 8, 10, 13, 120, 154, 201–2 n., 224, 283, 330, 357, 360, 362, 380. For their differences, see p. 289.
45 I am indebted to Mr A. Offer of Merton College, Oxford, for his advice on this matter.
46 G. Slater, *The English Peasantry and the Enclosure of Common Fields* (1907), pp. vi–vii.
47 A. H. Johnson, *The Disappearance of the Small Holder* (1909). See also, G. E. Mingay's introduction to the second edition of E. C. K. Gonner, *Common Land and Enclosure* (1966).
48 *AP*, p. xxiii.
49 *AP*, p. 121.
50 *AP*, p. 99.
51 *AP*, pp. 238–9.
52 *AP*, p. 102.
53 *AP*, pp. 169–70.
54 *AP*, p. 295.
55 *AP*, p. 131.
56 *AP*, pp. 161, 130.
57 *AP*, pp. 229, 289.
58 *AP*, p. 193.
59 *AP*, p. 257.
60 *AP*, p. 325.
61 *AP*, p. 347.
62 *AP*, p. 307.
63 *AP*, p. 184.
64 *AP*, pp. 390–1.
65 XI (1913–14), pp. 307–37 and 533–64. Reprinted as 'The assessment of wages in England by the Justices of the Peace', in W. E. Minchinton (ed.), *Wage Regulation in Pre-industrial England* (Newton Abbot, 1972), to which edition reference is made here.
66 'The assessment of wages by the Justices of the Peace', pp. 309, 336–7.
67 Ibid., p. 312.
68 Ibid., pp. 65–84.
69 Ibid., p. 66.
70 Winter, *Socialism*, ch. 6. Beveridge Papers, II.a.97, A. J. Tawney to W. H. Beveridge, 8 September 1914.
71 OUTCCM, 2 March 1918, 24 May 1919.
72 Winter, *Socialism*, pp. 172–9.

73 Durham Chapel Library. Henson Papers, Journals, vol. 25, p. 205, as cited in E. R. Norman, *Church and Society in England 1770–1970* (Oxford, 1976), p. 242.
74 Norman, *Church and Society*, pp. 279 ff.
75 Norman, *Church and Society*, p. 284. See also W. M. Pryke, 'COPED 1924', *Modern Churchman*, XIV (1924), pp. 49–59.
76 Norman, *Church and Society*, p. 299.
77 'The sickness of an acquisitive society', *Hibbert Journal*, XVII (1919), pp. 353–70.
78 M. Weber, 'Die protestantische Ethik und der "Geist" des Kapitalismus I–II', *Archiv fur Sozialwissenschaft und Sozialpolitik*, XX and XXI (1904–5), pp. 1–54 and 1–110.
79 J. M. Winter and D. M. Joslin (eds), *R. H. Tawney's Commonplace Book* (Cambridge, 1972), entry for 16 September 1912.
80 P. T. Forsyth, 'Calvinism and capitalism I–II', *Contemporary Review*, XCVII–XCVIII (1910), pp. 728–41 and 774–87, especially p. 728 n.
81 E. Troeltsch, *Protestantism and Progress*, trans. W. Montgomery (1912), pp. 132 ff.
82 Tawney Papers, Box on Usury.
83 W. Ashley, *An Introduction to English Economic History*, I, pp. 458–70.
84 'Religion and business. A forgotten chapter of social history', *Hibbert Journal*, XXI (1922), pp. 65–80.
85 'Religious thought on social and economic questions in the sixteenth and seventeenth centuries I–III', *Journal of Political Economy*, XXXI (1923), pp. 461–93, 637–74, 805–25.
86 T. S. Ashton, 'R. H. Tawney 1880–1962', *Proceedings of the British Academy*, XLVIII (1963), p. 470.
87 'Puritanism and capitalism' and 'The irreligion of capitalism', *New Republic*, 12 and 19 May 1926. Also, T. C. Barker, 'The beginnings of the Economic History Society', *Economic History Review*, 2nd ser., XXX (1977), p. 13.
88 R. H. Tawney (ed.), Thomas Wilson, *A Discourse upon Usury* (1925), p. 2. Hereafter cited as TW.
89 TW, p. 14.
90 TW, p. 16.
91 TW, p. 104.
92 TW, p. 16.
93 TW, pp. 59–60.
94 TW, p. 58.
95 TW, p. 81.
96 TW, p. 85.
97 TW, p. 143.
98 TW, p. 169.
99 Tawney Papers, Box on Usury.
100 R. H. Tawney, 'Religious thought on social and economic questions in the sixteenth and seventeenth centuries, I', *Journal of Political Economy*, XXXI (1923), p. 462 n. Hereafter referred to as 'RT, I', etc. R. H. Tawney, *Religion and the Rise of Capitalism* (paperback ed., 1966), p. 18. Hereafter referred to as *RRC*.
101 'RT, I', p. 462. *RRC*, pp. 18–19.
102 'RT, I', p. 462.
103 Tawney Papers, Box on Usury, draft lecture. 'RT, II', p. 670, *RRC*, p. 218.
104 *RRC*, p. 179.
105 'RT, II', pp. 655, 657.
106 *RRC*, pp. 188–9.
107 *RRC*, p. 114.
108 *RRC*, pp. 126–7.
109 *RRC*, pp. 225, 232, 238.
110 *RRC*, pp. 238, 239.
111 *RRC*, p. 211.
112 *RRC*, p. 116.
113 *RRC*, p. 226.
114 'Religion and economics', *Times Literary Supplement*, 29 April 1926.
115 H. R. Trevor-Roper, *Religion, the Reformation and Social Change* (1959), p. xi.

116 *RRC*, p. x.
117 *RRC*, p. 271.
118 Max Weber, *The Protestant Ethic and the Spirit of Capitalism*, trans. T. Parsons (1930), p. 29. Hereafter referred to as MW.
119 MW, pp. 48, 51–2, 54, 58.
120 'RT, III', p. 814. *RRC*, p. 225.
121 'RT, III', p. 819.
122 'RT, III', p. 808.
123 MW, pp. 105–6. Tawney Papers, Box on Usury, draft on Puritanism.
124 On which see Talcott Parsons' introduction to Max Weber, *The Sociology of Religion*, trans. E. Fischoff (1965).
125 MW, p. 181.
126 Tawney Papers, Box on Usury, draft on Puritanism.
127 Tawney Papers, Box on Usury, draft on Puritanism.
128 'The study of economic history', *Economica*, XIII (1933), p. 15.
129 C. H. Becker, M. Falski, P. Langevin, and R. H. Tawney, *The Reorganization of Education in China* (Paris, 1932).
130 *Land and Labour in China* (1932), pp. 32, 42–3. Hereafter cited as *LCC*.
131 *LLC*, p. 58.
132 *LLC*, p. 47.
133 *LLC*, p. 35.
134 Winter, *Socialism*, p. 44.
135 *LLC*, pp. 128–9.
136 *LLC*, p. 169.
137 *The Condition of China* (Newcastle upon Tyne, 1933), p. 16.
138 *LLC*, p. 74.
139 A. J. Tawney and R. H. Tawney, 'An occupational census of the seventeenth century', *Economic History Review*, V (1934), pp. 25–64.
140 I am indebted to Christopher Hill of Balliol College, Oxford, for making available to me a transcript of notes of the Ford Lectures Tawney delivered.
141 'The rise of the gentry', *Economic History Review*, XI (1941), p. 6.
142 'Harrington's interpretation of his age', *Proceedings of the British Academy*, XXIV (1941), p. 207.
143 R. H. Tawney, *Business and Politics under James I. Lionel Cranfield as Merchant and Minister* (Cambridge, 1958), pp. 196 n., 213.
144 Tawney, *Cranfield*, p. 188.
145 Tawney, *Cranfield*, p. 292.
146 Tawney Papers, Box: Papers Re Proposed Biography of Sidney Webb. Tawney was asked by the Passfield Trustees to prepare this book, but gave up the task when Margaret Cole produced her volume of essays entitled *The Webbs and Their Work* (1949). Tawney's annoyance was very pronounced.
147 Public Record Office. Cabinet Papers 117.40. Crystal to Tawney, 12 February 1941. Cabinet Papers hereafter referred to as CAB.
148 CAB. 117.40. Minute by Crystal, 19 March 1941.
149 CAB 117.40. Tawney to A. Baster, 7 August 1941.
150 CAB. 117.40. Postan to Baster, 21 August 1943.
151 CAB. 117.40. Baster to Sir Alfred Hurst, 23 August 1943.
152 Public Record Office. Foreign Office Papers 371.26187.A6429. Minute of F.T.A. Ashton-Gwatkin, Chief Clerk at the Foreign Office, 25 July 1941. Foreign Office Papers hereafter referred to as FO. For the full story of Tawney's venture in the diplomacy of labour, see J. M. Winter's introduction to R. H. Tawney, *The American Labour Movement and Other Essays* (1978).
153 FO 371.34153.A1821. F. E. Evans of Foreign Office to H. L. Ervin of Ministry of Information, 20 January 1943.
154 From lists in the possession of Mr Michael Vyvyan.
155 W. Citrine, *Two Careers* (1950), p. 98.
156 FO 371.30700.A7518. Minute by Harold Butler, 26 August 1942. FO

371.30700.A7967. Cable of Halifax to Foreign Office, 27 August 1942.

157 FO 371.30700.A8035. Eden to Churchill, 31 August 1942. FO 371.30700.A8035. Harold Butler to Halifax, 1 September 1942.

158 The memoranda may be found in:

(1) FO 371.513.A8009. 'Labour and the congressional elections', 1942, dated 12 August 1942.

(2) FO 371.30701.A8560. 'A note on the relations between the British and American labour movements', dated 3 September 1942.

(3) FO 371.30700.A9007. 'The American Labour Movement', dated 19 September 1942.

159 'Labour and the congressional elections', 1942, p. 15.

160 *The British Labor Movement* (New Haven, Conn., 1925).

161 'The American labour movement', p. 77.

162 'The American labour movement', p. 77.

163 'The study of economic history', p. 2.

164 E. P. Thompson, 'The moral economy of the English crowd in the eighteenth century', *Past and Present* (1971), pp. 76–136.

165 D. Hay *et al*, *Albion's Fatal Tree* (1975), and E. P. Thompson's forthcoming book, *Customs in Common*. The controversy over and influence of Thompson's *The Making of the English Working Class* (1964) raises obvious parallels with Tawney's work.

166 J. Hinton, *The First Shop Stewards' Movement* (1974), and R. Harrison (ed.), *The Independent Collier* (1978).

167 H. R. Trevor-Roper, 'The gentry 1540–1640', *Economic History Review* Supplement No. 1 (1953), and J. P. Cooper, 'The counting of manors', *Economic History Review*, 2nd ser., VIII (1956), pp. 377–89.

168 Trevor-Roper, *Religion, the Reformation and Social Change*, pp. 1–45.

169 J. H. Hexter, 'An historian and his sources', *Times Literary Supplement*, 24 October 1975.

170 E. Kerridge, *Agrarian Problems*, *passim*, and G. R. Elton, *The Future of the Past* (Cambridge, 1969).

171 I am indebted to Professor Donald Coleman, of Pembroke College, Cambridge, for his advice on this point.

172 L. S. Pressnell, *Country Banking in the Eighteenth Century* (1958), pp. 314–15.

173 A. Gerschenkron, *Economic Backwardness in Historical Perspective* (1960).

Editorial Note

R. H. Tawney considered the publication of an edition of his historical writings in the 1950s. After his death in 1962, he left his papers and notes to this edition to Mr. J. M. K. Vyvyan of Trinity College, Cambridge, his nephew and literary executor. Twelve essays concerning politics, education, and literature were published in 1964 under the title *The Radical Tradition*, edited by Rita Hinden. The job of producing an edition of the remaining historical writings was taken on by Professor David Joslin of the University of Cambridge, who died in 1970 before his work was completed. Professor W. H. B. Court of the University of Birmingham agreed to finish the preparation of this edition, but sadly he too passed away before doing so.

I have profited greatly from the critical comments on Tawney's writings which Professor Joslin and Professor Court left among their papers relating to this project. I have learned much as well from the notes passed on to me by Mr Vyvyan on his views, as well as those of T. S. Ashton and Tawney himself as to what should be included in such a volume of essays. The selection I have made, though, differs in one important respect from those of Joslin and Court. Their editions were to have included essays on social policy, education, and socialist ideas, as well as essays on history. While agreeing entirely about the unity of Tawney's views on these disparate subjects, I believe that a much-needed reconsideration of his work as an historian should include primarily his writings on economic and social history. This decision has meant the exclusion of several important essays which ought to be reprinted, such as his inaugural lecture as Director of the Ratan Tata Foundation, 'Poverty as an industrial problem', and a number of unpublished writings which are of considerable interest, such as his early essay 'The new leviathan' and other draft lectures to be found in Tawney's papers at the London School of Economics. There is every reason to publish a separate volume of Tawney's essays on education and social policy, which are undoubtedly important, but which are tangential to an evaluation of his work as an historian.

In deciding which of Tawney's historical essays to reprint, I have followed on the whole Tawney's own wishes. The long essay on 'The assessment of wages by Justices of the Peace' has been reprinted recently (see Introduction, n. 65) and has therefore not been included. Tawney's inaugural lecture at the London School of Economics, as well as his article on 'Harrington's interpretation of his age, and 'The rise of the gentry' (part I, chapters 1–3) can be found in collections still in print. I have decided none the less to republish them together on the grounds that any edition of Tawney's writings on history which did not include them would be unrepresentative of his work as a whole.

Limitation of space has required the exclusion of the only important historical essay written by Tawney which has yet to appear in print, his history of the American labour movement (see Introduction, pp. 30–3). This essay, written while Tawney was engaged in diplomatic work during the Second World War, is much longer than any of the writings included in this book. This essay will be published in a separate volume of Tawney's essays on labour history, which, it is hoped, will complement this edition.*

One of the problems in writing about Tawney the historian is that it requires a competence not only in the intellectual history of twentieth-century Britain, but also in the economic, political, social, diplomatic, and religious history of half a millennium and pertaining to several continents. Fortunately I have had the advice of a number of specialists in these varied aspects of Tawney's work. Many of them took the time to help on editorial problems and to comment on the introduction. In particular, I would like to thank the following people for their suggestions and criticisms: Volker and Marion Berghahn, Donald Coleman, Geoffrey Elton, Royden Harrison, Negley Harte, Christopher Hill, Peter Mathias, Harvey Mendelsohn, Avner Offer, Henry Pelling, Fritz Stern, Joan Thirsk, and Edward Thompson.

Permission to publish or republish the essays included in this book has been granted from: the editors of *Economica* for 'The study of economic history'; the British Academy for 'Harrington's interpretation of his age' and 'J. L. Hammond, 1872–1949'; Allen & Unwin for 'Max Weber and the spirit of capitalism'; the editors of *History* for 'A Berkshire farmer in the reign of James I'; the editors of

* R. H. Tawney, *The American Labour Movement and Other Essays*, ed. Winter, J. M., Harvester Press, 1979.

the *Economic History Review* for 'The rise of the gentry' and 'A history of capitalism'; the BBC for 'Devon and Dr Hoskins'; and the editor of the *Times Literary Supplement* for 'The church and the Stuarts'. For 'The abolition of economic controls, 1918–21', herein published for the first time in its original form, transcripts of Crown copyright records in the Public Record Office appear by permission of the Controller of H. M. Stationery Office.

Part I
Historical Essays

I

The Study of Economic History (1933)*[1]

No one can speak in this place on the Study of Economic History without recalling the names of those who have done so before him. The first book on the subject which I read was a volume in the library of classics by one of whom we are all the pupils, our encyclopædic chairman. The first lecture on it which I attended was by a research student of this School, later a master to whom a host of apprentices owed their instruction in the craft, George Unwin. The personality who gave it its place in our curriculum was Lilian Knowles, the most inspiring of teachers and most lovable of human beings. A student who inherits a corner of their estate must feel gratitude for their labours and humility at his own.

It is not only the memory of distinguished predecessors which fills me with diffidence. When I realised that the penalty of a Professorship was an Inaugural Lecture, I breathed a prayer to the bright goddesses of enterprise and self-help, who are ever at the elbows of teachers of this School. They frowned but did their best. 'Do not attempt,' they said, 'anything original or profound. It is not your line. Conform to the practice of the representative form, if, wretched historian, you know what that means. For once show real initiative. Study the addresses delivered on similar occasions by more illustrious persons. Aim at the median and you may hit the lower quartile.'

As always, when addressed by the voice of economic reason, I trembled and obeyed; but, as my researches proceeded, my despondency increased. If, as they inclined me to believe, one function of an Inaugural Lecture is to vindicate the claims of the department of knowledge represented by the lecturer against bold, bad men who would question its primacy, I am conscious of an incapacity for that entertaining branch of literature to be excused only, if at all, by a misspent youth. I came to the study of economic history, not as one dedicated from childhood to the service of the altar, but for reasons so commonplace that I am ashamed to admit them. When I reached years of discretion—which I take to mean the age at which a young man shows signs of getting over his education—I found the world surprising; I find it so still. I turned to history to interpret it, and have not been disappointed by my guide, though often by myself.

A student who is more interested in wild life than in museum specimens must be prepared to annoy gamekeepers by following it across country. If, in addition, he is an historian, with the historian's irreverent propensity for treating the most venerable institutions, from capitalism to university curricula, as historical categories, his need for indulgence is increased. He can only hope that he may be pardoned if he confesses to regarding what academic convention distinguishes as 'subjects,' not as independent entities, poised each in majestic isolation on its private peak, but as fluid and provisional divisions, with frontiers corresponding less to the articulations of the universe than to the exigencies of a world in which examinations last for three hours and a humane rubric requires that four, and not more than four, questions shall be attempted by candidates. It would be convenient if the question, Where is wisdom to be found? could be answered by referring the inquirer to the appropriate university department. But she appears to prefer the debatable land where titles are ambiguous and boundaries intersect; nor is her business much advanced by what in humbler spheres are known as demarcation disputes. So I hope that I shall not be thought less attached to the branch of knowledge which is my own, if I do not regard it as an appropriate object for proprietary defensiveness or patriotic fervour.

I

Since histories were first written, references to the work and wealth of mankind have found a place in them. But to distinguish between incidental allusions, which are forgotten as made, and the recognition of the significance of an aspect of life which leads to its systematic exploration, is the first canon of criticism; and to inflict upon you a history of Economic History is not my intention. If its springs are to be sought, they may be found, as far as England is concerned, in two movements in the century which gave both English economic life and English political institutions their decisive stamp. One of them, the attempt to offer a sociological explanation of the political breakdown, produced several *pièces de circonstance* and one masterpiece. But, when the stability of the edifice was assured, speculations as to its foundations fell out of fashion. While much of the best recent work in France has been prompted by curiosity as to the economic antecedents of the Revolution, the economic forces behind the English constitutional struggles continued to be almost ignored by historians till the theme was taken up in our own day by Russian scholars.

The highest landmark in the early history of English economic thought was the foundation of the Royal Society. The second influence found its motive in an attempt on the part of men closely in touch with the natural science of the day to apply an analogous technique to the investigation of contemporary economic phenomena, of which the paradox of Dutch prosperity, a pyramid balanced on its point, was the most arresting. A generation later the realisation that the quantitative methods employed, as a conscious innovation, by Graunt, Petty, King and Davenant to the study of the present could be applied with equal effect to throw light on the past, produced the work of Fleetwood, and later of Smith, Postlethwaite and Anderson, which links the Political Arithmetic of the seventeenth century to the statistical compilations of the early nineteenth. But it was an age of annalists and antiquarians, rather than of historians, and the giants of erudition, like Madox and Hearne, eschewed generalisation. The synthesis which proved, not for the last time, that the best fish are caught when poaching came neither from an historian nor an economist, but from a Professor of Moral Philosophy.

It is a truism that the central theme of *The Wealth of Nations* is historical. It is the emancipation of economic interests from the tyranny of custom, predatory class ambitions, and the obstruction of governments pursuing sinister ends in congenial darkness. The passages devoted to that vast movement, in which Smith, a good bourgeois, sees the clue to the progress of civilisation in Europe, are among the greatest attempts at philosophical history; and no one who studies his work, not in detached snippets of doctrine, but as composed by its author, will doubt that, without several generations of historical investigation, it could not have been written. His limitations are partly those of his generation, partly the penalty of any grand construction. He brings all things to one standard; finds the similarity of man's needs in different periods and climates more significant than contrasts of environment and circumstance; and, worlds apart as he is from the *naïveté* of his political popularisers, who selected their quotations to suit their interests, is not without complacency. Writing in the age before the deluge, in which it still seemed possible that the old régime might be reformed from above by men who were his friends, he is more conscious of the solidarity which rests on a rational appreciation of common interests than of unseen foundations and subterranean fires.

In the year before his death, the deluge came. When, a quarter of a century later, the waters receded, it was evident that, with a new society, a new history had been born. As always, it took its character from contemporary interests. In the study of economic development the decisive influences were three—the Revolution, Nationalism, and the progress of Capitalist industry, for which Blanqui coined the phrase that began as an epigram, continued as a platitude, and is now criticised as a fallacy. Of these England experienced the two first only at second hand. The serious achievements were those of continental scholars, of whom one, and not the least powerful, found his materials in London.

They came both from historians and from economists. In France the pioneers were the first. It was inevitable that men who were the heirs of the Revolution should inquire into the forces which had set the cataclysm in motion, and that, as they pressed their analysis, they should find the economic to be not the least important. Writers who did not accept Saint Simon's view, that the only history which matters is the history of industry, found themselves driven behind politics and the sacred formulæ of 1789 to the material foundations. Louis Blanc's propagandist *Histoire de dix ans* revealed the new influence, and the Revolution of 1848, with its doctrine of a fourth estate to be emancipated, underlined the lesson. De Tocqueville, whose *L'Ancien régime* appeared in 1855, has not usually been regarded as an economic historian; but his masterpiece is a watershed in the wild border region between economic and political history, where rivers have their source. The immense body of recent work by French and foreign scholars on the economic conditions of pre-revolutionary France, and the magnificent series of volumes in the *Collection de documents inédits sur l'histoire économique de la révolution française*, the publication of which was undertaken by the Government on the suggestion of Jaurès, are among the streams which descend from it.

The movement which in France started from the side of the historians came in Germany from men whose interests were primarily economic. In a country economically retarded and with a strong authoritarian tradition, doctrines of relativity, of successive stages of development, of an economic apprenticeship to be passed under the tutelage of the state, found a congenial climate. List, the journalist of genius who popularised the new ideas, was a propagandist who travelled light. In his treatment of English history, his favourite arsenal of arguments, he sees design where in reality there was nothing more recondite than a commonplace struggle of interests, ascribes to far-sighted statesmanship measures prompted by the necessities of an empty Exchequer, and selects as a golden example of mercantilist statecraft an episode which subsequent research has shown to be an unmitigated disaster. The book of Roscher, whose *Lectures on Political Science according to the Historical Method* appeared in 1843, was on a different plane. His materials were inadequate, and the title of his volume, like that of Knies, *Political Economy from the Historical Standpoint*, promised more than could be performed. The work of these scholars was important less for the new light which they threw on specific topics, than because they realised that the study of economic development requires a scheme and categories of its own, which do not coincide with those either of the theorist or of the political historian. Together with Hildebrand, they have the best title to be regarded as the fathers of the science as an academic discipline, with an assured status and a continuous tradition.

Judged, however, not by its immediate effect but by its influence in widening horizons and creating a ferment which would work, by action and reaction, on future generations, the most dynamic discovery of the forties was not made in a university. It was the conclusion reached by a young German journalist, in the process of revising Hegel's *Philosophy of Law*, that 'juristic relations and political forms are neither to be understood by themselves, nor explained by the general progress of the human mind, but are rooted in the material conditions of life,' and that 'the real foundations of which legal and political institutions are the superstructure are to be found in the relations into which men enter as producers.' To examine the implications of that conception of social development is a task for philosophers, who have the wings of an eagle, rather than for a pedestrian historian, and I shall not attempt it. But the significance of a pioneer is to be judged less by the number of professed followers who march under his banner than by his influence in determining the direction taken by subsequent explorers. In setting Capitalism in its place as one phase in the moving panorama of economic civilisation, with a pedigree to be investigated and a title to permanence not more assured than its predecessors, Marx opened a new chapter in historical discussion, which, two generations after his death, is still unclosed. His hints have become books by writers unconscious of plagiarism; and, if the verdict of Croce—that his effect is that of spectacles on the short-sighted—requires to be supplemented, it is, perhaps, only with the remark that there are defects of vision which are incurable by oculists. In so far as it is concerned with the economic foundations of society, serious history to-day whether Marxian or not, is inevitably post-Marxian.

For much of this ferment of ideas England supplied the text; from all of it she stood apart. In the period which the fashionable historian of his day described as that of 'the most enlightened generation of the most enlightened people that ever existed'—there were neither doubts as to social stability nor a grudge against history as an unfriendly stepmother, to set eyes scanning the economic past for clues to the economic future. The economic present was the province of a group of thinkers among whose virtues the capacity to see the characteristic achievements of their age as a strange, transitory episode was not the most conspicuous. Buckle in the fifties could describe *The Wealth of Nations* as 'probably the most important book that has ever been written'. But applause was not imitation; and, after Malthus, successors capable of developing the whole of Smith's estate had not been forthcoming. They were hardly to be expected.

Hence in England, while much of value was done in assembling materials, attempts at construction were few and feeble. Macaulay's famous third chapter, appropriately published in 1848, when its concluding pages on 'The Benefits derived by the Common People from the Progress of Civilisation' had a topical interest, was, for all its brilliance, less argument than ornament. Rogers, who produced the first volume of his *History of Agriculture and Prices* in 1866, laid all subsequent students under his debt by his great collection of data, which only now is being superseded by Sir William Beveridge and his colleagues. But, writing at a time when the institutions which supplied them had hardly yet been explored, he was stronger as an investigator than an interpreter. With a keen eye for facts, he took his doctrines second-hand from contemporary shop windows, where they had already gathered some dust, with the result that his generalisations not infrequently throw less light on the practice of earlier generations than on the prejudices of his own. The territory nearest to economic history where progress was first made was the province of the lawyers. Maine had opened in 1861 a brilliant chapter, which was continued by Vinogradoff, Maitland, and, in our own day, Professor Holdsworth. But the best work on English economic history continued down to the eighties to be done by Germans—Brentano, whose introduction to Toulmin Smith's collection of gild ordinances laid the foundations for all subsequent work on gild history, and who lived to publish three volumes on English economic development half a century later; Schanz, who first explained to English scholars the significance of the commercial politics and social crises of Tudor England; and Held, whose account of the Industrial Revolution appeared three years before Toynbee's well-known lectures and may profitably be compared with them.

Partly because the legal historians had been first in the field, partly through the example of German masters, the characteristic feature of the work of the two scholars who did most to give the subject a place in

English Universities was the strong institutional bias revealed when the first full-dress economic history of England appeared in 1882. Schmoller, who influenced both Cunningham and Ashley, had done much of his work on the mercantilist statecraft of the Prussian monarchy. He was somewhat heavily charged, it is perhaps fair to say, with the political assumptions natural to a German of his generation, and presented a picture of the part played by the state in economic progress, which, if a just corrective to a superficial individualism, would not always bear scrutiny. When his structure crumbled, with much else, laymen who knew economic history only through his interpretation of it, thought the blow irremediable. In reality, what had fallen was less his history than his theory. Against the latter a reaction had already been begun, not by theorists, but by historians.

It was a sign that interest had shifted from economic policy to economic evolution, that the significant problems were felt to lie in regions which elude the direct action of governments, and that a study which had crept into life as a *parvenu* between the elbows of economists and political historians was feeling its way towards a sociological interpretation of economic development which would find room within it for the contributions of both. The single most massive monument of the change is *Der Moderne Kapitalismus* of Werner Sombart, who took up again, on a higher plane of knowledge, the problems posed by Marx, and who emphasises his debt to him. But that impressive work is merely one peak on a continent; and, while some English reviewers of its concluding volumes sniffed nervously for heresy in the very words of its title, scholars of the most diverse opinions in half a dozen countries—Von Below, Strieder, Weber and Brentano in Germany, Sée and Hauser in France, and, a venerable name, Pirenne in Belgium, have attacked from different angles the problem of the antecedents, phases and characteristics of modern industrial civilisation which is its central theme. The nearest English analogy to the discussion is the argument of the last fifteen years on the interpretation of the economic history of the eighteenth and early nineteenth centuries, the leading parts in which have been played by Professor Clapham, the *doyen* of English economic history, whose book will be the foundation of all subsequent works on the nineteenth century, and by Mr. and Mrs. Hammond, whose brilliance conceals their scholarship from those critics—a great host—who believe that, in order to be scientific, it is sufficient to be dull. The volumes of our chairman and Mrs. Webb, of Professor Scott, Mr. Lipson, Mr. Ashton, Professor Nef and Professor Hamilton, and the recent admirable work by Mr. Wadsworth and Miss Mann, supply that debate with its indispensable background.

It would be tempting to illustrate the extension in the range of economic history by referring to the specialisms—business history, technological history, the history of the economic applications of natural science—to which, itself a specialism a generation ago, it has given birth; by comparing the works on the subject when this School was founded with the monograph literature and journals available to-day; or, most significant of all, by contrasting the economic innocence of the famous historians of last century with the permeation of recent general histories—consider only those of Halévy and Pirenne in Europe, and of Beard in America—by economic interests. But the study is still in its youth, and its greatest tasks, I am glad to say, are before it. Let me state briefly my view of the spirit in which it should approach them.

II

History, as I understand it, is concerned with the study, not of a series of past events, but of the life of society, and with the records of the past as a means to that end. Time, and the order of occurrences in time, is a clue, but no more; part of the historian's business is to substitute more significant connections for those of chronology. But time is the medium in which his data are embedded, and his relation to it is analogous to that of his fellow-workers in some other social sciences to space. He finds his materials strewn about it, or uncovers them by digging, as distant regions are ransacked for data by the anthropologist and sociologist. He finds also that those drawn from one epoch or civilisation possess, like the components of geological strata, certain common features, which distinguish them from those of periods preceding or following it, and he values these uniformities as one key to their interpretation. Since the evidence as to the character of a society derived from a single century is as misleading as that offered by a single locality, these materials, which are inaccessible to the intellectual villager who takes the fashion of his generation for the nature of mankind, are indispensable to him. They are indispensable, however, not because they relate to what is called the past, but because they are specimens cut from a continuous life of which past and present—itself the past before the word 'present' can be completed—are different aspects.

If society is to be master of its fate, reason conquer chance, and conscious direction deliver human life from the tyranny of nature and the follies of man, the first condition is a realistic grasp of the materials to be handled and the forces to be tamed. The historian serves, on his own humble plane, that not ignoble end. His object is to understand the world around him, a world whose cultural constituents and dynamic movements have taken their stamp and direction from conditions which the experience of no single life is adequate to interpret. He is pursuing that object as directly when he measures the skulls of palæolithic man, studies the financial institutions of the Roman Empire, or charts prices of wheat sold on a mediæval manor, as in investigating the antecedents of the latest economic crisis. If he visits the cellars, it is not for love of the dust, but to estimate the stability of the edifice, and because, to grasp the meaning of the cracks, he must know the quality of its foundations. In this sense, there is truth in the paradox that all history is the history of the present; and for this reason each generation must write its history for itself. That of its predecessors may be true, but its truth may not be relevant. Different answers are required because different questions are asked. Standing at a new point on the road, it finds that new ranges in the landscape come into view. It discovers that phenomena, which formerly appeared irrelevant, are a vital part of itself. It realises, in short, and sometimes realises too late, that what it supposed to be the past is in reality the present.

If, however, the business of the historian is not merely the harmless satisfaction of an antiquarian curiosity, but the study of society, he approaches that study from an angle of his own. Human societies are not the only societies; but biologists tell us that among their qualities is one which is unique. Unlike communities of ants and bees, they are subject to change, and to change which is primarily, not a biological, but a cultural, phenomenon. Hence, of necessity, they reveal their characteristics, not simultaneously, but successively. They are not static, but dynamic; time is one of their dimensions; and, if seen only in the flat, they are not seen at all. Just as an individual human being is not known, unless seen at different periods of his life and in varying social relations, so a civilisation is to be understood only by assembling the different aspects revealed in different phases of its growth. It acts in different ways at different times, and what is acting is, in spite of these differences, the same civilisation. To know it as it is, it is necessary to resist the illusion—it is not easily resisted—that it is in its essence what at one moment or another it appears to be.

When crises occur, that truism is self-evident. No one supposes that the characteristics of the peoples of England, France, and Russia are what intelligent observers supposed them to be in 1600, 1780 and 1910, or that the Europe which he knew in 1914 was the only Europe to be known. But it is equally relevant to the secular movements which alter social geology, and whose action is unseen till their effect is complete. 'This Island is blessed, sir, by Providence,' remarked Mr. Podsnap, 'to the Direct Exclusion of such Other Countries as there may happen to be. ... There is in the Englishman a combination of qualities, a modesty, an independence, a responsibility, a repose, combined with an absence of anything calculated to call a blush into the cheek of a young person, which one would seek in vain among the other Nations of the Earth.' Temporal, as well as national, frontiers produce their Philistines; and the provincialism which erects its generalisations from observations of one aspect of one type of human being in one kind of civilisation at one point in its development, without the qualifications by which judicious thinkers limit their conclusions, is a species of Podsnappery which, though obviously superficial, is not wholly extinct even among the elect. It is the rôle of the historian, by observing social behaviour in different conditions and varying environments, to determine the characteristics of different types of civilisation, to discover the forces in which change has found its dynamic, and to criticise the doctrines accepted in each epoch as self-evident truths in the light of an experience ampler than, without his assistance, any one of them can command. The rôle of the economic historian is to do so with special reference to the interests, which at the moment I need not more precisely define, concerned with the acquisition of a livelihood in a world of limited resources, the social groupings which arise from them, and the problems which they produce. It is ultimately to widen the range of observation from the experience of a single generation or society to that of mankind.

Experience does not yield instruction to simple inspection. It requires interpretation. Methodological discussions have some resemblance to those Chinese dramas the spectator of which, after listening for five hours to a succession of curtain-raisers, discovers that the performance is over at the moment when he hoped that it was about to begin; and I shall not inflict upon you a discussion of the logical problems of historiography. I will only say that the view on which interesting, if sometimes, perhaps, needlessly portentous, works have been written—the view that the subject-matter of history precludes generalisation—is not one which I share. Whether in its cruder version, which suggests that that subject-matter is a string of events, of which each is unique and all discontinuous, or in the subtler statement that the entities with which history deals—peoples, institutions, phases of civilisation—are collective wholes which can be intuitively grasped, but not analysed by reason, it seems to me to do violence to the procedure, not only of history, but of all other social sciences, and not only of science, but of ordinary human behaviour.

To say that a phenomenon—a bone found in a barrow, a political institution, an historical event—occurs in the same setting once and no more, is not to say that it is unique, but merely that it is individual. It is a platitude that identity in difference is the foundation of thought; and, so far from the fact that a phenomenon is individual precluding generalisation as to characteristics which it possesses in common with similar phenomena whose setting is different, it is precisely that fact which alone makes generalisation either possible or instructive. The generalisations of the historian, like those of the anthropologist and sociologist, take the form, it is true, not of propositions claiming universal validity, but of statements of the relations between phenomena within the framework of a specific epoch or civilisation. But, if relative to their context, which can be as large as a thinker has the capacity to make it, they are not less instructive within it. The historian need not be deterred from attempting, what in ordinary life is habitually done, the discovery of significant connections by comparison and analysis.

That is obvious when the field is limited, and the materials to be handled homogeneous in character. Whether the historian is dealing with a period, with the generation, for example, after 1815 or the critical forty years before the English Civil War, or with a problem, such as the causes which led to the precocious development of the great industry in England and have given English agriculture and rural society their distinctive stamp, light can obviously be thrown on the subject by the establishment of relations both within the region of strictly economic phenomena—monetary changes, prices, wages, rents, the growth of trade and public revenue—and, not less important, between that region as a whole and political and intellectual movements which appear at first unconnected with it. The same method is valid, if more difficult to apply, on a larger scale. Nothing, indeed, could be less appropriately described as unique and self-contained than the stages in the economic development of European countries. Nationality is a category which is applicable only to a late phase in the history of Europe, and which to certain of its most important aspects is, except with large qualifications, not applicable at all. It has, of course, its significance, which the historian must explain; but the idea that any department of economic life, except the policy of governments, can be adequately interpreted in terms of it is an illusion to be discarded. No European nation has worked out its economic destiny in isolation. All have lent and all have borrowed. The economic civilisation of each is a cosmopolitan achievement which is the creation of its neighbours hardly less than of itself.

Whatever he thought of the generalisations in which it has been attempted to formulate the characteristics of that common evolution—whether or not we accept theories such as that which suggests that large-scale enterprise has a continuous history in Europe from the later Roman Empire, in which the landmarks are Byzantium, Venice and North Italy, South Germany, and the Low Countries; or that economic development is marked by a rhythmic movement of long alternating phases of expansion and contraction; or that economic organisation has passed through recurrent stages in which mastery over the processes of economic life oscillates between the poles of collective control from below and authority exercised from above; or that European history is the record of the rise, conflicts and decline of successive classes; or that the critical accelerations and retardations in the development of different countries are the result of tidal movements launched by alterations in the price-level; or that the main impetus to social change has come from the growth and shifting of population—there is no doubt of the part played in giving a common stamp to European economic life, not only by similarities of environment, but by migration, rivalry and direct imitation. Whether, in short, he agrees, or not, with diffusionist theories of pre-history, the economic historian, who begins where it ends, while not ignoring other factors, must pay his tribute to diffusionism. In such circumstances, comparative study reveals relations of similarity and contrast without a grasp of which neither the past evolution of economic society nor its present characteristics can be understood. It is not only, of course, within the limits of Western economic civilisation that comparison is instructive. A student is not likely to make much of the sharply contrasted Industrial Revolutions now taking place in China and Russia, if unacquainted with the conditions which produced different versions of the corresponding movement in England, Germany and the United States, and retarded it in France. Nor, perhaps, will he be unaided in understanding some of the peculiarities of industrial civilisation in Europe if he reads with discrimination such a study of a pre-industrial society as is contained in the admirable book of Dr. Raymond Firth on the economic life of the Maori.

Since the sources for economic history are vast and still largely unworked, the historian must be an investigator. But research is a means, not an end, and it is less important to discover new materials than to see the meaning of old. In handling them, he must naturally learn from both the economic theorist and the sociologist. Except as a story embalmed, with other legends, in the mausoleum of text-books, the issue between theorists and historians was never a serious affair. In Germany, where methodological discussions are popular, it struck some sparks. In England, if it arose at all, it was a skirmish of camp-followers, and is now long dead. It is obvious that the historian must be interested in theory, for more than one reason. Theories have a history, sometimes drab, sometimes exciting, sometimes merely morbid. The children of the conditions which they are formulated to explain, they reveal the traits of mortality most unmistakably when, with the *naïveté* of youth, they claim to be immune from it, and overcome the contingencies of this transitory life only by acquiring sufficient sophistication to recognise and admit them. It is the pious duty of the historian, who guards the tombs of the long line of their ancestors, without forgetting to reserve a place for those of their descendants, to explain to their exponents the peculiar combinations of circumstances which made possible their birth and occasioned their demise.

Not only, however, does he watch by the cradle of theories and follow their bier, he is interested in them also for reasons less altruistic. Correctly employed, the expression 'economic theory' should include, on the analogy of other sciences, all concepts found useful in the analysis and systematisation of economic phenomena. Part of the historian's work is done with such concepts. Not all, of course, are equally serviceable to him; nor can he restrict himself to the doctrines most prominent in the canonical books of the economic scriptures, if only for the reason that it is precisely the interaction between the economic and non-economic aspects of society which, as the example of Adam Smith should be sufficient to remind us, is a central part of his theme. But, in so far as he uses concepts formulated by economists, as for some purposes he must, he must obviously seek enlightenment from those who are their masters. No one supposes that legal history can be written without a knowledge of law, or military history without some familiarity with strategy, or ecclesiastical history without an acquaintance with the organisation and doctrines of churches; no one should suppose—though many apparently do—that the political historian can dispense with an analytical study of the phenomena which fall within the province of the political scientist. It would be equally irrational to imagine that those aspects of human affairs which are the special concern of the economic historian can be handled without some tincture of the technique devised by economic theorists.

In so far as there is a divergence between his outlook and theirs, it arises less from differences of interpretation with regard to those matters with which both are equally concerned, than from the fact that the nature of his work makes it necessary for him to take account of considerations which the theorist, with his more specialised interests, may properly treat lightly. Thus, for one thing, the historian cannot ignore the part which is played in economic development by forces other than economic. Their significance can, of course, be over-emphasised. They have been over-emphasised in my judgment by some scholars who have brought to their subject the categories of political history; and it might fairly be argued—to take a very different example—that the brilliant work of Max Weber, at any rate in the essays by which it is most widely known in England, sought in the region of ideas and psychology an interpretation of movements susceptible of simpler explanations. The fact remains, however, that the civilisation of an age forms a connected whole the different elements of which interact, and that, as a consequence, economic causation does not work in a straight line which can be traced without reference to other forces which twist and divert it. The plane on which evolution takes place is determined, in short, by factors, both positive and negative—legal systems, governmental policies, scientific and cultural attainments, class organisation, and, not least, the most neglected factor in social development, the institution of war—which, if rooted in economic conditions, can hardly be described as directly economic. An account of it which ignores them is necessarily abstract and artificial.

For another thing, the historian's scale of magnitudes is different from that of the theorist, and the difference of scale throws into relief different aspects of the landscape. The geography of the explorer is not that of the surveyor, though the latter is part of it. Working, as he does, with a large map, the historian is compelled to take account of Alps and steppes which can be provisionally neglected by those who operate more intensively in a narrower field. The difference is illustrated by the familiar contrast between the degrees of emphasis laid by economic historians and economic theorists on the institutional structure. Its importance depends partly on the length of the period which is under review. The theorist, concerned with short segments of time, over which legal and political systems may be assumed to be constant, may reasonably, for his own purposes, take them for granted, as the historian normally ignores climatic and geological changes which are of vital importance to the student of pre-history. These systems, however, are historical products; they have changed in the past, and will change in the future. In so far as it assumes the existence of any one of them, the conclusions of economic theory, some of its exponents would agree, if valid in that context, are less cogent outside it. Unless purely formal, they are true *rebus sic stantibus*; with modifications in institutions and social psychology, they require to be modified. The question, it may be observed in passing, whether such modifications are possible or to be desired, the question of the permanence or merits of any particular social order, is one which the theorist who takes this view of his subject—others, of course, may be taken—properly regards, *qua* theorist, as not within his province. It is permissible to reach conclusions by assuming as a premise an existing body of institutions. It is illegitimate to argue as to the merits of the institutions by appealing to conclusions based on the assumption of their existence.

Economic historians have sometimes made too much of the institutional side of their subject; but they cannot ignore the masonry which canalises and deflects economic currents. They are concerned, not merely with the market, but with the forces behind it. They cannot investigate the rise of new forms of economic enterprise without reference to the conditions which have given enterprise its opportunity, or understand historical changes in the distribution of wealth without a study of corresponding changes in the institution of property, the class-structure of society, and the policy of states. Even were they persuaded by Professor Simkhovich that one factor in the decline of the Roman Empire was the exhaustion of the soil, it would still be necessary for them to turn to the great work of Professor Rostovtseff to study the collapse of organisation which made irreparable the effect of economic strains.

Nor, if the generalisations of historians contain a large element of contingency, are they on that account devoid of light or fruit. It is natural that the plain man who resides in all of us should regard as inevitable and immutable the economic arrangements most familiar to himself; he has always done so, and presumably always will. But, in the world as known to science, there is no such phenomenon as an 'economy' in general, any more than there is a law, religion or art which exists in independence of time and space. There are only particular economic, as there are particular legal and religious, systems. It is these particular systems which alone can be studied, because they alone exist. The individual valuations and their expression in price relationships which I understand—though I speak with diffidence—to be the special concern of the theorist, take place within a framework fixed partly by nature, partly by legal and customary arrangements, partly by the cultural and intellectual level of the society concerned. The relevance of his generalisations to any particular set of conditions can be determined only when the special features of those conditions have been investigated.

To say this is not, of course, to question their value; truths do not cease to be true because they are formal. It is merely to recall the commonplace that the tension between human wants and the limited resources available for satisfying them takes place, not in a vacuum, but in a specific cultural environment, by which the character both of the wants and of the resources is determined. If, for example, the formula that earnings correspond to marginal productivity be accepted, the question of practical importance is where the margin stands. The answer to it can be given only by a study of the objective conditions, from the law of inheritance to the organisation of industry and the system of education, which determine the accessibility of different occupations and the supply of workers competing for entrance to each. The law of diminishing utility is, doubtless, illustrated by the savage, who, having eaten one missionary, finds his appetite for a second temporarily jaded, not less than by a produce exchange in London or

New York, or by the familiar procedure of exchanging nuts for apples, which is so common a transaction of every-day economic life. In so far, however, as it is true of both, it throws a somewhat less brilliant light on the special characteristics which are distinctive of each, on the conditions which cause different societies to choose different diets, and on the forces which cause a transition to take place from one plane of economic civilisation to another.

It is these distinctive conditions and forces which are the special province of the historian, as formal analysis is that of the theorist. In practice, of course, it is necessary to employ the methods of both. A student unpractised in analysis would be as impotent to unravel the morbid monetary history of the sixteenth and seventeenth centuries as that of our own day, which compared with it, is lucid; but, unless his grasp of analytical methods were supplemented by some knowledge of the special financial and political conditions of the Europe of the Renaissance, his interpretation of that history would be more hypothetical than realistic. It would obviously be presumptuous for him to consider questions relating to the distribution of wealth in different periods and societies, without having familiarised himself with the doctrines on that subject enunciated by theorists; but his account of its peculiarities in England and France would be somewhat unsubstantial, unless he knew something of the development of land tenure, industry and taxation in the countries in question, by which, among other factors, it has, in fact, been determined. To discover grounds of contention between sciences whose procedure is so different, while much of their subject-matter is the same, requires a more than ordinary degree of megalomania or muddle-headedness. Since neither is conceivable in the children of light, the most plausible explanation of such differences as may have occurred in the past is the mediæval *suadente diabolo*—the intervention of the Prince of Intellectual Darkness.

Conceived in this manner, economic history obviously has close affinities with sociology. The sciences differ, it is true, in two important respects. The concern of the sociologist, as I understand his work, is primarily with the general. It is to produce a classification of societies and institutions, and to do so without more than a passing reference to the particular context in which historically they occur. The concern of the historian begins with the particular, though it does not end with it. His business is to systematise the turbulent world of concrete facts; and, while for that purpose he must make a large use, and should make a larger one, of hypotheses such as those formulated by the sociologist, he is more concerned than the latter in testing their applicability to specific situations. The sociologist brings the result of his researches to one plane; he is more interested in types than in the order in which they occur. To the historian change, or the absence of change, is a crucial aspect of life, and to establish a sequence, not merely of events, but of phases or stages of development is, therefore, vital to him. These, however, are differences of emphasis, not of substance; and, if the starting-point of the sociologist and the historian is different, their objective is the same. Both are engaged in the attempt to determine the characteristics of different types of civilisation, and to discover the causes which produce a transition from one to another; both use for that purpose analysis and comparison; and, if the sociologist must be something of an historian in assembling his materials, the historian must learn from the sociologist the critical use of the concepts by which alone they can be made to yield light. In reality, as a glance at the work of the most eminent of both is sufficient to show, the sciences meet in their higher ranges.

It would be presumptuous to suggest that sociologists have not exhausted the possible services of history to their subject. But I do not feel the same diffidence in expressing the view that the future of history, and, in particular, of economic history, depends on its ability to acquire a more consciously sociological outlook. The advance of historical technique during the last half-century has been impressive. But, especially in England, progress in methods of investigation has not, in my judgment, been accompanied by a corresponding progress in methods of treatment and interpretation.

For one thing, historians, with certain conspicuous exceptions, have continued to employ unanalysed concepts—nation, state, political power, property, progress, commercial supremacy, and a host of similar *clichés*—with an exasperating *naïveté*. If critical in their use of sources, they have been astonishingly uncritical of the formulæ employed to interpret the data derived from them. Such scrupulousness as to facts and casualness as to categories is as though a judge should be a master of the law of evidence, and then base his decisions on the juristic notions of the tenth century. For another thing, with certain brilliant exceptions, they have preferred burrowing to climbing. They make a darkness, and call it research, while shrinking from the light of general ideas which alone can illumine it. In the third place, the narrative form which descends from the chronicle, and which is still the commonest method of organising historical material, is not adequate to a large range of problems facing the historian to-day. It has its uses, sometimes very magnificent ones; but, as the greatest of early historians long ago discovered, it is too simple a procedure to reveal effectively the relations between different elements in a complex situation, the explanation of which is a large part of the business of economic history. In these matters the practitioners of that branch of knowledge must learn, not only from the sociologists, but from the legal historians, whom the nature of their subject-matter compelled from the start to make a large use of comparison, hypothesis and argument.

The task before them—I do not refer to subjects needing specialised research, which are inexhaustible, but to the major problems for which research supplies the data—are of a kind to make such methods indispensable. I will give only two examples. Economic history should be, of all forms of history, the least national, for economic civilisation is an international creation. But the corollaries of that truism have still to be applied. What is needed is nothing less than a complete change of emphasis. Instead of national economic histories, containing incidental references to international economic relations, we require histories which will take as their main theme a comparative treatment of movements and problems common to several different countries—comparative studies, for example, of the rise of the great industry or of agricultural development—and treat phenomena peculiar to particular nations against that larger background. Most persons—to give a second illustration—must have felt a certain sense of unreality in reading much that is described as political history. It says so much, and explains so little. But, in so far as its defects are those of conventionality and abstraction, they are not to be corrected by placing another conventional abstraction, labelled economic history, side by side with it. Having caricatured political and religious development by isolating it from its economic and social background, we must not proceed to repeat that blunder under the guise of correcting it, or ignore the effect on the economic aspects of life of changes in the world of politics and religion. The only adequate history is *l'histoire intégrale*, and the limitations of specialisms can be overcome only by a treatment which does justice at once to the economic foundations, the political superstructure and the dynamic of ideas. Such a history is, doubtless, remote. But there is no reason why savages should have all the science. It is possible to conceive economic historians and sociologists preparing the way for it by combining to treat economic and social organisation—forms of property, class structure, economic enterprise—in some modern period with the same detachment and objectivity as anthropologists bring to the investigation of similar phenomena in more primitive societies.

III

I am conscious that to many persons Economic History, as I have attempted to portray it, will appear to lack most of the qualities which give History its charm. I am not indifferent, I trust, to its literary aspects; nor am I disposed to dispute Professor Trevelyan's statement that what is significant is that men did the thing they did, not why the thing was done. At the moments when I forget that I am a teacher in a School of Economics, I confess to an unregenerate pleasure in the clang of decisive action, and in the noise which human beings make in the rare hours when they rise to it. But I do not think that a man will be less touched by the opening chapters of Michelet for having studied the economic paths which led to the precipice, or less stirred by Froude's picture of Robert Aske riding home for the cub-hunting to find his way barred by the floods and the rebels, because he knows the conditions which for a thousand years made the social problem of Europe, not the wage-earner, but the peasant. It is permissible to hope that science and art are not finally irreconcilable.

Notes

**Economica*, XIII (1933), pp. 1–21. [Tawney's later corrections have been added in some places. Ed.]

1 Inaugural lecture delivered at the London School of Economics and Political Science on 12 October 1932. The Chair was taken by the Right Hon. Lord Passfield.

2

Harrington's Interpretation of His Age (1941)*

Few political thinkers have undergone sharper vicissitudes of reputation than the author who is the subject of my present lecture. In his own day an oracle, not only to his followers, but to opponents who accepted his analysis even when shocked by his deductions from it; praised in the next century by Hume; accorded the compliment of respectful criticism by Montesquieu; cited with approval by Burke; a pioneer to whom the fathers of Republicanism in America and France the more readily acknowledged their debt because, with what seemed inspired prescience, he had foretold the independence of the first and the ascendancy of the second—'the learned and ingenious speculator' Harrington enjoyed a prestige far below that of Locke, but above that accorded by his countrymen to most other theorists who took politics as their theme.[1] Five editions of his complete works were produced in just over seventy years. He continued for a century after his death to exercise the influence which belongs to the exponent of doctrines whose practical relevance is still unexhausted.

He did not retain it. Across the great divide of the French Revolution and the smoke of the expanding industrialism of England, his Utopia of agrarian democracy was a fading mirage. Partly for that reason; partly because a treatment and terminology criticized by contemporaries as exotic struck posterity as artificial to the point of exasperation; partly because the revival of interest in the England of the Stuarts found its favourite themes in passages of the story which to Harrington had been incidents in a more general movement, he slipped from his pedestal, and passed from the ranks of the prophets to those of the eccentrics. Macaulay does not mention him. Carlyle would probably have placed him among the apostles of 'constitution-pedantries and parchments'.

Masson does justice to the Harringtonian Republicans, but touches lightly on their intellectual parent. Later scholars have redressed the balance. Sir Charles Firth pays a tribute to the light which is thrown on political history by Harrington's theory of property; Acton, Maitland, and Dr. Gooch have placed him high among the masters of political wisdom.[2] Only one of his books, however, has been reprinted since 1771, and the first good edition of it, by a Swedish scholar, is less than twenty years old. After the account of his influence outside England contained in the valuable work of Mr. Russell Smith,[3] it is needless for me to dwell on that aspect of the subject. But Harrington's originality consisted primarily in his analysis of the constitutional consequences of English economic development in the century and a half preceding the Civil War. With the fuller knowledge of that development which we now possess, we are in a better position than in the past to compare his interpretation of events with those given by his contemporaries, and to see in their proper perspective the theories of the first English thinker to find the cause of political upheaval in antecedent social change. From what sources were they derived? What light do they throw on the breakdown of his age?

It is of the nature of political thought that much of its best work is topical. It achieves immortality, if at all, not by shunning the limitations of period and place, but by making them its platform. We know that the first book of Harrington had been long on the stocks; nor need we take too literally his subsequent statement, made under examination in the Tower, that it had been completed in response to the appeal of a group in the army who had besieged the Protector with demands for a Commonwealth, and, when snubbed with the retort that neither he nor they knew what, if anything, the term meant, had turned to Harrington to provide a working model to convince him.[4] But the story, if over-dramatized, is true in spirit. The *Oceana*, the long restatement of its argument in *The Prerogative of Popular Government* and *The Art of Landgiving*, and the eighteen shorter controversial pieces, which form with them his legacy, were crowded into a space of less than four years between September 1656 and February 1660. All, including the most ambitious, were tracts for the times. Their target was the problems of 'Rome or London, not fool's paradise'; and, while their author believed that he had discovered a principle of universal validity, it was the relevance of that principle to the issues of a particular crisis which turned him temporarily from a student into a propagandist and pamphleteer. The most insistent of the questions of the day did not need to be stated. It was that which had moved Cromwell, who did not love paper constitutions, to prick up his ears when the Petition and Advice made much of the word 'settlement', and which caused Harrington himself to enumerate eight different essays in political architecture in seventeen years, with the obvious expectation of seeing several more.[5] Constantly sought, and as constantly receding, stability, finality, permanence, an end of 'disputes about Government, that is to say, about notions forms and shadows',[6] had already, when his earliest work appeared, become an obsession, and remained a hope, though an ever more forlorn one, when he published his last. The civic temper, which was one of the noblest qualities of his age, burned strongly in him. He was convinced that he had hit on a political secret of vital importance to mankind in general and to England in particular. It was with the object of persuading his fellow-countrymen to act on it that he became an author.

He approached his theme by an unfamiliar path. There are large blanks in his life as told by Wood,[7] and later, with some additional material derived from his sisters, by Toland; but the main influences which set their mark on him are plain enough from his writings. 'If God', wrote Fuller in 1648, 'should have no more mercy to us than we have charity one to other, what would become of us?'[8] We hear too little in most books on the period—the latest, and one of the best, that of Professor Allen,[9] is an exception—of the men who refused to take part in the Civil War, not through cowardice or indifference, but on grounds of principle. Like his friend, Andrew Marvell, though not quite for Marvell's reasons, Harrington was one of them. After unsuccessfully contesting a seat in the autumn of 1640, he made no attempt to enter Parliament, and declined to subscribe to the creed of any party. He met reproaches of lack of public spirit with the answer that his political detachment was among his chief qualifications for writing on politics.[10]

Hobbes had spoken scathingly of young gentlemen persuaded that they knew the meaning of liberty, because they had read in the classics of kings branded as tyrants;[11] but the taunt that Harrington was a paper-reformer, who judged the world from his study, missed the mark. His six years on the Continent had not been the conventional scamper, but the occasion of a serious study of the history and constitutions of half a dozen states, pursued in the spirit of what to-day would be described as scientific research. Made a member, on his return, of the Privy Council Extraordinary; later in constant attendance on the King during a critical two years; related to a score of different families on both sides of the struggle; with his most intimate friend an active politician, a cousin who was a member of most of the Councils of the Commonwealth and Protectorate, and a brother in the City when the City was a power—he would have suffered from an imbecility which no critic ascribes to him if his experiences had left him a political innocent. A niche in public life was not easily found by an enemy of monarchy who was a friend of the King; a Republican who denounced the Republic as, not a commonwealth, but an oligarchy; an enthusiast for toleration to whom wars of doctrine, as he had seen them in Germany, were an abomination, and the rule of the saints a contradiction in terms; an aristocrat who, while rating high the public role of an educated gentry, epitomized the pre-war politics of most of his class as a settled determination to prevent the Crown from interfering with their hunting and the lower orders with their shooting.[12] It is not surprising, perhaps, that Harrington should have been denounced as an atheist and a democrat, have been dogged by secret service men under Cromwell and imprisoned under Charles, and have suffered the confiscation of his papers under both. But the reasons which first isolated him from public affairs, and then drew him into contact with them, were not merely personal. The intellectual movement which accompanied the Revolution passed through two distinct stages. The first was repugnant to him. He was in sympathy with the second.

The zeal for regeneration, which found expression in the official affirmation of popular sovereignty at the birth of the Commonwealth, in the attacks launched by the democratic movement in the army and in London on a Parliament whose declarations were belied by its actions, in the programmes of law reform, land reform, ecclesiastical reform, political, economic, and social reconstruction that beat on the new régime for the better part of four years, was genuine, but short-lived. To those who had hailed the Republic as the dawn of a new era, the relapse into the light of common day was a cruel blow. Its effects can be felt in the descent from triumphant confidence to something like despair, which makes the later political writings of Milton—Parliament, Protector, and people tried in turn and found wanting—a study in disillusionment. But the reaction which shocked the idealists as the victory of Mammon had its positive side. Its counterpart was the growth of a new climate of thought, of which the progress of Natural Science and the recognition accorded it were the most important product, but which left its mark on the attitude to the world of men, as well as of nature.

Realism; objectivity; the appeal to experience; the conviction that expediency is a surer basis for government than natural right and interests than ideals; the attempt to discover, beneath the shifting sands of controversy, the operation of impersonal, constant, and, it might be, measurable, forces, which, to be controlled, must be understood—such were the notes of the new temper. In spite of his irreverent jest, made not without provocation, at Dr. Wilkins and his disciples, with 'their excellent faculty of magnifying a Louse and diminishing a Commonwealth';[13] in spite, also, of the fanciful form in which he cast his speculations, Harrington found in that increasingly naturalistic outlook some affinities with his own. The fragment, *The Mechanics of Nature*,[14] written during his last illness, does not deserve Toland's eulogy; but the standpoint from which he wished his work to be judged was shown by his description of it as 'political anatomy', and by his comparison of himself with Harvey.[15] His circle included half-a-dozen future members of the Royal Society, in addition to his brother. His central conception, that institutions are not accidental, or arbitrary, or susceptible of change at will, but are the necessary consequence of causes to be discovered by patient analysis, was all in the spirit of the New Learning of the day. One attempt to introduce that spirit into a field hardly yet touched by it was made by the rising school of Political Arithmeticians, with their deliberate application to economic phenomena of the quantitative methods of Natural Science. Harrington made another. 'No man', he wrote, 'can be a politician'—by which he meant a student of politics—'except he be first a historian or a traveller.'[16] The path which he chose was comparative history.

It is unfortunate for Harrington's reputation that the only one of his works easily accessible to-day should be at once the most ambitious and the least convincing. When defending his views against criticism, he could write with force and directness, while his *System of Politics delineated in short and easy Aphorisms*[17] reveals him as a master of the art of pregnant epigram. In the *Oceana* he attempted a literary masterpiece; he did not succeed. It is the most highly finished of his productions, but it is also the most laboured and artificial. Its theme is the reconstruction by a constituent assembly of the political system of 'the blessed and fortunate' island of Oceana, at a time when, after a Civil War, it had come to be governed by a single council miscalled a parliament. Of the two main divisions into which the book falls, the first—the 'Preliminaries'—is concerned with the antecedent causes of the crisis; the second, and longer, with the constitution adopted as a remedy for it. The latter shows Harrington's faults as a writer at their worst. It is remorselessly exhaustive, puts every button on every uniform, wearies the reader with digressions, harasses him with a needlessly technical terminology, and, in an effort at dramatic effect, puts much of its doctrine into the mouths of imaginary statesmen, whose speeches are meant to give life to the argument, but are sometimes of a woodenness that makes one regret that he did not find room among his characters for Colonel Pride.

Oceana is, of course, England, and much of the matter in the book is important, as revealing the author's diagnosis of the diseases of his own country. If the ballot was borrowed from Venice, the principle of rotation in office from Athens, and the devices of indirect election and of the separation of the functions of debating and voting from municipal precedents, the first was an obvious specific for the notorious English scandal of electoral corruption, the second was pointed for contemporaries by the awful example of the later days of the Long Parliament, the third and fourth were intended to allay alarms aroused by the agitation for a democratic franchise, while maintaining the principle of a popularly elected chamber. The kernel, however, of Harrington's constitutional programme is contained in articles which would not, at first sight, be expected to appear in a constitution. It consists in the famous provisions abolishing, within limits, primogeniture, requiring each owner of real property producing an income of more than £2,000 to divide it equally among his heirs, and forbidding him to purchase additional land which will raise his income above that figure, and to give or receive marriage portions exceeding £1,500.

These proposals, later slightly modified to spare existing life-interests, were regarded both by Harrington and by his critics as the keystone of his system. The debates on them in his fictitious constitutional convention are the longest and liveliest. The introductory sections of the book are planned so as to lead up to them. They are the author's chief prescription for the feverish oscillation between extremes which was the malady to be cured. But the proposals themselves are less significant than the conception behind them. The first part of the *Oceana* and the bulk of his other writings are intended to establish one general conclusion. In the former that conclusion is somewhat overshadowed by the author's stage-machinery, though even there it is sufficiently obvious to make the common description of the *Oceana* as a Utopia a misnomer for a work whose purpose is not to paint a picture of a state laid up in Heaven, but to point a moral from English history; in the latter it is plainly the dominant *motif*. It is that the revolution of his day had been determined by changes in social organization which passed unnoticed till too late; that the old régime had been destroyed neither by the errors of the ruler on whom the Tower of Siloam[18] fell, nor by the intransigence of the Parliament, but by impersonal forces too strong for both; and that political stability was not to be expected till political institutions were brought into accordance with economic realities. Forms must be adapted to social facts, not facts to forms. If a customer complains that a suit does not fit, it is absurd for the tailor to tell him that he must fit his body to it. It is equally absurd for lawyers to make an idol of a system of real property law inherited from the past, when, by a process of natural development, society has outgrown it.

Maitland[19] remarks that Harrington differed from most contemporary political theorists, including the greatest, in basing his arguments not on the nature of Man, but on the specific characteristics of particular societies of men. His preference for mere 'empiricals' to 'undeniable principles and the deductions from them' was an offence to his critics; and, given their premises, the reproach was just. The most famous political work of the century had appeared five years before his own, and Harrington's comments upon it contain his answer to the charge. Hobbes is right, he thinks, in finding the essence of the state in power, not in paper constitutions, but the analysis given in the *Leviathan* is, he argues, incomplete. Power is not an abstraction suspended in the air 'by geometry'; it rests on military force, and behind military force stands the economic system which supports it. 'An army is a beast with a great belly.'[20] The ox knoweth his master's crib; and, if the resources needed to maintain troops in the field are in the hands, not of the prince, but of his subjects, then the prince, whatever the theorists may say, must rule by consent or not at all, for, if he attempts to rule otherwise, he will discover that words are a poor answer to blows. That the task of the political scientist is not to impose on a nation a government selected from a gallery of ideal constitutions, but to determine the government which actual conditions make at once possible, and, on a long view, inevitable, is the central article of Harrington's creed. His appeal, in short, is to history, and it is his reliance on historical arguments which is the characteristic feature of his thought. He was not learned, in the sense of Selden or the great antiquarians, but he was widely read. Neither knowledge nor time permits me to examine in detail his authorities and his use of them. It is sufficient to say that he had a good first-hand knowledge of the classical literature of Greece and Rome, of the historians of Venice, Contarini, and Gianotti, and, above all, of Macchiavelli; that his picture of the consequences of the barbarian invasions was taken either from Procopius, or, more probably, from the use made of him by Grotius, in his *History of the Goths*; and that his conception of feudal society, which was important to his argument, was derived mainly from Selden, Coke, and Prynne. For information on recent and contemporary European affairs, he relied partly on his own experience, partly on the numerous works of travel and observations which appeared in his own day, such as Overbury's *Observations ... upon the State of the 17 Provinces* and the account of Turkey in Sandys's *Travailes*. He makes, it appears, several errors of fact; but he remains throughout on a realist, not to say pedestrian, plane, is unseduced by the allurements of the Book of Daniel, conducts no skirmishes with the Old Dragon, and, even when writing on the history of the Jews, contrives to keep his head.

The reader who survives his discussion of the constitution of the Sanhedrim is unlikely to reproach him with lack of sobriety.

If, however, Harrington's method is historical, his history has a purpose. With not only the English Civil War but the Thirty Years War beneath his eyes, he is convinced that in Europe as a whole, as well as in England, the world is out of joint. The key which he applies to the disorders of both—at once a generalization from experience, a principle of interpretation, and a programme of reform—is contained in his famous formula, the Balance of Dominion or Balance of Property, which, since property confers power, are, on a long view, two terms for one fact. Societies, he argues, may be classified in different ways; but, as far as their internal well-being is concerned, one division of them is fundamental. Given that they are crossed—a point which, like most of his contemporaries, he assumes as self-evident—by sharp lines of class stratification, the crucial question is the relations, particularly in respect of property, between the successive stories of the pyramid. Different property systems have different types of government as their necessary consequence. Great demesnes in the hands of a prince become the foundation of an absolute monarchy; mixed monarchy arises when the estates of the nobility overshadow those of the rest of the nation and enable them to deal on equal terms with the ruler; a wide distribution of land among the mass of the population produces the popular sovereignty properly known by the term 'Commonwealth'.[21] But the distribution of property is subject to change. There are longer or shorter periods, therefore, in which political systems and economic facts drift apart. When the Crown, for example, sheds its estates, but continues to claim the power which formerly it owed to them; or when the nobility is bought out by a rising middle class, but will not abdicate its privileges; or when the unprivileged masses lose their hold on the land, but cling, nevertheless, to rights which they can no longer enforce, the result—whether tyranny, as in the first case, or oligarchy, as in the second, or anarchy, as in the third—is an interlude of dislocation. The only possible remedy for the resulting disorders is the reconstruction of political institutions in accordance with the requirements of the changed social structure.

Such a crisis, Harrington thinks, has now overtaken both the Continent and England. The Roman world, though it crumbled from within, through the curse of *latifundia*, before shattered from without, had known how to maintain a political system in which private were subordinated to public interests, and the principle of which was 'the rule of laws not of men'.[22] The feudal societies which rose on its ruins, with the organized inequality which he calls 'the Gothic Balance', and their dispersion of sovereignty in private hands, had as their characteristic the rule of men, not of laws, in the sense that the idea of the common good was submerged beneath a welter of particular and incompatible ambitions. Their equilibrium, when they succeeded in establishing one, had been of its essence unstable. Their much-vaunted representative institutions had been, at best, a long wrestling-match between king, nobility, and people, with different victors in different countries, and, at worst, as destructive as gunpowder. They had prepared an explosion, and the explosion had at last occurred.

> What is become of the Princes ... in Germany? Blown up. Where are the Estates, or the power of the people in France? Blown up. Where is that of the people of Aragon and the rest of the Spanish kingdoms? Blown up. On the other side, where is the King of Spain's power in Holland? Blown up. Where is that of the Austrian Princes in Switz? Blown up.... Nor shall any man show a reason that will be holding in prudence why the people of Oceana have blown up their king, but that their kings did not first blow up them.[23]

For England, though a particular case of a general rule, is a highly peculiar one. Her political destiny, like that of other countries, has been determined by her social history; but her social history has flowed in a channel of its own. Partly for economic reasons; partly through the policy of a dynasty uncertain of its title, conscious that the great houses, which had brought it in, could also throw it out, and bent, therefore, on ensuring its future by the creation of a counterpoise, the successor of feudalism in England had been neither the absolutism of France nor the commercial republicanism of the Netherlands, but a society in which property in land, while remaining the basis of political power, had floated from its moorings, and had given birth, as it shifted and disintegrated, to a new type of State. Encouraged by the growth of an active land-market to turn estates into cash; stripped of their military force by the dissolution of their private armies, and of their hold on their tenants by the protection given tenant-right; overshadowed by new families founded on ecclesiastical wealth, the petty sovereigns of the past had become the courtiers, the *entrepreneurs*, or the bankrupts of the future. But, if the nobility had been the first victims of the rise of a *bourgeois* society, they were not the last. In deliberately depressing them, the monarchy exorcized one danger but created another. Haunted by the fear of feudal revolts, which remained to the end the Tudor nightmare, it had courted the middle classes in country and town, without reflecting on the possibility that its allies might one day aspire to be its masters. Now, deprived by its own action of the buttress which only a powerful aristocracy could offer it, it found itself face to face with a new force 'so high and formidable unto their princes that they [have since] looked pale' on it—the rising power of the House of Commons. As a result of the new wealth of the gentry and yeomanry, the shadow of the approaching revolution could already be discerned in the later years of Elizabeth. Her successors lacked the arts by which she had beguiled the monster, and, in attempting to arrest its encroachments, only taught it its strength. Thus the fall of the monarchy was hastened by the measures taken by the Tudors to preserve it. Its collapse was not a matter for surprise, but as natural and inevitable as the death of an individual. It was not the Civil War which had destroyed the old régime, but the dissolution of the social foundations of the old régime which had caused the Civil War.[24]

The same forces, Harrington argues, as acted then, have acted since, and are acting as he writes, with the result that whereas, under Henry VII, the nobility and clergy together may have owned three-quarters of the land of the nation, to-day some nine-tenths of it is in the hands of other classes. As a consequence, popular sovereignty is not a theory or an aspiration; it is already a reality in all but name. Under the influence of classical studies, the examples of the Netherlands and Venice, and an unshakeable assurance of the political virtues of the mass of his fellow-countrymen, he had fallen in love with the Republican ideal. Now hard facts, it seems, confirm his preferences, for they prove that a Republic is not only the best form of government, but the only form possible in the England of his day.

> The course of England into a Commonwealth is both certain and natural. The ways of nature require peace; the ways of peace require obedience to the laws; laws in England cannot be made but by parliament; parliaments in England are come to be mere popular assemblies; the laws made by popular assemblies ... must be popular laws; and the sum of popular laws must amount unto a Commonwealth.[25]

In such circumstances, the question whether there is a Restoration or not is of minor importance. What matters is not words, but facts. Though the king may return, the monarchy of the past will not return with him, for his friends will be as determined as his enemies to draw its teeth and cut its claws. The business of the statesman, therefore, is not to perpetuate civil strife by attempting the impossible task of making history run backwards. It is to accept the results of developments which he is powerless to reverse, to stabilize by legislation the social situation created by them, and to adjust the political system to the conditions which it imposes.

> That empire follows the balance of property [wrote the earliest editor of Harrington's complete works] is a noble discovery, whereof the honour belongs solely to him, as much as those of the circulation of the blood, of printing ... or of optic glasses to the several authors. It is incredible to think what gross and numberless errors were committed by all who wrote before him ... for want of understanding this plain truth, which is the foundation of all politics.[26]

The first reaction of the modern reader is apt to be less favourable. Wearied by the pertinacity with which Harrington harps on a few darling themes, he is tempted to dismiss them as the extravagances of a doctrinaire unable to escape from the charmed circle of his own paradoxes. There is something in the criticism; but phrases whose remorseless reiteration arouses suspicion ought not to prejudice the verdict on Harrington's thought. The truth is that his terminology, if not actually common form, was at any rate in the fashion.

Partly as a metaphor borrowed from business accountancy, and later encouraged by analogies suggested by science, the terms balance, over-balance, equipoise, counterpoise had become familiar categories of thought, and their employment in political discussion was already well established. Before the death of Elizabeth, Malynes—to mention no earlier economist—had applied them to trade; Overbury, in the early years of James I, to the relations of power between States; Bacon to both and to the social system as well; while, at the very moment when Harrington was writing, the necessity of a 'balance' or 'a balancing power' was the argument of Cromwell.[27] The words employed by him, therefore, to express his key-conceptions, were not the laboured formulae of a pedant, but firmly fixed in current usage. Nor was his extension of the conception to property in land and the class-relations based on it a surprising departure. A reader of Aristotle's *Politics* could hardly fail to be struck by his remarks on inequality of possessions as a cause of sedition. The part played by agrarian agitation in Roman history was a commonplace made familiar by Plutarch in his lives of the Gracchi, and by Cicero in his Orations on the subject. Raleigh had referred to the combined justice and inexpediency of an 'agrarian law'; and a speaker in the House, in defending episcopacy in May 1641, had warned his fellow-members that, if that bulwark fell, the next demand might well be 'for a *Lex Agraria*, the like equality in things temporal'.[28] Harrington, who was more interested in the victory of his ideas than in claiming paternity for them, underlined his obligation to Greek and Roman writers, and, above all, to the modern whom alone he thought worthy to be set side by side with them. Macchiavelli, 'the only politician of later ages', had left his mark on the thought both of Raleigh and of Bacon. Still a byword for unscrupulous cynicism to most of Harrington's contemporaries, to Harrington himself he was an idol. He influenced him in three ways. He confirmed, if he did not supply, Harrington's conception of society as a mechanism moving, not arbitrarily, but in obedience to laws, which it was the first duty of the political scientist not to praise, or to denounce, but to explain. He helped to supply him with spectacles through which the history of the classical world and of modern Italy could be read. Though Macchiavelli had not himself employed the phrase 'the balance of property', the idea expressed by it was, Harrington held, implicit in his thought. In insisting that any given type of state, whether principality or republic, could be stable only if it rested on the economic foundation appropriate[29] to it, he had hinted at considerations, which, when developed and systematized, became the theory of the *Oceana*.

The use made by Harrington of that theory as a key to the crisis of his own country and day is, of course, a different question. The aspects of history which it omits are too obvious to require emphasis; but, here again, to dismiss his interpretation as the freak of an isolated eccentric is to forget that, whatever the criticisms to be made on it, it was not without support in contemporary opinion. We cannot now trace the evidence for his statement that views similar to his own as to the erosion of the economic basis of the monarchy had been canvassed in governing circles under Elizabeth;[30] but it is not necessary on that account to seek, with Mr. Russell Smith, the source of his argument in events so recent, and so extraneous to the main currents of English development, as the Cromwellian settlement of Ireland and the pathetic, but futile, agitation of the Diggers in England.[31] The truth is that, if the solutions which Harrington proposed were his own, the problems which they were designed to meet had attracted the attention of thinkers for two generations before he set pen to paper.

Few rulers have acted more remorselessly than the early Tudors on the maxim that the foundations of power are economic. They had made the augmentation of the royal demesne, and the protection of the peasant cultivator, two of the keystones of the New Monarchy. By the later years of Elizabeth, the former policy was crumbling badly, and the latter, always unpopular with the larger landowners, was encountering an ever more tenacious opposition. As a result partly of the new strains encountered by both, but still more of changes in the economic environment, opinion became conscious of a shift in the balance of social forces. A discussion began which continued for the greater part of a century, and in which Harrington's work is one landmark, but no more. The decline in the position of the nobility through personal extravagance and political ineptitude; the readjustment of rents in favour of landlords as long leases fell in; the continued plunder of ecclesiastical property; the impoverishment of the Crown as royal estates melted; the rise in the income of a gentry in process of conversion to up-to-date methods of land management, and quick to seize the opportunity of rising on the ruins of ancient fortunes—such were the common themes. Bacon, Raleigh, Goodman, Selden, the Venetian Embassy in London in the instructive reports which it wrote for its Government, select for special emphasis different passages in the story, but point to identical conclusions.[32] A precocious statistician who wrote with the aid of official sources, Thomas Wilson the younger, the nephew of Elizabeth's Secretary of State, attempted to express in figures the result of the change in the distribution of wealth which, in common with them, he held to have been taking place. In a book[33] composed in 1601, when the most sensational changes were still in the future, he estimated that the aggregate income of some 16,000 families of gentry was approximately three times that of the peerage, bishops and deans and chapters, and richer yeomen combined. It is not surprising that a quarter of a century later, in 1628, it should have been said that the House of Commons could 'buy the Upper House thrice over'.[34]

To examine at length the forces which were changing the structure of English society would take us too far afield; but it may be noted that the picture drawn by political theorists and men of letters is confirmed by recent work on the economic history of the period. Behind the complexities of detail which at first confuse the eye we can discern a three-fold process of decay, growth, and stabilization, which profoundly modified the contours of the social landscape. In a period of sensational monetary depreciation, the economy of many noble landowners was an obsolete anachronism. With heavy overheads in the shape of great establishments, troops of servants and retainers, cumbrous administrative machines, their expenses steadily rise. Managing their properties on conservative lines, drawing part of their revenue from majestic, but unremunerative, franchises, with interests of a dozen different kinds scattered over a dozen different counties, they find their real incomes not less steadily diminishing. Given such conditions, a crisis is hardly to be avoided; and, in the difficult years between the accession of Elizabeth and the meeting of the Long Parliament, the number of such families which encounter one is not small. Some weather the storm, ruthlessly curtailing their expenditure and rationalizing their estate-management, amid cries of lamentation from dismissed serving-men and rack-rented tenants. Many of them are too wedded to routine, too immersed in amusements or politics, not infrequently too impoverished or easy-going, to be capable of effecting it. The game, they say to themselves, is almost up; but the world may change again, and, at worst, the old ways will last their time. So they plunge into debt, at first borrowing small sums from friends or tradesmen, then mortgaging their estates wholesale to *nouveaux riches* in the City. Ultimately, unless they retrieve their fortunes by marrying money, they sell.

They have no difficulty in finding buyers. For the new economic climate, which struck one type of landowner with paralysis, was to another a forcing-house. Professor Pirenne, in a well-known essay,[35] has argued that the capitalists of each successive era are normally recruited, not from those of the preceding one, but from individuals of humble origin, who fight their way upwards; form in time a new plutocracy; relapse, having done so, into dignified torpor, and in their turn are superseded. There are periods when somewhat the same alternation of progression and stagnation can be observed in the history of the landed classes. The three generations before Harrington wrote were one of them. The progress of internal unification; the growing population of the larger towns such as Bristol, Norwich, and, above all, London; the progressive permeation of rural districts by the decentralized industry of the day, with the result of creating deficiency areas which could be fed only from the surplus of other regions—all provided an expanding market which the business farmer could exploit. The long upward movement in prices, which hit the landed *rentier*, meant a rising income for the agricultural *entrepreneur* who managed his demesnes, not to meet domestic needs, but to produce wool and grain in bulk. The great redistributions of property by acts of authority, which were characteristic of an age when the financial system of the past was crumbling, worked in the same direction. They at once accelerated the rise of new wealth and stabilized it, when achieved.

They had taken place at intervals on an impressive scale—first with the confiscation of monastic lands yielding a net income put by Dr. Savine[36] at approximately £110,000; then with sales of Crown property at the three crises of Elizabeth's reign, realizing in all some £807,000; then with further sales to the value of nearly twice that figure, roughly a million and a half (£1,425,000), under her two successors.[37] On the precise effect of these grandiose transactions much detailed work still remains to be done, and we must speak with due reserve. Such knowledge, however, as we possess suggests that it was neither the leviathans nor the minnows, neither the owners of great estates nor the peasant cultivators, but the intermediate stratum of country gentry and their connexions, who were their principal beneficiaries. It is the latter, for example, who in the few counties for which figures have been put together, acquire between two-thirds and three-quarters of the monastic manors confiscated at the Dissolution, and who—a fact even more significant, since it shows their superior staying-power—have absorbed nine-tenths of them by the beginning of the next century.[38] It is they who appear—though here our evidence is scantier—to take much of the land off the hands of the financial syndicates employed to underwrite sales of Crown property under James I. It is they, again, who purchase some two-thirds of the estates sold by the Commissioners who handled the same business under his son.[39] The last, and not the least sensational, chapter in the story was still to come. In spite of previous alienations, the land still remaining to the Crown in 1640 was no trifle, and when, at the crisis of the Civil War, Parliament threw it on the market, the sum realized was in the region of £2,000,000.[40] The transaction was followed by the sale of the estates of the bishops and of deans and chapters; and, that, again, by the confiscation of some properties of malignants, and the forced sale of others by their owners to pay fines and taxation. Dr. Tatham[41] has shown that half the purchases of episcopal property were made by gentry in the provinces or the capital, just under a third by London tradesmen and merchants, and rather less than one-tenth by yeomen and husbandmen. No equally full analysis has been made of the buyers of Crown estates at the same period; but such sample figures as we owe to Dr. Madge[42] suggest somewhat the same story. The land settlement of 1660 was based on the principle that confiscated lands should return to their former owners, so that, in theory, the Crown and the Church recovered what they had lost. In practice the difficulties of complete restoration appear to have been almost insuperable; while, in the case of lands sold, even though sold under duress, restoration was not attempted. The general results, therefore, of the extensive redistribution of property which had taken place during the interlude of revolution were qualified, but not reversed, by the limited measure of resumption which closed it.

It was movements of that order, denounced by some as fostering the evil known as 'a parity', and applauded by others as a symptom of prosperity more widely diffused, which were the background of Harrington's thought and the premise of his proposals. Burke[43] compared him with Siéyès; but the ingenuities of his political mechanism are less significant than the analysis which impelled him to construct one; and, if later analogies are to be sought, his affinities are less with the architects of constitutions than with the thinkers who have attempted to depict their conception of the society of the future as a necessary deduction from the facts of social history. His interpretation of his age has the weakness of all theories which rely on one key. The range of his vision is not equal to its acuteness. He simplifies the springs of political action to fit his formula for manipulating them; has an unshakeable confidence in the magic of institutions; and, while propounding a scheme for a national Church, with tolerance for Dissenters, which resembles in principle that accepted in the future, habitually underestimates the dynamic power of religious conviction.

Within his own limits, however, he stands on firm ground. The modern criticism that he ignores the revolutionary effects of the expansion of trade was rarely heard in his own day. Contemporaries were aware that the sharp division between the landed and commercial classes which obtained in most parts of the Continent had no parallel in England. Accustomed to a society in which substantial landowners were not a parasitic *noblesse*, but what a French admirer[44] of their business activities applauded as *bons bourgeois*, and in which most successful business men were themselves substantial landowners, they saw nothing paradoxical in doctrines which found the clue to the transference of political power in changes in the distribution of real property intimately affecting both. In reality, Harrington's analysis found favour in quarters where his practical proposals were regarded with repugnance, for common experience appeared to confirm it. It was natural enough, no doubt, that officers floated upwards by the acquisition of Crown estates should protest against the establishment of a hereditary second chamber on the ground that 'the gentry ... now have all the lands';[45] that, in the year of anarchy which followed Cromwell's death, Harrington's proposals should have been pressed on Parliament as one port in the storm;[46] and that, after his death, his most intimate friend, Henry Neville, should have restated[47] the argument of the *Oceana* in the light of the political experience of the quarter of a century since its publication. That personalities so different in political sympathies as Sir Edward Walker, a theologian like Thorndike, and Whigs such as Algernon Sidney and Burnet[48]—to mention no others—should have agreed in endorsing the view that the political crisis of their age had social roots offers more significant evidence that men not predisposed to welcome Harrington's theories were none the less impressed by the facts which suggested them.

If, however, within a generation of his death, his main thesis was on the way to become a commonplace, it was a commonplace from which different conclusions were drawn than those which it had first been formulated to support. He had foretold that, were the monarchy restored, England would be governed, nevertheless, not by a king but by her landowners, and in substance, if not in form, that prophecy was fulfilled; but the effects of its fulfilment did not correspond with his hopes. The latest study[49] of the land-system in the two generations following 1688 has suggested an explanation which, though partial, is of a kind which would have appealed to the author of the *Oceana*.

The economic tide, which for more than a century had favoured the disintegration of great estates, now, it appears, turned and ran the other way. Hard hit by war taxation, the smaller squires and country gentry, whose advance had been the theme of earlier writers, were selling out. Large properties, which could stand the strain better, instead of dissolving, were coalescing into larger, which, once formed, were stabilized by the extension of entails and the more favourable attitude to the practice shown by the judiciary. The general tendency, Mr. Habakkuk argues, was to strengthen 'the stable and conservative elements in society' through an increase in 'the number of great proprietors and the area of land owned by them'. If that view is correct, Harrington's political ideals received their *coup de grâce* from forces of the kind once invoked as their ally. At the moment when his theory that property does rule was at once confirmed and superseded by Locke's demonstration that property ought to rule, the practical significance of both doctrines was transformed by a shift in the centre of social gravity—a shift which Harrington would have deplored, and Locke, perhaps, welcomed, but which neither could foresee.

Notes

* *Proceedings of the British Academy*, XXIV (1941), pp. 199–223.

1 Hume, Essay xvi; Montesquieu, *Esprit des Lois*, Eng. trans. (1878), i, p. 174; Burke, *Works*, v, p. 341. For Harrington's remarks on American colonies and France, see *James Harrington's Oceana*, ed. with notes by L. B. Liljegren (Lund and Heidelberg, 1924), pp. 20 and 197. All subsequent references to the *Oceana* are to this edition.

2 D. Masson, *Life of Milton*, v, pp. 481–5; C. H. Firth, *The House of Lords during the Civil War*, pp. 28–32; Acton, *Lectures on Modern History*, p. 204; F. W. Maitland, *Collected Papers*, ed. H. A. L. Fisher, i, pp. 21–2; G. P. Gooch, *English Democratic Ideas in the Seventeenth Century* (1927 ed.), pp. 241–57.

3 H. F. Russell Smith, *Harrington and his Oceana: a study of a Seventeenth Century Utopia and its influence in America* (1914).

4 'The Life of James Harrington', in *The Oceana and other works by James Harrington, with an Account of his Life*, by John Toland, 1771. Subsequent references to works by Harrington other than the *Oceana* are to this edition.

5 'Politicaster', in *Works*, p. 549.

6 Marchmont Needham in *Mercurius Politicus*, March 26–April 2, 1657, quoted by Firth, *The Last Years of the Protectorate*, i, p. 158.

7 *Athenae Oxonienses*, iii, pp. 1115–26.

8 Thomas Fuller, *A Sermon of Contentment* (1648).

9 J. W. Allen, *English Political Thought, 1603–1660*, vol. i, 1603–44 (1938).

10 'Politicaster', in *Works*, p. 549.

11 Hobbes, *Behemoth*, in Maseres, *Select Tracts relating to the Civil Wars in England*, pt. ii, p. 478.

12 *Oceana*, p. 58, and 'Valerius and Publicola' in *Works*, p. 448 (Oligarchy); *Oceana*, pp. 38, 55–6, and 'Valerius and Publicola', pp. 457–8 (wars of religion and rule of the Saints); *Oceana*, pp. 35, 117–18, and 'A Discourse showing that the Spirit of Parliaments ... is not to be trusted for a settlement', etc., in *Works*, p. 575 (the gentry).

13 'Life of James Harrington' in *Works*, p. xxi.

14 Ibid., pp. xxxviii–xl.
15 Ibid., p. 175.
16 *Oceana*, p. 13.
17 *Works*, pp. 465–82.
18 'The Art of Law-giving', in *Works*, pp. 366–7.
19 Maitland, *Collected Papers*, i, p. 22.
20 *Oceana*, p. 16.
21 *Oceana*, pp. 14–15, 32–3.
22 Ibid., pp. 12–13.
23 Ibid., pp. 47–8, 124–5.
24 'The Art of Law-giving', Book I, chap. ii, in *Works*, pp. 365–7; *Oceana*, pp. 47–50.
25 'The Art of Law-giving', Book III, Preface, in *Works*, pp. 405–6; 'A Word concerning a House of Peers', in *Works*, pp. 441–2; 'Political Aphorisms', in *Works*, p. 486.
26 'The Life of James Harrington', in *Works*, p. xv.
27 G. de Malynes, *A Treatise of the Canker of England's Commonwealth* (1600); Overbury, *Observations on his Travels* (1609), quoted by G. N. Clark, *The Seventeenth Century*, p. 136; Bacon, 'Of the true Greatness of the Kingdom of Britain', in *Works* (Bohn ed.), pp. 502 sqq., and *Essays*, xix, 'Of Empire'; Speech iv in Carlyle's *Letters and Speeches of Oliver Cromwell*. For suggestive remarks on the various applications of the conception of a 'balance', see Clark, op. cit., pp. 26–7, 135–8, 214.
28 Raleigh, 'A Discourse ... of Wars' in *Works*, ed. T. Birch, ii, pp. 65–6; E. Waller, speaking May 27, 1641, quoted by E. Bernstein, *Cromwell and Communism*, p. 54.
29 E.g. *Discorsi*, Book I, ch. iv. See *Oceana*, pp. 17–18.
30 'The Art of Law-giving', Book I, ch. ii, in *Works*, pp. 365–6, where the views in question are attributed to Sir Henry Wotton, 'which tradition is not unlike to have descended to him from the Queen's Council'.
31 Russell Smith, op. cit., pp. 26–9.
32 Bacon, 'Certain Observations upon a libel published this year 1592', in *Works* (Bohn ed.), i, p. 385; Raleigh, *Works* (ed. T. Birch), i, pp. 206–7; Goodman, *The Court of King James I* (ed. J. Brewer), i, pp. 311, 290–1, 322–3; Selden, *Table-Talk*, under 'Land'; *Cal. S.P. Ven.*, 1603–7, no. 729; 1617–19, no. 658; 1621–3, no. 603.
33 Thomas Wilson, *The State of England Anno Dom. 1600* (ed. F. J. Fisher, Camden Misc., vol. xvi, 1936).
34 *Court and Times of Charles I*, i, p. 331.
35 H. Pirenne, *Les Périodes de l'histoire sociale du capitalisme*, Brussels, 1914.
36 A. Savine, 'English Monasteries on the Eve of the Dissolution', in *Oxford Studies in Social and Legal History* (ed. by Vinogradoff), vol. i.
37 The facts as to these sales are summarized by S. J. Madge, *The Domesday of Crown Lands*, pp. 40–2, 48–60.
38 A table summarizing Savine's conclusions as to the grantees of monastic lands under Henry VIII is given by H. A. L. Fisher, *Political History of England, 1485–1547*, App. ii. Some evidence as to the tendency of monastic and Crown lands in certain counties to pass into the hands of the gentry will be found in a forthcoming article by the writer on 'Some Factors in the Rise of the Gentry, 1558–1640', in the *Econ Hist. Rev.*, vol. xi, no. 1, 1941.
39 A summary of the sale of Crown Lands under James I is contained in Lans. MSS., vol. 169, art. 51, f. 110. The Cranfield MSS., for permission to examine which I am indebted to Lord Sackville and Professor A. F. Newton, give facts as to the resale of some of the lands bought by one group of 'contractors'. Particulars of the sales between 1625 and 1634 are given in Add. MSS., 18795, ff. 2–22.
40 S. J. Madge, op. cit., p. 256, gives the figures as £1,993,952 17*s*. 0$^1/_2$*d*.
41 'The Sale of Episcopal Lands during the Civil War and Commonwealth', in *Eng. Hist. Rev.*, xxiii, pp. 91–108. Dr. Chesney, 'The Transference of Lands in England, 1640–1660' (*Trans. R.H.S.*, 4 to ser. xv, pp. 181–210), gives figures which suggest that the business world played a much larger part as buyers of sequestered properties.
42 S. J. Madge, op. cit., p. 220.
43 *Works*, v, p. 242.
44 Pierre Coste, *De l'éducation des enfants* (1695). Coste's book was a translation of Locke's

Thoughts on Education.

45 Th. Burton, *Diary*, iii, pp. 132–3.

46 'A Proposition in order to the proposing of a Commonwealth or Democracy', in *Works*, p. 586; Gooch, op. cit., pp. 255–6; Russell Smith, op. cit., pp. 85–108.

47 In his *Plato Redivivus* (1681).

48 Sir Edward Walker, Garter King at Arms, *Observations upon the Inconveniences that have attended the frequent Promotions to Titles of Honour*, etc. (1653); H. Thorndike, *Theological Works*, v, pp. 440–2, 339, 371–3; Algernon Sidney, *Discourses concerning Government* (1750 ed.), pp. 311–13; G. Burnet, *History of his own Times* (1815 ed.), i, p. 12.

49 H. J. Habakkuk, 'English Landownership 1680–1740', in *Econ. Hist. Rev.*, vol. x, no. 1, Feb. 1940.

3

The Rise of the Gentry 1558-1640, and Postscript (1941 and 1954)*[1]

The first French translator[2] of Locke's *Thoughts on Education* introduced it with the remark that foreign readers, in order to appreciate it, must remember the audience to whom it was addressed. It was composed, he explained, for the edification of an element in society to which the Continent offered no exact analogy, but which had become in the last century the dominant force in English life. To M. Coste, in 1695, the triumphant ascent of the English gentry—neither a *noblesse*, nor a bureaucracy, but mere *bons bourgeois*—seemed proof of an insular dynamic of which France, with the aid of his translation, would do well to learn the secret. His compatriots, a century-and-a-half later, hailed the effortless survival of the same class in an age which had seen *seigneurs* in flight from their castles, and even *junkers* cajoled into some semblance of concessions, as an example of social stability as eccentric as it was remarkable, and marvelled at the depth to which the tree had struck its roots. De Tocqueville in the 'forties, de Lavergne in the 'fifties, Taine in the 'sixties and 'seventies, wrote in a mood of reaction; but they had some excuse for opening their eyes.[3] In spite of the influx in the interval of Scots, Nabobs, some merchants, a few bankers, and an occasional industrialist, not less than one in every eight of the members sitting for English and Welsh seats in the last un-reformed House of Commons, and one in five of the House of Lords, belonged to families which, two centuries before, had given representatives to the House of Commons in the Long Parliament.[4] Ten English counties had been blessed in 1640 with some sixty-two leading landowners, masters of six or more manors apiece. Of those in the whole ten one-half, of those in five just under two-thirds, had descendants or kin who owned 3,000 acres or upwards in 1874.[5]

I

The political rôle of this tenacious class has not lacked its eulogists. It has itself, however, a history, which is not only political, but also economic; and the decisive period of that history is the two generations before the civil war. 'Could humanity ever attain happiness,' wrote Hume of that momentous half-century, 'the condition of the English gentry at this period might merit that appellation.' Contemporary opinion, if more conscious of the casualties of progress, would have been disposed, nevertheless, to endorse his verdict. Observers became conscious, in the later years of Elizabeth, of an alteration in the balance of social forces, and a stream of comment began which continued to swell, until, towards the close of the next century, a new equilibrium was seen to have been reached. Its theme was the changing composition, at once erosion and reconstruction, of the upper strata of the social pyramid. It was, in particular, since their preponderance was not yet axiomatic, the increase in the wealth and influence of certain intermediate groups, compared with the nobility, the Crown and the mass of small land-holders. Of those groups the most important, 'situated,' as one of its most brilliant members wrote, 'neither in the lowest grounds ... nor in the highest mountains ... but in the valleys between both,'[6] was the squirearchy and its connections.

Holding a position determined, not by legal distinctions, but by common estimation; kept few[7] and tough by the ruthlessness of the English family system, which sacrificed the individual to the institution, and, if it did not drown all the kittens but one, threw all but one into the water; pouring the martyrs of that prudent egotism, their younger sons, not only into the learned professions, but into armies, English and foreign, exploration and colonisation, and every branch of business enterprise; barred themselves by no rule as to *dérogeance* from supplementing their incomes from whatever source they pleased, yet never, as in Holland, wholly severed from their rural roots, the English gentry combined the local and popular attachments essential for a representative rôle with the aristocratic aroma of *nobiles minores*, and played each card in turn with tactful, but remorseless, realism. Satirists[8] made merry with the homely dialect, strong liquor and horse-coping of the provincial squire; but, in spite of the Slenders and Shallows, the mere bumpkins of the class, for whom the French invented a special name, were not too distressingly conspicuous. Its failures, instead of, as on the Continent, hanging round its neck and helping to sink it, discreetly disappeared with the disappearance of their incomes. Its successes supplied the materials for a new nobility. They provided more than one.

Inconsistencies were inevitable in speaking of a class freely recruited from below, in a society where the lines of social stratification were drawn, not, as in most parts of the Continent, by birth and legal privilege, but by gradations of wealth. The elasticity which such peculiarities conferred has often been applauded, but they were not favourable to precise classifications; nor was precision in demand. There were moments, it is true, when it was convenient to stand on an hereditary dignity, authentic or assumed; did not the arch-leveller of the age, free-born John himself, win one of the earliest of his famous collection of judicial scalps by refusing to plead to an indictment drawn against 'John Lilburne, yeoman'?[9] There were voices from the past which, when the crash came, hailed the fall of the monarchy as the inevitable nemesis of a general downward slide towards the abyss of social 'parity,' and reproached the professional custodians of traditional proprieties with opening to fees doors which a prudent rigour would have locked.[10] But agricultural, commercial and industrial interests were, in most parts of the country, inextricably intertwined. Mere caste had few admirers—fewer probably among the gentry militant of the early seventeenth century than among the gentry triumphant of the early eighteenth—and that note was rarely heard. Common sense endorsed the remark that 'gentility is nothing but ancient riches,'[11] adding under its breath that they need not be very ancient. Sir Thomas Smith had said that a gentleman is a man who spends his money like a gentleman.[12] Of the theorists rash enough to attempt a definition, few succeeded in improving on that wise tautology.

In spite, nevertheless, of ambiguities, the group concerned was not difficult to identify. Its members varied widely in wealth;[13] but, though ragged at its edges, it had a solid core. That core consisted of the landed proprietors, above the yeomanry, and below the peerage, together with a growing body of well-to-do farmers, sometimes tenants of their relatives, who had succeeded the humble peasants of the past as lessees of demesne farms; professional men, also rapidly increasing in number, such as the more eminent lawyers, divines, and an occasional medical practitioner; and the wealthier merchants, who, if not, as many were, themselves sons of landed families, had received a similar education, moved in the same circles, and in England, unlike France, were commonly recognised to be socially indistinguishable from them. It was this upper layer of commoners, heterogeneous, but compact, whose rapid rise in wealth and power most impressed contemporaries. Literature celebrated its triumphs. Travelled intellectuals sought to polish its crudities. Manuals[14] written for its edification laid the foundations of a flattering legend. Education, the professions, the arts, above all, architecture, reflected its influence. Nor were there wanting observers who discerned in a changing social order the herald of a new state.

Interpretations of the political breakdown of the age, of a kind which to-day would be called sociological, have commonly received short shrift from historians. The tougher breed which experienced it has some right to an opinion. It was disposed to take them seriously. Once thought has been stirred by a crisis, the attempt to pierce behind controversial externals to the hidden springs of the movement is in all periods common form. The influence in the second half of the century of doctrines which sought one of the dynamics of revolution in antecedent economic change is not, therefore, surprising. But the disturbance of the social equilibrium had excited the curiosity of a generation which could only guess at its political repercussions. Theories canvassed in the 'fifties in the Rota Club had faint fragmentary anticipations before Harrington had started on his travels, and when Neville was still a schoolboy.

The facts were plain enough. The ruin of famous families by personal extravagance and political ineptitude; the decline in the position of the yeomanry towards the turn of the century, when long leases fell in; the loss, not only of revenue, but of authority, by the monarchy, as Crown lands melted; the mounting fortunes of the residuary legatee, a gentry whose aggregate income was put even in 1600 at some three times that of peers, bishops, deans and chapters, and richer yeomen together, and who steadily gathered into their hands estates slipping from the grasp of peasant, nobility, Church and Crown alike—such movements and their consequences were visible to all. Not only a precocious economist like Thomas Wilson the younger, the nephew of Elizabeth's Secretary of State, but men of greater eminence; Bacon; Cranfield; Selden; the shifty, but not unintelligent, Goodman; those artists in crying stinking fish, the Venetian embassy in London; Coke, most amiable and most futile of secretaries of state, who begs Buckingham, of all people, to save Crown lands from the spoiler—wrote footnotes on the same theme.[15]

The man who saw deepest into the moral of it all was primarily neither a theorist nor a politician, though he had the gifts of both. He was a great man of action, perhaps the greatest of his age. The doctrine that political stability depends on the maintenance of that Balance of Property, which was later to become a term of art, was not, in essence, novel. It was implicit in the conception of society as an organism, requiring the maintenance of a due proportion between its different members, which was part of the medieval legacy. But it is one thing to repeat a formula, another to apply it. Raleigh's dialogue, composed, it seems, in 1615, just after the central crisis of James' reign, was the first attempt to state the relevance of that conception to the changing circumstances of his day, and to deduce from it the need, not for mere conservatism, but for reform. The argument with which his country gentleman confutes the noble parasite is no abstract disquisition on constitutional formalities. It is a deduction from social history. The centre of social gravity has shifted; political power is shifting with it. The Earl who could once put a thousand horse into the field cannot now put twenty-five; if the greatest lord lifts a finger, he will be locked up by the next constable. The commons to-day command most of the wealth, and all the weapons. It is they, not the heirs of the feudal past, who hold the keys of the future. It is with them; with their natural leaders, the gentry; with the House of Commons, which is their organ, that the monarchy, if it is wise, will hasten to make its peace.[16]

II

These hints of political deductions from the fact of social change must not now detain us. In considering the character of that change itself, the right point of departure is that which Raleigh suggests. To speak of the transition from a feudal to a bourgeois society is to decline upon a *cliché*. But a process difficult to epitomise in less hackneyed terms has left deep marks on the social systems of most parts of Europe. What a contemporary described in 1600 as the conversion of 'a gentry addicted to war' into 'good husbands,' who 'know as well how to improve their lands to the uttermost as the farmer or countryman,'[17] may reasonably be regarded as an insular species of the same genus.

It was a precocious species, which later, when its survival was assured, was to be the admiration of foreigners, but which for long found few imitators; nor was it accomplished without anguish. The movement passed through the three familiar stages of breakdown, reconstruction and stabilisation. If one aspect of the first phase consisted in the political and legal reforms[18] by which the Tudor State consolidated its power, another aspect was economic. Jolted sharply by the great depreciation; then squeezed by its masters to find the means for new styles in fashion and display; then pulled by expanding markets, when expedients adopted to stave off catastrophe were discovered, once systematised, to pay dividends beyond hope, agrarian society was everywhere under strain. The ability of nature to cause confusion with her silver is greatly inferior, we now know, to that of human art; and, in view of the dimensions of the movement, the lamentations provoked by it seem to-day overdone. But, in judging the effects of this most un-revolutionary of monetary revolutions, three truisms must be remembered. It broke on a world which had known within living memory something like a currency famine. The society which experienced it was crossed by lines of petrification, which make modern rigidities seem elastic. Except for brief intervals, the movement was continuous, on the Continent for some three generations, in England for nearly four. The wave of rising prices struck the dyke of customary obligations, static burdens, customary dues; rebounded; struck again; and then either broke it, or carved new channels which turned its flank.

More than one country had known a dreadful interlude, when anarchy was not remote. In most it was discovered, when the worst was over, that the land system which came out of the crisis was not that which had gone into it. The key, as usual, was finance. The items comprising the landowner's revenue change their relative importance. The value of all customary and non-commercial payments tumbles down;[19] that of the more elastic sources of income increases. Some groups can adapt themselves to the new tensions and opportunities; others cannot. The former rise; the latter sink. Examples of both are to be found in every stratum of society. There are grounds, nevertheless, for thinking that what Professor Bloch has called *la crise des fortunes seigneuriales*[20] was felt more acutely, and surmounted with greater difficulty, by the heirs of ancient wealth, with its complex and dispersed interests, and large public responsibilities, than by men of humbler position or more recent eminence. Contemporaries noted the turn of the wheel in their superb prose. 'How many noble families have there been whose memory is utterly abolished! How many flourishing houses have we seen which oblivion hath now obfuscated . . . ! Time doth diminish and consume all.'[21] But time was not the chief destroyer.

Such a family, inheriting great estates, often inherited trouble. Its standards of expenditure were those of one age, its income that of another. 'Port'—the display becoming in a great position—was a point of honour; who would wish to be thought, like Lord Dencourt, to 'live like a hog'?[22] 'What by reason,' wrote a close observer, 'of their magnificence and waste in expense, and what by reason of a desire to advance and make great their own families,'[23] the life of a considerable part of the aristocracy was apt to offer an example of what a modern economist has called 'conspicuous waste.' Other regalities might have gone; what remained, and, indeed, increased, was a regal ostentation. The overheads of the noble landowner—a great establishment, and often more than one; troops of servants and retainers; stables fit for a regiment of cavalry; endless hospitality to neighbours and national notabilities; visits to court, at once ruinous and unavoidable; litigation descending, like an heirloom, from generation to generation—had always been enormous. Now, on the top of these traditional liabilities, came the demands of a new world of luxury and fashion. With the fortunes resulting from inflation and booming trade all standards are rising. London, rapidly advancing in financial and commercial importance, with a court that under James is a lottery of unearned fortunes, exercises a stronger pull. Town houses increase in number; visits to the capital are spun out; residential quarters are developed; to the delight of dress-makers, something like a season begins to emerge. Culture has demands to which homage must be paid. New and more costly styles of building; the maintenance of a troop of needy scholars and poets; collections of pictures; here and there—an extreme case—the avenues of posturing nudities which Bacon saluted at Arundel with ironical dismay—'the resurrection of the dead!'[24]—all have their votaries. Public duties, in some cases, complete what private prodigality has begun. They yielded some pickings; but, under Elizabeth and her two successors, more than one bearer of a famous name was brought near to ruin by the crowning catastrophe of a useful career.

So towering a superstructure required broad foundations. Too often they were lacking. The wealth of some of the nobility, and especially of the older families, was not infrequently more spectacular than substantial. It was locked up in frozen assets—immobilised in sumptuous appurtenances, at once splendid and unrealisable. More important, the whole structure and organisation of their estates was often of a kind, which, once a pillar of the social system, was now obsolescent. Side by side with more lucrative possessions, their properties included majestic, but unremunerative, franchises—hundreds, boroughs, fairs and markets; a multitude of knights' fees, all honour and no profit; free-holds created in an age when falling, not rising, prices had been the great landowners' problem, and fixed rents were an insurance; hundreds of prickly copyholds, whose occupants pocketed an unearned increment while the real income of their landlord fell. What was the use, a disconsolate peer expostulated with the Queen, of pretending to relieve his necessities by the gift of a manor whose tenants were protected by law against an increase in rents, and by custom against an increase in fines?[25] That cheerless condition was to be expected in properties which Elizabeth thought suitable for presents; but it was not, unfortunately, confined to them. The administrative machine which controlled a great estate had some of the vices of a miniature State department. It was cumbrous, conservative, difficult to divert from its traditional routine to new and speculative enterprises. The very magnitude and wide dispersion of the interests concerned—property of a dozen different kinds in a dozen different counties—made drastic reconstruction a formidable business, which it needed an exceptional personality to force through. It is not surprising that inherited opulence should sometimes have lacked the initiative to launch it.

Such difficulties confronted all conservative landowners, both peers and commoners, in proportion to the magnitude of their commitments and the rigidity of their incomes. The most that can be said is that the former usually carried more sail than the latter, and found it, when the wind changed, more difficult to tack. Mere majestic inertia, however, was an expensive luxury. As the tension tightened, something had to go. What went first was an aspect of life once of the first importance, but to which justice to-day is not easily done. The words 'hospitality' or 'house-keeping,' its ordinary designation, were the description, not of a personal trait or a private habit, but of a semi-public institution, whose political dangers, once a menace to the State, were a thing of the past, but whose social significance had survived little abated. As the centre of a system of relations offering employment, succour, a humble, but recognised, niche to men helpless in isolation, the great household had performed somewhat the same rôle as was played, till yesterday, by the informal communism of the family system in China, and its break-up was attended by the same symptoms of disintegration as have followed in the Far East the shattering of ancient social *cadres* by western industrialism. The stream of lamentations voiced by popular opinion, conservative moralists, and the Government itself, all strike the same note. Their burden is that, as expenses are cut down, staffs reduced, and household economy put on a business footing, a cell of the social organism is ceasing to function. The plight of younger brothers, put off, like Orlando 'with the stalling of an ox,' or compelled—to the public advantage, but to their own exasperation—to take 'to letters or to arms,'[26] is a footnote to the same story; it is not a chance that attacks on primogeniture become more vocal at the moment when once prosperous families are feeling the pinch. The social dislocation, if exaggerated, was not a trifle; but the relief to the landowner was not proportionate to it. Since his real income, in default of other measures, continued to decline, it was, at best, only a respite.

The materials for generalisation have hardly yet been put together; but to say that many noble families—though not they alone—encountered, in the two generations before the Civil War, a financial crisis is probably not an over-statement. The fate of the conservative aristocrat was, in fact, an unhappy one. Reduced to living 'like a rich beggar, in perpetual want,'[27] he sees his influence, popularity and property all melt together. Some, like Lord Howard of Effingham and the Earl of Sussex, part with their estates to their creditors, or sell outlying portions to save the remainder. Some resort to half-obsolete claims on their tenants, with which, as a Lancashire landlord remarked, the victims comply, 'if not for love, then for fear';[28] claims resembling, in their pedantic and exasperating legality, those most criticised in the Crown, but which—so merciful is history to the victors—are commonly ignored in the case of private landowners. Some, like the Berkeleys, do both. The sixth earl,[29] for whom his admiring biographer—a lover of honorific titles—could find no more appropriate name than Lord Henry the Harmless, combined with the style and establishment of a medieval potentate the sporting tastes of a country gentleman; periodical plunges into the world of fashion in London; the maintenance of a *salon* as a concession to culture; and an heirloom in the shape of a lawsuit, which when he inherited it had already lasted a century, and which in 1609, four years before his death, he steered at last, with cries of self-congratulation, to a disastrous victory. While continuing to manage his Gloucestershire estates with a conservatism as agreeable to his tenants as it was fatal to himself, he sinks ever deeper into debt to tradesmen, to scriveners, to merchant-bankers; sells land outside the county to the value of £60,000; and ends his life in a maze of financial expedients, charged with a slightly exotic odour, as of the Seine rather than the Severn—collecting an aid from his freeholders to knight his eldest son, releasing his customary tenants from irksome obligations that had elsewhere long vanished, and raising a benevolence to pay for the ruinous results of his triumphs as a litigant. Other landowners again—Lord Compton, Lord Noel, Lord Willoughby, the Earl of Holderness—restore their fortunes by marrying City money.[30] Others, with a pull in the right quarter, plant themselves on the preposterous pension list of the Crown, angle—an odious business—for 'concealed lands,' or intrigue, with a kind of amateurish greed, for patents and monopolies.

Whether their embarrassments were increasing it is impossible to say; some debts, it is fair to remember, represented reproductive expenditure on development and improvements. But soundings, wherever taken, show much water in the hold. The correspondence of Burleigh,[31] in the last decade of Elizabeth, reads like the report of a receiver in bankruptcy to the nobility and gentry. A few years later, when, with the opening of the great boom which began in 1606, things should have been better, Cranfield, no financial leviathan, had a score of them in his books, while, to judge by stray references, Hicks the silk-man and banker—later Lord Campden—and Herriott, the goldsmith, may well have had more. Rubens, no stranger to the costly futilities of courts, still retained sufficient naïveté to lift his eyebrows at the orgy of extravagance and peculation—'business, public and private, sold cash down, over the counter'[32]—which distinguished that of James. Clarendon's[33] account of the notabilities of his day is a catalogue of splendid spendthrifts. When, in 1642, all went into the melting-pot, the debts owed to the City by Royalists alone were put, in a financial memorandum, at not less than £2,000,000.[34] Of the commercial magnates who, a few years later, scrambled for confiscated estates, not a few, as Dr. Chesney[35] has shown, were creditors entering on properties long mortgaged to them. It was discovered, not for the last time, that as a method of foreclosure war was cheaper than litigation.

III

For, if the new world had its victims, it had also its conquerors. That 'the wanton bringing up and ignorance of the nobility force the prince to advance new men that can serve, which ... subvert the noble houses to have their rooms themselves,'[36] had been noted with uneasiness in the early years of Elizabeth, when suggestions were considered for redressing the balance. Half a century later, the consequences of the movement were visible to all, and there could be no question of reversing it. 'The age was one,' writes Miss Wake in her account of Northamptonshire under James, 'which had recently seen the rise of the solid middle class of lesser landowning gentry on the ruins of the ancient aristocracy. The families were few which ... managed to survive the turbulent end of the middle ages ... Many of the knights and squires belonged to families of local and extraneous origin who had made money early in the previous century by the law, trade, or sheep-farming.'[37] That picture is true of more counties than one. The conditions which depressed some incomes inflated others; and, while one group of landowners bumped heavily along the bottom, another, which was quicker to catch the tide when it turned, was floated to fortune. The process of readjustment was complex; but two broad movements can be observed, affecting respectively the technique of land-management and the ownership of landed property.

While the crisis of depreciation was not confined to one country, the English response to it had a character of its own. Partly for economic reasons, partly owing to the political and military conditions of a frontier region, parts of Eastern Europe had met the emergency by a servile reaction which gave villeinage a new life. In East Prussia, in particular, the great estate, half farm, half fortress, swollen by the holdings of evicted peasants, and worked by its owner with the aid of *corvées*, became the dominant institution, against which the reforming monarchy, when it took the matter up—not to mention its successors—would for long struggle in vain. France had felt the same tightening of the screw, but the French escape from the *impasse*—if it was an escape—took the opposite direction. Precluded by law from evicting the *censitaires*—the customary tenants—French landowners had been thrown back on the policy of a more remorseless exaction of customary dues, of which the last desperate gamble, when the clock had almost struck, was to be denounced under the name of the feudal reaction, but which in fact, other avenues being blocked, had gone on piecemeal for centuries. In England, as elsewhere, it was necessary for landlords, if ruin was to be averted, to play to the score; but the tune called by English conditions was neither the despotism of the *Junker* nor the half-abdication of the *Seigneur*. English agriculture had as its setting a commercial, increasingly individualistic society, in process of an industrialisation that was more than merely local. Landowners learned—when they did learn—from their environment, and cured their wounds with a hair of the dog that bit them. Fixed incomes falling, and profits rising, who could question that the way of salvation was to contract interests as a *rentier*, and expand them as an entrepreneur? The experts, at any rate, felt no doubts on the subject. Business is booming. They cry with one accord, 'Go into business and prosper.'

Business methods and modernisation, the fashionable specific, have different meanings in different ages. The stage at which matters stood under the early Stuarts was that, not of crops and rotations, but of marketing, management, tenures, the arrangement of holdings, and reclamation. If modern analogies are sought, they are to be found in the sphere, not of cultivation and breeding, but of rationalising the administration of estates and improving their lay-out. The problem was, in the first place, a financial one. Certain sources of income were drying up; a substitute must be found for them. Several lines of attack were possible, but the most characteristic were four. First, customary payments dwindling, the landlord could revise the terms on which his property was held, get rid of the unprofitable copyholders when lives ran out, buy out small freeholders, and throw the land so secured into larger farms to be let on lease. Rent at this period is an ambiguous category; but leasehold rents were certainly rising—on the view of Thorold Rogers[38] six-fold in half a century, on the estimate of a contemporary[39] five-fold in rather less, on the evidence of some estate documents about three- to four-fold. Second, instead of, or in addition to, letting, he could expand his own business activities, run his home-farm, not to supply his household, but as a commercial concern, enlarge his demesnes, and enclose for the purpose of carrying more stock or increasing his output of grain. Third, if he had the means, he could invest capital in bringing new land into cultivation, clearing woodlands, breaking up waste, draining marshes. Finally, he could supplement his agricultural income by other types of enterprise, going into the timber trade, exploiting coal, iron and lead, speculating in urban ground-rents.

Naturally, none of these departures was without abundant precedents. Naturally, again, the particular policy, or combination of policies, adopted depended both on local circumstances and on individual resources. But the tendency of all was the same. In each case, whatever the particular expedient used, the emphasis of the up-to-date landowner is increasingly thrown on the business side of land-management. He relies for his income on the rents or profits derived from it.

The situation confronting the landed classes in the half-century before the Civil War resembled in miniature that of 1850–70. Not only were prices rising, but, with the progress of internal unification, the development of specialised semi-industrial areas, and the growth of urban markets, demand was expanding. The advice to put estate management on a business footing was, in such circumstances, sound; but not everyone could take it, and not all who could would. Then, as now, rationalisation might look easy on paper, but was, in fact, no simple matter. Then, as now, therefore, what appeared at first sight a mere pedestrian improvement in methods of administration set in motion, as it developed, subtle social changes. It was to be expected that men with the resources and ambition to play the part of pioneers should gain at the expense of groups, whether below them or above, less qualified by means and traditions to adapt themselves to a new climate. The well-to-do yeoman, the *kulak* of the day, might maintain, or even improve, his position; but the extension of demesne farms, the upward movement of rents and fines, and encroachments on commons, combined in parts of the country to tilt the scales against the humbler peasants. To that chapter of the story, whose local diversities still remain to be worked out, but of which the outlines are known, must be added another, of which historians have said less, but by which contemporaries were impressed. There was a struggle for survival, not only between large landowners and small, but between different categories among the former.

It was primarily a struggle between economies of different types, which corresponded more closely with regional peculiarities than with social divisions. There are plenty of gentry who stagnate or go downhill. It would be easy to find noble landowners who move with the times, and make the most of their properties; the sheep-farming of Lord Spencer; the enclosures of Lords Brudenell, Huntingdon and Saye and Sele; the coal-mines of the Earl of Northumberland and the Earl of Wemyss; above all the grandiose reconstruction carried through by the Russells, are cases in point. The smaller the part, nevertheless, played by passive property, as compared with active enterprise, the larger the opportunities of rising; and the increased rewards to be reaped by the improving landlord favoured classes still ascending the ladder compared with those already at the summit. The charms of established wealth might be represented by an Earl of Newcastle, with a rent-roll of £22,000, or an Earl of Pembroke, with the ninety-three manors, four boroughs and estates scattered over ten counties from Middlesex to Yorkshire, which gave him, at his death in 1630, the reputation of one of the richest peers in England.[40] But, when experiment and innovation were the order of the day, the cards were in other hands. They were all on the side of the enterprising country gentleman.

Professor Kosminsky has described the owners of 'small and medium-sized estates' in the thirteenth century as 'all people less intimately involved in the economic system of feudalism, and early subject to capitalist transformation.'[41] It is the representatives of much the same indeterminate middle class, with interests large enough to offer a secure base for manoeuvre, but not so large as to be top-heavy, who, three centuries later, are quickest, when the wind shifts, to trim their sails. Such a man was not tempted by great possessions into the somnolence of the *rentier*; was less loaded than most noble landowners with heavy overhead charges in the shape of great establishments; did his work for himself, instead of relying on a cumbrous machine to do it for him; owned, in short, his property, instead of being owned by it. Usually, unless one of the minority of active administrators, he was freer from public duties in his county, and more immune to the blandishments of London. The problem confronting him, if he undertook reconstruction or development, was of manageable dimensions. It demanded practical experience of farming, common sense, attention to detail, not the rarer gifts of the business strategist.

Under the pressure of an environment in motion, several types emerge. Some strike no roots; others survive and become fixed. There is the gentleman farmer, leasing land, till he makes money, without owning it, and not infrequently—since the thing is his profession—running several farms at once. There is the man who works his land as a commercial undertaking—a John Toke in Kent, buying Welsh and Scottish runts to finish on Romney marsh for the London market; a Robert Loder in Berkshire, all piety and profits; a Sir Thomas Tresham in Northamptonshire, selling everything, from rabbits supplied on contract to a poulterer in Gracechurch Street, to wool to the value of £1,000 a year, whose dual rôle as a leader of the Catholic cause in England and the most hated encloser in his much disturbed county is a point on the side of those who dismiss as a mare's nest the alleged affinities of economic and religious radicalism; a Sir John Wynn in North Wales, cattle breeder, tribal chieftain, land-grabber, scholar, and prospector for minerals unknown to science, with the vanity of a savage and the credulity of his beloved alchemists, whose dealings with his tenants were too much for his own class, and cost him his seat on the Council of Wales. There are families like the Pelhams and Twysdens, living mainly on rents, but doing on the side a useful trade in grain, hops, wool and iron in local markets and in London.[42] Each type has its own idiosyncrasies, but none is in land for its health. All watch markets closely; buy and sell in bulk; compare the costs and yields of different crops; charge the rent, when custom allows, which a farm will stand; keep careful accounts. Mr Fussell's[43] description of one of them—'before all things a business man'—is true of all.

It was agricultural capitalists of this type who were making the pace, and to whom the future belonged. Nor, if land supplied the base from which they started, were their interests confined to it. The lament that 'it is impossible for the mere country gentleman ever to grow rich or raise his house, he must have some other profession,'[44] was uttered at a moment when pessimism was pardonable, and was too pessimistic. It is true, however, that many of the class, whether of necessity or by choice, were up to the eyes in other branches of business. Naturally, they turned first to the industries native to their own districts—iron in Sussex and the Forest of Dean; tin in Cornwall; lead in Derbyshire and North Wales; coal in Nottinghamshire, Durham and Northumberland; textiles in a dozen counties. But their business connections were not merely local. The habit of investment was spreading rapidly among the upper classes, and the starry host of notabilities, who lent lustre to the Virginia and East India Companies, contributed less to its development than did the web woven by the humbler ventures of hundreds of obscure squires. Some of them, too, held shares in those much advertised undertakings. More had relations in the City, and sent their sons into business. An increasing number—for the current did not run only one way—had been in business themselves.

'See,' wrote Codben to Bright, 'how every successful trader buys an estate!'[45] The remark might have been made with equal truth under James I. The movement from trade into land had long been an old story. Each successive generation made its bow to the proprieties by affecting surprise at it. It was not so long, indeed, since a statesman, alarmed at the crumbling of the social pyramid, had proposed to shore it up, by fixing a legal maximum to the real prooerty which vulgar persons, like mere merchants, might buy.[46] Thirty years later that pose had worn thin. The Government of the first two Stuarts continued, on a more majestic scale, the Elizabethan policy of turning Crown estates into cash. So far from deprecating the acquisition of land by the business world, it threw land at its head. It was not surprising that a successful merchant, who had made his pile in trade, should prefer to the risks of commerce the decorous stability of what was regarded as a gilt-edged investment. By the middle years of James, if not, indeed, earlier, it is difficult to find a prominent London capitalist who is not also a substantial landowner; even such dubious cosmopolitans as Van Lore and Burlamachi, like Pallavicino before them, feel obliged to astonish the natives by setting up as country gentlemen. Fortunes made in law went the same way. Whether it is true or not, as was alleged, that leading barristers[47] were making, in the later years of Elizabeth, £20,000 to £30,000 a year, there was general agreement that their emoluments were not trifling. Their profession had taught them what, properly handled, land could be made to yield; naturally, they used their knowledge. Popham, who speculated heavily in Crown lands; Ellesmere, who left his son £12,000 a year; the odious, but indispensable, Coke, were all substantial landowners; the last, indeed, with his fifty odd manors, was well up in the first flight. In the 'twenties, the inroads of the London plutocracy on the home counties gave rise to complaints; and what was true of the neighbourhood of London was hardly less true of the environs of other growing cities, for example Bristol.[48] In such conditions, the social categories used to distinguish the landed and trading classes, which in France and Germany remained terms with a legal significance, lost in England any claim to precision which they may once have possessed. The landowner living on the profits and rents of commercial farming, and the merchant or banker who was also a landowner, represented, not two classes, but one. Patrician and *parvenu* both owed their ascent to causes of the same order. Judged by the source of their incomes, both were equally *bourgeois*.

IV

The advance of the classes representing a more business-like agriculture was accompanied by a second movement, which at once reflected its influence and consolidated its results. That movement was the heightened rapidity with which land was changing hands. The land-market deals in a form of capital, and, in many societies, the most important form. The article which it handles is not merely a commodity, but an instrument of social prestige and political power. It is most active, therefore, when a rise in incomes swells the surplus for investment, and when wealth, in addition to increasing, is passing into new hands. Commercial expansion, industrial progress, discovery and invention, but also financial recklessness, revolution and war, have all at different times set the wheel spinning with heightened speed. In the age of Elizabeth and her two successors, economic and political conditions combined to mobilise real property, while the hostility of the courts to entails gave both forces free play.[49] The former, apart from occasional severe depressions, acted continuously, and with increasing force, to augment the demand for it. The latter, by periodically bringing fresh blocks of land into the market, supplied recurrent opportunities for profitable speculation.

The economic causes which lent property wings need no lengthy explanation. By depreciating fixed incomes, and inflating profits, rising prices sapped the reluctance of conservative owners to sell, and heightened both the eagerness and the ability of the business classes, whether agriculturalists or merchants, to buy. The very customary arrangements—fixed freehold and copyhold rents, and, sometimes fixed fines—which, if maintained, threatened ruin, could be turned by a bold policy of innovation from a liability to an asset. Involving, as they did, the existence of a wide margin between the actual receipts from a property and its potential yield, they offered, like an old-fashioned company which has survived into a boom, a golden opportunity for a remunerative reconstruction. Given a knowledge of the ropes, manors could be refloated as easily as mills, with results as agreeable to those who got in on the ground floor, and equally unpleasant to everyone else. To the purchaser with the capital and capacity to undertake it, modernisation was as profitable as it was unpopular with his tenants. If himself a farmer, he sold his produce in a rising market. If he dealt in land as a speculation, he could count on reselling at a profit. If he bought to hold, he could feel a reasonable confidence that he would leave to his heirs an estate appreciating in value. In the event, many bought for a committee of enemies at Goldsmiths Hall. But none foresaw the war.

Our first formal accounts of the land-market seem to be subsequent to the Restoration.[50] The picture then drawn is of a stream of mortgages and sales in London, which, owing to its financial resources, had the bulk of the business, even from the remotest counties, in its hands. Before the end of the previous century, however, it had been realised that the increased volume of transactions raised some awkward problems. The later 'seventies and early 'eighties appear to have been a period of exceptional activity. There were complaints of malpractices, and legislation was passed to check them. An Act of 1585 voided fraudulent conveyances, imposed heavy penalties on the guilty parties, and required all mortgages to be entered with the clerks of recognizances, who were to keep a record, which intending purchasers could inspect on payment of a small fee.[51] The last provision appears to have remained a dead letter, but the issue raised did not die down. The unorganised condition of the market was thought to depress prices, and a patent was granted in 1611 for the establishment of a public office, which was to have as part of its business the provision of facilities for dealing in real property and the recording of transactions. Copyholds—it was an advantage to set against their inconveniences—were transferred publicly in the court of the manor, so that encumbrances on them could not be concealed. It was natural that it should be asked whether the purchaser of a freehold could not be given similar security. Registration of title, advocated and opposed on the same grounds as to-day, was being urged from the left by the 'forties and found later a place in the abortive programmes of land reform prepared during the interregnum.[52]

Long before that date, a second unpleasant symptom of the increased scale of the business had attracted general comment. Lawyers were not beloved by laymen; 'Peace and law,' wrote an indignant country gentleman, who had seen much of the tribe, 'hath beggared us all.'[53] The portentous inflation of the legal profession—the figures of men called to the bar at Gray's Inn and Lincoln's Inn rose[54] by almost two-thirds between 1591-1600 and 1631–40—was ascribed largely to the new opportunities open to the conveyancer. Nor, perhaps, is it without significance that it was in 1612, towards the end of the greatest orgy of speculation seen since the Reformation, that another body of practitioners which handled the same business, the growing trade of scriveners, applied for a charter of incorporation.[55] 'Sell not thy land; ... rather feed on bread and water than be the confusion of thy house,'[56] might be the motto of parents. Things were in the saddle and rode their sons. The earliest version of 'clogs to clogs in three generations' was applied, not to Lancashire mills, but to Lancashire land.[57] The rapid absorption by absentee aliens of estates in Northamptonshire and Nottinghamshire was noted with disfavour under James I, and much the same statement as to properties in Berkshire was made half a century later by Fuller; while nearly two-thirds of the gentry owning land in Bedfordshire in 1620 were said to have sold it and left the county by 1668. The oft-quoted remark that half the properties in conservative Staffordshire had changed hands in sixty years does not, in the light of such evidence, appear too unplausible.[58] The passing of familiar names, the break-up of patriarchal households, the unpleasantness of the *parvenus* who rose on their ruins, provided dramatists with materials for satire and moralists for sermons. If Sir Petronel Flash and Sir Giles Overreach were successful as parodies, it was that the nauseous reality was not too grossly caricatured.

Lamentations that the oaks are shedding their leaves are a piece of sentimental common form, too fashionable in all ages to throw much light on any one of them. Rising classes, like crowned heads, have always known how to grab and weep at once; nor, once in possession of the title-deeds, are they at a loss for a pedigree. In reality, the Bladesovers of England, repeatedly submerged beneath a flood of new wealth, have been refloated not less often, with undiminished buoyancy, as wealth has found a way to make novelty venerable. The statistical evidence of the dimensions of the movement has not yet been put together, nor is it often in the form most instructive to posterity. Contemporaries commonly thought in terms, not of acreage, but of manors; they spoke of a man owning manors, or selling them, much as to-day he might be said to hold, or to dispose of, large investments, in order to convey an impression, not to record precise facts. The category, needless to say, is a highly ambiguous one, embracing estates varying widely in magnitude, value and organisation. At best, it covers only one species of real property, and that not the most marketable. In the two generations before the Long Parliament such property seems, nevertheless, for what the fact is worth, to have changed hands with fair rapidity. Of 2,500 odd manors in seven counties, whose owners can be traced, just under one in three were sold once in the forty years between 1561 and 1600, and rather more than one in three between 1601 and 1640. In the case of the six hundred odd in Hertfordshire and Surrey, which felt the wash of the London whirlpool, the figure in the second period was over 40 per cent.[59]

The only continuous register of sales of smaller parcels of land, which naturally came into the market more often, seems to be that supplied by the records of the Office of Alienations.[60] The land which it handled, being subject to awkward financial obligations to the Crown, was not attractive to purchasers. But the average sales per decade described a rising curve, in rough correspondence with the movement of foreign trade, which helped to determine the surplus available for investment. In the expansion of the 'seventies and early 'eighties the figure bounded up; declined with the slump which began on the eve of the Armada; rose again with the beginning of recovery at the turn of the century; reached the highest point yet attained in the boom of 1606–16; and fell sharply with the depression of the early 'twenties. It ended at a level which, from 1630 to 1639, stood well above twice that at which it had started. It is not, perhaps, an exaggeration to say that for two generations there was an intermittent real estate boom. Naturally land values bounded up. An observer who stated in the later years of Elizabeth that they had risen tenfold[61] within living memory over-stated his case; but there was general agreement that the rise had been impressive. Not much weight can be attached to the fact that under James I some Crown land was sold at the fantastic price of forty-five[62] years purchase, for such land—it was one of its attractions—was notoriously under-rented. Twenty-eight[63] years purchase, however, was quoted in the later 'twenties as the price at which some estates were then changing hands.

This mobilisation of property, the result of commercial expansion and inflation combined, was not peculiar to England. As Professor Bloch and M. Raveau have shown, a similar reshuffling of possessions was occurring at the same time in France.[64] But in England the results of an accelerated economic tempo were heightened by adventitious causes. The state threw its weight into the scales, and permanently depressed them. Intending to buttress its own foundations, it released currents which, in the end, carried them and it away.

Periodical redistributions of land by acts of public policy, to the gain or loss now of this class, now of that, are not the astonishing departure from pre-established harmonies which they appear to their victims. In one form or another, they are a recurrent feature of European history, whose repeated appearance lends colour to the view which sees in them, not an accident, but the prelude to a new era. The decorous story of England is no exception to that rule. In the century and a half between the Reformation and Restoration, such a redistribution took place on a scale not seen since the Conquest. There were two immense confiscations, the result of revolution and civil war, and a steady alienation, under financial duress, of estates formerly used to provide a revenue for public purposes.

The opening act of the drama is not here in place. But the story which had begun with the Dissolution had not ended with it. Like taxation, the fruits of confiscation do not always rest where they first light. It is an error to suppose that, when James skipped happily on to his throne of thorns, the results of that great transaction were already ancient history. Property producing a gross income equal to about half the then yield of the customs had been cut adrift from its moorings, and added to the acreage available for acquisition by influence or enterprise. When the first fever of speculation was over, it had continued to float from hand to hand in the ordinary way of business, coming at intervals to anchor only again to resume its exciting voyages. Nor had the Crown's interest in the matter ceased with the mere act of confiscation and the sales which followed it. For one thing, though it had disposed within a decade of the greater part of the spoils, those which it retained remained substantial. For another, part of the land with which it parted had not been sold outright, but had been leased for terms of years, and ultimately returned to it. In the third place, part of that which it sold came back to it later through escheats and confiscations. Two generations later, therefore, it still owned, as a result of the Dissolution, a great mass of property, which could be leased, mortgaged or sold, and which, when the Court of Augmentations was wound up in 1554, had continued to be administered by the Augmentations office of the Exchequer. A vast deal in Chantry lands brought temporary relief to the financial embarrassments of the early years of James. His son was disposing of monastic estates within a decade of the Long Parliament.

The continued redistribution of monastic property in the century following the Reformation was as momentous, therefore, as that which accompanied it. The transference to lay hands of part of the land owned by bishops and by deans and chapters—'their wings ... well clipt of late by courtiers and noblemen, and some quite cut away'[65]—has been studied in detail only during the Interregnum, but the statements of contemporaries suggest that the scale on which it took place under Elizabeth was not inconsiderable. Nor was it only ecclesiastical property which came into the market in large blocks. Few rulers have acted more remorselessly than the early Tudors on the maxim that the foundations of political authority are economic. They had made the augmentation of the royal demesnes one of the key-stones of their policy.[66] They had enjoyed, as a consequence, not only a large revenue from land, but the extensive economic patronage which great estates conferred, and had been powerful as Kings partly because unrivalled as landowners. A shrewd foreigner remarked, as he watched in the next century the headlong plunge downhill of the Crown finances, that the Stuarts were on the way to be overshadowed in wealth by their subjects before they were overthrown by them.[67] There was some substance in the view, hinted more than once under James, that the New Monarchy was undermined by reversing for three generations the financial policy which had helped to establish it. Each of the three great crises of Elizabeth's reign carried its own block of Crown estates away; she sold in her forty-five years land to the value, in all, of some £817,000. Her two successors inherited the nemesis of living on capital, as well as of rising prices and of their own characters. They sold in thirty years nearly twice as much. In spite of half-hearted attempts to tie his hands, alienations of property under James reached about £775,000, and those of Charles I, in the first decade of his reign, over £650,000.[68] The estates remaining to the Crown, when the Long Parliament met, were still, of course, substantial; but how ruinously they had been dilapidated can be shown by a comparison. Between 1558 and 1635 Crown lands to the value of some £2,240,000 had been thrown on the market. When, in the crisis of the Civil War, the remains were swept together and put up to auction, the sum realised, it seems, was under £2,000,000.[69]

V

What, if any, were the social consequences of these portentous landslides? Did they, while changing, or reflecting a change in, the fortunes of individuals, leave unaltered the distribution of property between different groups? Or was the set of social forces such that some classes gained, while others lost? Is there truth in the suggestion of a later political theorist that 'two parts in ten of all those vast estates' of the nobility, 'by the luxury and folly of their owners, have ... been purchased by the lesser gentry and commons,' and that 'the crown-lands, that is the public patrimony, are come to make up the interest of the commons'?[70]

As to the tendency of private transactions, little can at present be said. Some great estates can be seen disintegrating, and others being formed. A comparison of the distribution at different dates of certain categories of property reveals the results. But the threads in the intricate skein leading from the first stage to the last can rarely be unravelled.[71] The dealings in monastic and Crown lands left a trail which is easier to follow. Much is still obscure; but enough is known to suggest certain provisional conclusions.

The natural starting-point, in considering the former, is the classification of grantees made, some thirty years ago, by Dr. Savine.[72] His figures suggest that the lion's share of the spoils had passed, in the first instance, to two categories of persons. The first, the peers, received the largest individual grants; the second, the gentry and their connections, the largest aggregate share. What is known of the subsequent history of the land in question suggests that the second of these groups had the greater survival value. Properties dispersed, like the acquisitions of some noble grantees, over half-a-dozen different counties, were more readily sold than smaller and more compact estates, to which their owners were bound by strong local attachments. The squirearchy was less exposed to the vicissitudes which ruined some aristocratic families; while, keen farmers and business men as many of them were, they were in a better position to reap the fruits of commercial progress and improved methods of agriculture. Hence while, as a class, they had gained most by the Dissolution, they not only succeeded in retaining their acquisitions, but continued to add to them in the course of the next century.

'As the Gibeonites,' wrote Fuller, 'though by their mouldy bread and clouted shoes pretending to a long peregrination, were but of the vicinage; so most of those gentry [*sc.*, in the later years of Henry VIII], notwithstanding their specious claims to antiquity, will be found to be ... low enough in themselves, did they not stand on the vantage ground heightened on the rubbish of the ruins of monasteries.'[73] The settlement of monastic estates into the hands of the most progressive element in rural society may be illustrated by the course of events in one small corner of the country. In Gloucestershire, Northamptonshire and Warwickshire about 317 manors, together with a mass of miscellaneous property—tithes, rectories and land in different places—appear to have changed hands at the Dissolution.[74] Of the manors, which are more easily traced than the smaller acquisitions, between 250 and 260 passed into the ownership of individuals, the remainder being obtained by bishops, deans and chapters, colleges and other corporations. The nobility had done fairly, though not immoderately, well; twenty-six[75] peers had acquired monastic property of some kind, and seventeen had secured just over forty manors. Crown officials, like Saddler and Kingston, the two largest grantees of Gloucestershire estates; big business, in the persons of Gresham, Sharington and Stump; and an ubiquitous group of professional speculators, had all got their share; while a number of smaller men picked up crumbs from the cake. The bulk of the property had gone, however, not to influential aliens, but to well-known local families. In Gloucestershire the beneficiaries had included Chamberlains, Poynzs, Thynnes, Throckmortons, Tracies, Dennises, Porters, Comptons and Botelers; in Northamptonshire Montagues, Knightleys, Kirkhams, Cecils and Fermors; in Warwickshire Knightleys, Aglionbys and Throckmortons. Precision is impossible; but it is probably not an exaggeration to say that from one-half to two-thirds of the property acquired by individuals had passed to men of this type and to humbler members of the same class. In so far as there had been competition between national notabilities and tenacious local interests, local interests had won.

Their victory became steadily more decisive in the course of the next century. Compared with the adventurers who dealt in properties that they had never seen, the local gentry were a settled population confronting mere marauders. As the revolution receded, and its first turmoil died down, their strategic advantage—the advantage of a settled base—asserted itself with ever-increasing force. Political convulsions shook down the estates of one group of absentees; financial embarrassments sapped the staying-power of another. As each over-rigged vessel went on the rocks, the patient watchers on the shore brought home fresh flotsam from the wreck. Long after the last monk had died, they were adding to their abbey lands, and, if not admitted on the ground floor, became shareholders at one remove. In Gloucestershire the estates of Cromwell, Northumberland and the Seymours drifted, some quickly, some gradually, into the hands of the Duttons, Winstons, Dorringtons and Chamberlains. The property of the Earl of Pembroke, who browsed juicier pastures elsewhere, passed, soon after its acquisition, to the Dennises and Comptons. The lands of Sir Thomas Gresham came by marriage to the Thynnes, and those of Lord Clinton and Sir Robert Tyrwitt to the Heydons; while, of the eight manors secured by Sir Anthony Kingston, more than half had passed by 1608 to other families, in particular, the Baynhams and Sandys. Sir Ralph Sadler's descendants continued to be considerable landowners in the county; but the property acquired by him from the Abbey of Winchcombe, and four of the six manors taken from the college of Westbury-on-Trim, had left them by that date, some passing to the Actons and Bridges, others to less well-known families. In Northamptonshire, of the property acquired by peers at the Dissolution, some, by the beginning of the next century, had returned to the Crown; most of it had come to Kirkhams, Hattons, Spencers, Andrews, Stanhopes, Cradocks, Griffins and Ishams. In Warwickshire, the families who gained most by later re-shuffles were the Leighs, Dilkes, Throckmortons and Spencers. The general result in these counties, in spite of the reputation of Northamptonshire as the Dukeries of the age, was that, of the forty odd manors which had gone to peers at the Reformation, those remaining to them two generations later numbered only six, while the remainder swelled the fortunes of rising middle-class families. Something between two-thirds and three-quarters of the manors secured by private persons had gone originally to the squirearchy. By the early years of the next century, the proportion in their hands was over nine-tenths. Thus the ultimate consequences of the Dissolution, if similar in kind to its immediate effects, were different in degree. In this part of England, at any rate, it did not so much endow an existing nobility, as lay the foundations of a new nobility to arise in the next century.

'It is owing,' writes Dr. Chambers in his study of Nottinghamshire, 'to the elimination of these factors, the monasteries, the copyholders, the Crown, and the Church, as rivals to the gentry, that Thoroton is enabled to place them on the pedestal of unchallenged local supremacy.'[76] The full effects of the dismemberment of Crown estates before the Civil War still remain to be worked out; but enough is known to suggest that it is not of one county alone that his statement is true. The individuals into whose hands the land in question passed fell, between 1600 and 1640, into three main categories. Part of it was acquired by the peasants on Crown estates; part, in the first instance, by syndicates of speculators, who bought land in large blocks, subdivided, and resold it; part by well-to-do landowners and business men. The Government's dealings with the first class in parts of Lancashire and Yorkshire have been described by Dr. Tupling.[77] Their social effects were not without interest; but, as a solution of the financial problem, that method of disposing of Crown property was of worse than dubious value. It involved prolonged higgling with obstinate copyholders; years of surveying, hearings before commissions, and litigation; the extraction from thousands of petty transactions of sums which, in the end, were liable to be unimpressive. What the Government wanted was to get large tracts of land taken off its hands for prompt and substantial payments. If it was to secure that result, it must clearly look elsewhere than to the cautious avidity of impecunious peasants.

These reasons caused the best market for Crown property to be found, not among the smaller cultivators, but in the classes who could afford to deal on a large scale. Many well-to-do families had been interested in particular estates long before they came to be offered for sale. Among the lessees of Crown lands in the first decade of Elizabeth, appear, side by side with humble members of the Royal Household, distinguished civil servants and statesmen, like Smith and Cecil, judges and law officers of the Crown, and leading country gentlemen.[78] Down to, and after, the beginning of the century, much of the property in question was notoriously under-rented.[79] As a consequence, a would-be purchaser could offer a figure which appeared on paper impressive, but which in fact, especially if he bought to reconstruct, was money in his pocket. In such circumstances, it was natural that prosperous landowners, who already held Crown land on lease, should welcome the prospects of acquiring the freehold. The Irish war had brought one great opportunity. The accession of James was the occasion of a second. The great deals in Crown property were financed largely on credit;[80] one leading speculator professed to have raised £80,000 in the City, and to have burned his fingers. The boom in trade, which began with the peace of 1605, meant easy money. With a debt which by Michaelmas, 1606, was over £550,000, and showed signs of mounting, fresh spoils were in the offing. As usual, it was complained that Scots got more that their fair share; but there is no sign that the higher civilisation was backward in the scramble. 'At court,' wrote a future secretary of state, shocked—not for the last time—by the magnitude of the depredations, 'every man findeth way for his own ends.'[81] Coke was not alone in thinking that the thing threatened to become a ramp.

The dimensions of the business, and the anxiety of the Government to realise without delay, prompted the adoption of a technique which, if not new in principle, was now practised on a novel scale. The traditional expedient of sale through Special Commissions brought in, between 1603 and 1614, just over £180,000. What was done, in addition, was to use the financial machinery of the City. The procedure was somewhat analogous to the underwriting of a Government loan to-day by a group of issuing houses, except that what was involved was an actual transference of property. Instead of itself dealing with prospective purchasers, the Crown disposed of land wholesale to financial syndicates, who paid cash down, retained as much as they wanted for themselves, and peddled the remainder over a period of years. One group, for example, took over in 1605–6, and again in 1611, a mass of tithes, priory lands and chantry lands; a second just over 400 Crown mills, with the land attached to them; several others different blocks of property. The 'contractors,' as they were called, included, in addition to certain guinea-pigs in the shape of courtiers and officials, the leading business magnates of the day, such as Garway and Jones, two farmers of the Customs; Hicks, the silk merchant and banker; the masters and prominent members of certain city companies; and—the man who plunged most heavily, being engaged in seven separate deals to the value of £137,055—Arthur Ingram, the controller of the Customs. The separate bargains made with these syndicates between 1605 and 1614 numbered seventeen, and the total sum thus obtained—apart from sales direct to individuals—amounted to just under half a million.[82]

The capitalists concerned bought primarily, of course, not to hold, but as a speculation, unloading partly on the subsidiary rings of middlemen, whose names also are known, partly on the public, at the best price they could get. It was complained in the House in 1614 that they made 100 per cent., and skinned purchasers alive.[83] The procedure adopted masked the personalities of the ultimate beneficiaries; but, wherever the latter can be traced, while part of the land goes in small lots to obscure peasants or craftsmen in Devonshire, the Isle of Wight and elsewhere, the bulk of it is seen passing, as would be expected, to people of substance, such as leading lawyers, country gentlemen and business men.[84] The same tendency can be traced in greater detail in the transactions of the next reign. The most imposing deals were two. In the first place, a Commission[85] was set to work, which, between 1625 and 1634, disposed of property to the value of £247,597. In the second place, with a view to settling outstanding debts and to raising a further loan, the Crown transferred to the City Corporation land valued at £349,897.[86] The City marketed it gradually during the next twelve years, using the proceeds to pay the Crown's creditors.

The purchasers concerned in the first of these transactions numbered 218, and the value of the land which can be traced £234,437. The comment of a foreigner—that most of the property went to courtiers who had secured promises for it in advance—exaggerated the part played by influence, as distinct from money; but, in emphasising that the sales of Crown land under Charles, when the financial system of the monarchy was tottering to its fall, were, to an even greater extent than under his predecessors, a deal between the Crown, big business and the richer country gentry, he put his finger on a vital point. For obvious reasons of speed and economy, the policy of the Commission was to sell in large blocks. Lots of £1,000 and upwards, accounting for four-fifths of the land sold, went to less than one-third of the purchasers. The scale of the transactions naturally narrowed the market. Five merchants got one-tenth of the total; twenty-seven peers between one-quarter and one-third; a group of a hundred and thirty-three knights, esquires and gentlemen rather more than half. The second and larger deal, in which the City was the auctioneer, differed from the first only in the fact that the business world had a larger hand in it, and the nobility a smaller, the latter acquiring about one-tenth of the land and the former one-quarter. But the bulk of it went in the same direction as before. Among the three hundred and fifty odd purchasers the squirearchy and its dependants formed the largest group, and acquired well over half the total. It is not exaggeration, in fact, to say that, apart from purchases effected through other channels, these two transactions alone had the effect that, in the course of something over fifteen years, several hundred families of country gentry added to their possessions land to the value of £350,000 to £400,000. Nor is that the whole story. Much of the property was sold as undeveloped land to men who, when the time came, would seize the chance to develop it. If an exasperated official, who put the difference in value between the two at twenty-fold,[87] over-stated his case, we know from other sources—for example, the margin between old rents and improved rents on private estates—that the difference sometimes ran into hundreds per cent. It was this margin—not merely the price at which Crown land was transferred, but the prospective increment of rack-rents, enclosure, exploitation of timber and minerals—which must be considered in estimating the gains accruing to its purchasers.

To complete the picture of property passing from the Crown to its wealthier subjects, it would be necessary, in the first place, to take account of further less obtrusive changes, which went on side by side with these grandiose deals. The process of piecemeal disintegration associated with the dubious business of 'concealed lands,' and with gifts and grants, such as the concessions of 'drowned lands' to persons willing to reclaim them, still awaits its historian. Even the famous matter of the forests made little noise till near the end, when it made too much. The *de facto* transference of possessions involved in the absorption by neighbouring landowners of the last alone would seem not to have been a trifle. 'The King loseth daily by intrusions and encroachments';

'wholly converted to the private benefits of the officers and private men'; '[private] claims do swallow up the whole forest, not allowing his Majesty the breadth of one foot'[88]—such lamentations, though uttered before the question entered politics, may sound like the voice of official pessimism; but the routine returns of encroachments contained in the records of some forest courts make them appear not unplausible. It would be necessary, in the second place, for the purpose of obtaining a comprehensive view, to compare the course of events in England with the history of those parts of the Continent where matters went a different way. Leaving these further questions, however, on one side, what significance, if any, it may be asked, is to be attached to the movement of which the dull transactions described above are specimens?

VI

Its financial consequences are obvious; they were those which led Hobbes to make his comment on the futility of attempting to support a State by endowing it with property subject to alienation.[89] The effect on the peasants of recurrent orgies of land speculation, if less conspicuous, is equally certain. In the third place, such figures as we possess suggest that the tendency of an active land-market was, on the whole, to increase the number of medium-sized properties, while diminishing that of the largest.[90] Mr. Habakkuk has shown in a striking article[91] that 'the general drift of property in the sixty years after 1690 was in favour of the large estate and the lord,' and has explained the causes of that movement. During the preceding century and a half the current, as he points out, appears to have flowed in the opposite direction, with the result that, as the number of great properties was levelled down, and that of properties of moderate size levelled up, the upper ranges of English society came to resemble less a chain of high peaks than an undulating table-land. Is it too incautious, in the fourth place, to regard as one symptom of the change in the distribution of wealth the acquisition of new dignities by members of the class which gained most from it? Of 135 peers in the House of Lords in 1642, over half had obtained their titles since 1603. They included some lawyers and merchants, but the majority of them were well-to-do country gentlemen. The creation by the Stuarts of a *parvenu* nobility, like the sale of baronetcies to knights and esquires with an income from land of £1,000 a year, if politically a blunder, showed some insight into economic realities. It owed such fiscal utility as it possessed to the existence of a social situation which such expedients could exploit.

Nor, finally, were political attitudes unaffected by the same influences. With the growth of speculative dealings in land, the depreciation of the capital value of certain categories of real property by the antiquated form of land-taxation known as the feudal incidents became doubly intolerable. The more intimately an industry—agriculture or any other—depends on the market, the more closely is it affected by the policy of Governments, and the more determined do those engaged in it become to control policy. The fact that *entrepreneur* predominated over *rentier* interests in the House of Commons, was, therefore, a point of some importance. The revolt against the regulation by authority of the internal trade in agricultural produce, like the demand for the prohibition of Irish cattle imports and a stiffer tariff on grain, was natural when farming was so thoroughly commercialised that it could be said that the fall in wool prices alone in the depression of 1621 had reduced rents by over £800,000 a year. The freezing reception given by the Long Parliament to petitions from the peasants for the redress of agrarian grievances is hardly surprising, when it is remembered that one in every two of the members returned, up to the end of 1640, for the five Midland Counties which were the disturbed area of the day, either themselves had been recently fined for depopulation or belonged to families which had been.[92] The economic reality behind the famous battle over the forests was the struggle between more extensive and more intensive methods of land utilisation, to which the increased profitableness of capitalist farming lent a new ferocity. Most of the attitudes and measures, in fact, which were to triumph at the Restoration can be seen taking shape between the death of Elizabeth and the opening of the Civil War.

To attempt an answer which went beyond these commonplaces would, perhaps, be rash. But it is not presumptuous to address the question to contemporaries; and some of them have left us in little doubt as to their opinion. Mr. Russell Smith,[93] in his interesting study of Harrington, has suggested that the thesis as to the political repercussion of changes in the distribution of landed property, which is the central doctrine of the *Oceana*, if partly inspired by a study of Roman history, derived its actuality from the English confiscations in Ireland under the Act of 1642 and the Diggers' movement in England. In reality, it was needless for Harrington to look so far afield as the first, or in spheres so humble as the second. In so far as he was in debt to previous writers, his master was Macchiavelli; but the process from which he generalised had been taking place beneath his eyes. His own relatives had been engaged in it.[94]

Had he shared the modern taste for figures, he would have found little difficulty in supporting his doctrine by some casual scraps of statistical evidence. He would have observed, for example, had he taken as a sample some 3,300 manors in ten counties, that out of 730 held by the Crown and the peerage in 1561, some 430 had left them (if new creations[95] are ignored) by 1640, while an additional 400 had been acquired by the gentry. He would have discovered that, as a consequence, the Crown, which in 1561 owned just one-tenth (9 per cent.) of the total, owned in 1640 one-fiftieth (2 per cent.); that the peers held one-eighth (12.6 per cent.) at the first date, and (ignoring new creations) one-sixteenth (6.7 per cent.) at the second; and that the share of the gentry had risen from two-thirds (67 per cent.), when the period began, to four-fifths (80 per cent.) at the end of it. His remarks on the social changes which caused the House of Commons 'to raise that head which since hath been so high and formidable unto their princes that they have looked pale upon those assemblies,' and his celebrated paradox, 'Wherefore the dissolution of this Government caused the war, not the war the dissolution of this Government,'[96] were based on his argument as to the significance of a 'balance' of property; and that argument took its point from his belief that in his own day the balance had been altered. To the sceptic who questioned its historical foundations, he would probably have replied—for he was an obstinate person—by inviting him either to submit rebutting evidence, or to agree that there was some *prima-facie* reason, at least, for supposing that, in the counties in question, the landed property of the Crown had diminished under Parthenia, Morpheus and his successor by three-quarters (76 per cent.), and that of the older nobility by approximately half (47.1 per cent.), while that of the gentry had increased by not much less than one-fifth (17.8 per cent.).[97]

In reality, however, as far as this side of his doctrines were concerned, there were few sceptics to challenge him. To regard Harrington as an isolated doctrinaire is an error. In spite of its thin dress of fancy, his work was not a Utopia, but partly a social history, partly a programme based upon it. Contemporaries who abhorred the second were not indisposed to agree with the first, for it accorded with their own experience. The political effect of the transference of property appeared as obvious to authors on the right, like Sir Edward Walker, whose book appeared three years before the *Oceana*, as to Ludlow, to that formidable blue-stocking, Mrs. Hutchinson, and to Neville, on the left.[98] If, in 1600, it could be said[99] that the richer gentry had the incomes of an Earl, and in 1628 that the House of Commons could buy the House of Lords three times over,[100] the argument advanced in some quarters in 1659 that, since the Peers, who once held two-thirds of the land, now held less than one-twelfth, the day for a House of Lords was passed, was not perhaps, surprising.[101] It overstated its case; but a case existed.

The next generation, while repudiating Harrington's conclusions, rarely disputed his premises. Dryden was not the only person to see political significance in the fact that

> The power for property allowed
> Is mischievously seated in the crowd.

Thorndike complained that 'so great a part of the gentry as have shared with the Crown in the spoils of the monasteries think it in their interest to hold up that which ... would justify their title in point of conscience'; that the result had been 'a sort of mongrel clergy of lecturers'; and that 'it is visible that the late war hath had its rise here.' Temple defended the plutocratic composition of his proposed new Council with the remark that 'authority is observed much to follow land.' Burnet wrote that the Crown had never recovered from the sales of land by James I, not merely for the reason of their effect on the revenue, but because they snapped the links which had kept the tenants of the Crown 'in a dependence' upon it; Sidney that the nobility, having sacrificed 'the command of men' to the appetite for money, retained 'neither the interest nor the estates' necessary to political leadership, and that, as a consequence, 'all things have been brought into the hands of the Crown and the commons,' with 'nothing left to cement them and to maintain their union'; an author—possibly Defoe—with the *nom-de-plume* of Richard Harley, that the 'second and less observed cause' of the troubles of his youth was 'the passage of land from its former possessors into the hands of a numerous gentry and commonalty'; Davenant that the case for a resumption, at any rate of recent grants, was overwhelming, though it would be prudent to try it, in the first place, in Ireland.[102]

The moral for Governments desirous of stability was drawn by a writer[103] who borrowed Burnet's name, and whose father—if the ordinary ascription is correct—had had much to say half a century before on the effects of the transference of land in his own county of Gloucestershire. He condemned the book of Harrington—'calculated wholly for the meridian of a Commonwealth'—but quoted its doctrines, and propounded a policy, which, but for his Republicanism, Harrington himself might have endorsed. The cause of all the trouble, he wrote, had been the reckless alienation of the estates of the Crown and nobility. Salvation was to be found by reversing the process. The Crown should by purchase gradually build up a new demesne, which should remain inalienable; and—'since a monarchy cannot subsist without a nobility'—should confine new peerages to persons with estates worth at least £6,000 a year and entailed on their heirs. Of these proposals, the first had long been impracticable, the second was superfluous.

Notes

* *Economic History Review*, XI (1941), pp. 1–38, and 2nd ser., VII (1954), pp. 91–7.

1 The omission of some references, which should have been inserted, and the incompleteness of some others, require an apology. They are due to circumstances which, since the article was written, have made it difficult to consult some of the sources used. [The reference is to the Blitz. Ed.]

2 Pierre Coste, *De l'education des enfants* (1695).

3 de Tocqueville, *L'ancien régime* (trans. by H. Reeves) pp. 15, 72, 77, 85; L. de Lavergne, *The Rural Economy of England, Scotland and Ireland* (trans. 1855), chaps. ix and x; H. Taine, *Notes sur l'Angleterre* (1872).

4 *Official Return of Members of the House of Commons* (1878).

5 The counties concerned are Herts, Beds, Bucks, Surrey, Hants, N. Riding of Yorks, Worcs, Glos, Warwick, Northants. The facts for the first seven in 1640 are taken from the lists of manors and their owners given in the V.C.H., and for the last three from Sir R. Atkyns, *The ancient and present state of Gloucestershire*; Dugdale, *Antiquities of Warwickshire*; J. Bridges, *History and Antiquities of Northamptonshire*. Those for 1874 are taken from John Bateman, *The Acreocracy of England, a list of all owners of three thousand acres and upwards ... from the Modern Domesday Book*.

6 Sir W. Raleigh, *Concerning the Causes of the Magnificency and Opulency of Cities*.

7 Thomas Wilson, *The State of England Anno Dom. 1600* (ed. F. J. Fisher, Camden Miscell., vol. xvi, 1936), p. 23, put the number of gentlemen at '16,000 or thereabouts,' plus some 500 knights. For the purposes of this article, no distinction is drawn between knights and gentry.

8 Samuel Butler, *Characters and Passages from Notebooks*, ed. A. R. Waller, and J. Earle, *Micro-Cosmographie* (1628). See G. Davies, *The Early Stuarts, 1603–1660*, pp. 264–72.

9 *The Examination and Confession of Captain Lilbourne* (B.M. E.130/33). I owe this reference to Miss P. Gregg.

10 See, for the tendency towards a 'parity,' Sir Edward Walker, *Historical Discourses upon Several Occasions* (1705), and, for the laxity of heralds, the same writer's *Observations upon the Inconveniences that have attended the frequent Promotions to Titles of Honour and Dignity since King James came to the Crown of England* (1653).

11 *Hist. MSS. Com., MSS. of the Duke of Portland*, vol. ix, p. 5.

12 *De Republica Anglorum* (ed. L. Alston, 1906), pp. 39–40, 'and, to be shorte, who can live idly and without manuall labour, and will bear the port, charge and countenance of a gentleman, he shall be ... taken for a gentleman.'

13 Th. Wilson, *op. cit.*, pp. 23–4, gives £650–£1,000 a year as the income of a gentleman in London and the home counties, and £300–£400 as the figure for the remoter provinces. He describes knights as men of £1,000–£2,000 a year, but cites some with incomes of £5,000–£7,000.

14 E.g. H. Peacham, *The Complete Gentleman*, 1622; R. Braithwaite, *The English Gentleman*, 1633.

15 Thomas Wilson, *op. cit.*, pp. 18–24; Bacon. 'Certain Observations upon a libel published this present year 1592,' in *Works* (Bohn ed.), Vol. I, p. 385; Dr. G. Goodman, *The Court of King James I*, ed. J. Brewer, Vol. I, pp. 311, 290–1, 322–3; Selden, *Table Talk*, under 'Land' (see also under 'Knight Service'); *Cal. S.P. Ven., 1603–7*, No. 729, 1617–19, No. 658, 1621–3, No. 603, 1629–32, No. 374; *Hist. MSS. Com., MSS. of the Earl of Cowper*, Vol. I, p. 129.

16 *The Works of Sir Walter Raleigh, Knt.*, ed. by Tho. Birch (1751), Vol. I, p. 9 (where the metaphor of a scales is used) and pp. 206–7.

17 Thomas Wilson, *op. cit.*, p. 18.

18 See the admirable article by Miss Helen M. Cam, 'The Decline and Fall of English Feudalism,' in *History*, vol. xxv, Dec. 1940, and *Trans. R.H S.*, N.S., vol. xx, R. R. Reid, 'The Rebellion in the North, 1569.'

19 For the fall in the value of one item, profits of Courts, see *Cottoni Posthuma* (1651 ed.), p. 180, where it is stated that on Crown estates 'the casual profits of courts never paid to the present officers their fees and expenses,' and that in 44 Eliz. the costs of collection exceeded the receipts by £8,000. For a similar condition on a private property see *Bedford MSS.*, 'Answere to my L. Treasurer's demands, and what may growe to the payment of my late lordes debts,' April 20, 1586, 'the profyttes of Courtes will not be much moare than to answer the stuerdes and officers' fees, and in some places the same will not be discharged with their profyttes.' I am indebted to Miss G. Scott Thomson for a transcript of this document.

20 M. Bloch, *Les Caractères originaux de l'histoire rurale française*.

21 *Harl. Misc.*, vol. ii, pp. 515 *sq*, 'The Mirror of Worldly Fame,' 1603, chap. iii.

22 Clarendon, *History of the Rebellion*, Vol. VI, p. 58.

23 Bacon, 'Of the True Greatness of the Kingdom of Britain,' in *Works* (Bohn ed.), Vol. I, p. 507.

24 L. Aikin, *Memoirs of Court of King James I*, p. 300.

25 *Bedford MSS*, 'Reasons to move her Mat[s] gracious consideration towards the Erle of Bedf.', February 1579. I am indebted to Miss G Scott for a transcript of this document.

26 Thomas Wilson, *op. cit.*, p. 24.

27 *Hist MSS. Com., MSS. of Duke of Portland*, vol. ix, p. 5.

28 *Chetham Misc.*, vol. iii, pp. 6–7, 'Some Instructions given by William Booth to his stewards ...'

29 John Smyth, *Lives of the Berkeleys*, Vol. II, pp. 265–417, and Smyth Papers in the Gloucester Public Library.

30 Lord Compton married the daughter of Sir John Spencer, Lord Mayor in 1594, who died worth £300,000 (some said £800,000), Goodman, *op. cit*, Vol. II, pp. 127–32; Lord Noel a daughter of Sir Baptist Hicks, mercer, *Court and Times of Charles I*, Vol. ii, p. 355; Lord Willoughby a daughter of Alderman Cockayne, 'who brought him £10,000 in money ... £1,000 a year pension out of the Exchequer, and a house very richly furnished,' *ibid*, Vol. II, p. 220; the Earl of Holderness another daughter of Cockayne, with £10,000 as portion, *Cal. S.P.D. Jas. I, 1623–5*, CLXX, 54.

31 *See Hist. MSS. Com., MSS of the Marquis of Salisbury, passim*. Some references to the indebtedness of the nobility will be found in Thomas Wilson, *A Discourse Upon Usury*, Introduction, pp. 31–42.

32 Max Roose et Ch. Ruelens, *Correspondence de Rubens et Documents Epistolaires*, Vol. V, p. 116, '... molti altri, signori e ministri ... sono sforzati a buscarsi la vita come possono, e per cio qui si vendono gli negoci publici e privati a dinari contanti.'

33 E.g. *History of the Rebellion*, Vol. I, pp. 131–6, 115–26, 131, 167, 170; Vol. III, pp. 27, 93, 95, 283.

34 *S P D Chas. I*, CCCCXCVII, No. 59, March 1642–3.

35 H. E. Chesney, 'The transference of lands in England, 1640–60,' in *Trans. R.H.S.*, 4th ser., Vol. XV, pp. 181–210.

36 *Hist. MSS. Com., MSS. of the Marquis of Salisbury*, Vol. I, pp. 162–5.

37 *The Montagu Musters Book, 1602–1623*, ed. by Joan Wake (Vol. VII of the Publications of the Northamptonshire Record Society), Introduction, pp. xiv–xv.

38 Th. Rogers, *A History of Agriculture and Prices*, Vol. V, p. 812.

39 *Harl Misc.*, III, pp. 552 *sq.*, 'The present state of England,' by Walter Carey, 1627.

40 Marg. Duchess of Newcastle, *Life of the Duke of Newcastle* (Everyman ed.), pp. 98–100; *Abstract of Wilts Inquis. p/m.*, pp. 97–101; Clarendon, *History of the Rebellion*, Vol. I, pp. 120–6.

41 E. A. Kosminsky, 'Services and Money Rents in the Thirteenth Century,' in *Econ. Hist Rev.*, Vol. V, No. 2, April, 1935.

42 *The Account-book of a Kentish Estate, 1616–1704*, ed. by Eleanor C. Lodge (1927); *Robert Loder's Farm-Accounts*, ed. G. E. Fussell (Camden Society); Add. MSS., 39836, and *Hist MSS Com, Report on MSS in Various Collections*, Vol. III, 1904 (Tresham papers); Wynn Papers in Nat. Library of Wales, Aberystwyth, and published *Calendar of Wynn Papers*;

Add. MSS., 33142 (agricultural accounts of the Pelhams) and 33154 (accounts relating to iron); Add. MSS., 34167–77 (Twysden papers).

43 *Robert Loder's Farm-Accounts*, Introduction.

44 *A Royalist's Note-book, the Commonplace Book of Sir John Oglander of Nunwell, 1622–52*, ed. Francis Bamford, p. 75.

45 Quoted by O. F. Christie, *The Transition to Democracy*, pp. 147–8.

46 *Hist. MSS. Com., MSS. of the Marquis of Salisbury*, Vol. I, pp. 162–3, 'Considerations delivered to the Parliament, 1559.' See for earlier complaints King Edward VI's *Remains*, 'Discourse Concerning the Reformation of many Abuses,' and F. J. Fisher, 'Commercial Trends and Policy in Sixteenth-Century England,' in *Econ. Hist. Rev.*, Vol. X, No. 2, p. 110.

47 Thomas Wilson, *op cit* , p. 25.

48 *S.P.D., Jas.I*, XXII, No. 63, contains complaints of the purchase of Suffolk manors by Londoners. For Bristol see *S.P.D. Chas I*, XXXV, No. 43, Sept. 8, 1626, and W. B. Willcox, *Gloucestershire 1590–1640*, p. 105.

49 The attitude of the Courts is well summarised in Mr. H. J. Habakkuk's article, 'English Landownership 1680–1740,' in *Econ. Hist. Rev.*, Vol. X. No. 1, Feb. 1940.

50 *Harl. Misc.*, VII, pp. 488–93, 'Reasons and Proposals for a Registry ... of all Deeds and Incumbrances of Real Estate,' etc., by Nicholas Philpott, 1671; *ibid*, pp. 493–501, 'A Treatise concerning Registers ... of Estates, Bonds, Bills, etc., with Reasons against such Registers,' by William Pierrepoint.

51 27 Eliz. Cap. IV. An earlier Act requiring the enrolment of sales of land had been passed in 1536. For an example of enrolments under it in one county, see Somerset Record Society, Vol. LI, 'Somerset Enrolled Deeds,' by Sophia W. B. Harbin.

52 *Harl. Misc.*, VI, p. 72, 'A word for the Army and two words for the Kingdom,' by Hugh Peters, 1647; *ibid.*, VII, pp. 25–35, 'A Rod for the Lawyers,' by William Cole, 1659.

53 *A Royalist's Note-Book*, etc., p. 14. An earlier complaint on the same subject is contained in Th. Wilson, *op. cit.*, pp. 24–5.

54 For Gray's Inn see Harl. MSS., 1912, no. 16, f. 207b, and for Lincoln's Inn *Records of Lincoln's Inn*, 'The Black Books,' Vol. II.

55 *Cal. S.P.D., Chas. I*, CXCIV, p. 87, June 20, 1631.

56 *A Royalist's Note-book*, p. 212.

57 *The Dr. Farmer Chetham MSS* (Chetham Society, 1873) pp. 122–3.

58 *Hist MSS Com., MSS of Duke of Buccleuch*, Vol. III, p. 182 (Northants); J. D. Chambers, *Nottinghamshire in the Eighteenth Century*, pp. 6–7; Thomas Fuller, *The History of the Worthies of England* (1840 ed.), Vol. I, p. 140; *Harl. Soc. Pub* , Vol. XIX, 1884, pp. 206–8 (Beds); Sir Simon Degge in Erdswick's *Survey of Staffordshire*.

59 The counties concerned are Surrey, Herts, Beds, Bucks, Hants, Worcs and N. Riding of Yorks. The figures, which I owe to the kindness of Mr. F. J. Fisher, are taken from the lists of manors and their owners given in the V.C.H. They exclude transfers of leases, and transfers due to marriage, gift, inheritance, forfeiture, or other non-commercial transactions.

60 Excheq. Accounts, Alienations Office, *Entries of Licenses and Pardons for Alienations*.

61 Cotton MSS., Otho E. X., no. 10, ff. 64–78 (*c.* 1590).

62 Lans. MSS., vol. 169, art. 51, f. 110, Contract made with Sir Baptist Hicks and others, Dec. 19, 18 Jas. I (by which land with an annual value of £1,000 was sold for £45,000).

63 *S P D Chas. I*, CIX, 44, quoted by W. R. Scott, *English Joint Stock Companies*, Vol. I, p. 192. As Professor Scott points out, the price of land reflected not only the annual rent, but casualties, such as fines.

64 Marc Bloch, *op. cit.*, pp. 140–5; Paul Raveau, *L'Agriculture et les classes paysannes dans le Haut-Poitou au xvi*^{e} *siècle*, especially chap. II.

65 Thomas Wilson, *op. cit.*, pp. 22–3.

66 F. C. Dietz, *English Government Finance, 1485–1558*.

67 *Cal. S.P. Ven., 1603–7*, No. 709; 1617–19, No. 658; 1621–3, No. 603; 1629–32, No. 374.

68 For sales of Crown land under Elizabeth, see *S.P D. Jas. I*, XLVII, Nos. 99, 100, 101, and S. J. Madge, *The Domesday of Crown Lands*, pp. 41–2; under James, Lans. MSS., Vol. 169, art. 51; under Charles I, Add. MSS. 18705, ff. 2–22, and *S.P.D Chas. I*, CXXIV, 51; and under the two last, and 1649–56, Madge, *op cit* , pp. 47–64.

69 Madge, *op. cit.*, p. 256.
70 Henry Neville, *Plato Redivivus* (1763 ed.), p. 39.
71 One example may be given. John Smythe (*Lives of the Berkeleys*, Vol. II, pp. 356–61) gives particulars of property sold by Lord Henry Berkeley between 1561 and 1613 to the value of approximately £42,000. Sales of 25 manors and of the lease of one manor, realising £39,279 odd, were made to 13 persons (7 knights or baronets, 5 esquires and the trustees of a peer), the remainder, to the value of £2,789, going to 25 other persons of unspecified condition. Thus (i) 38 owners succeeded one; (ii) over nine-tenths of the property sold was acquired by purchasers relatively high in the social scale.
72 Dr. Savine's figures are printed in H. A. L. Fisher's *The Political History of England, 1485–1547*, App. ii, pp. 497–9.
73 Thomas Fuller, *op. cit.*, Vol. I, p. 60.
74 The following account of the fate of monastic property in three counties does not pretend to complete accuracy. It is based mainly on Sir Robert Atkyns, *The Ancient and Present State of Gloucestershire*, and *Men and Armour in Gloucestershire in 1608* (London, 1902, no editor stated), a list compiled by John Smythe from the Musters roll of 1608; J. Bridges, *History and Antiquities of Northamptonshire*; and Dugdale, *Antiquities of Warwickshire*.
75 I.e., eliminating duplication arising from the fact that several peers acquired monastic property in more than one of the three counties in question.
76 J. D. Chambers, *op cit* , p. 4.
77 G. H. Tupling, *The Economic History of Rossendale* (Chetham Society, N.S. Vol. 86, 1927).
78 The source of this statement is a list of lessees of Crown land 1–12 Eliz., contained (I think) in *S P.D Eliz.*, CLXVI, but the reference has been mislaid. The list includes among others, Sir William Cecil, Sir Thomas Smith, Anthony Brown (Justice of the Common Pleas), David Lewis (judge of the Court of Admiralty), Sir Francis Knollys, Sir Maurice Berkeley, Sir Henry Jernigan, Sir Walter Mildmay, Sir Gervase Clifton, Richard Hampden, etc.
79 Bacon, 'Discourse in the Praise of his Sovereign' in *Works* (Bohn ed.), Vol. I, p. 371. For statistical evidence of under-renting, see S. J. Madge, *The Domesday of Crown Lands*, pp. 55–6.
80 This was so, e.g., in the case of Lionel Cranfield's speculation of 1609. His ledger shows that he and his partners borrowed £529 from Sir John Spencer, £427 from Lady Slanye, and £209 from Thomas Mun. I am indebted to Lord Sackville and Professor A. P. Newton for permission to examine the Cranfield papers.
81 *Hist. MSS. Com , MSS. of the Earl of Cowper*, Vol. I, p. 50.
82 A summary of these transactions, with the names of the principal contractors, is contained in Lans. MSS., Vol. 169, art. 51, f. 110. *S.P D. Jas. I*, Vols. XL to LXXV, contain many references to the subject.
83 *C.J* 1614, April 18, speech of Mr. Hoskyns.
84 I take these particulars from the Cranfield MSS. For the deal in which he was specially engaged see *S.P.D. Jas. I*, XLV, No. 159 (articles between the Commissioners for the sale and demise of Crown Lands and John Eldred and others, contractors for purchase of the same).
85 Add. MSS., 18795, ff. 2–22.
86 *Cal. S.P.D Chas I*, 1628–9, CXXIV, 51. The sale of land to the City was the result of a contract made in 1628 with Edw. Ditchfield and other trustees acting on behalf of the Corporation. Particulars as to the subsequent sale by the City of the properties concerned are contained in the Royal Contract Deeds in the Guildhall.
87 *Cal. S P.D., Jas. I*, CXI, No. 80, Dec. 15, 1619. Sir T. Wilson to Master of Rolls. 'The King was greatly deceived in the Chantry lands which he granted to discharge that debt, for he passed the lands with £5,000 or £6,000 a year at the old rents, which are now worth 20 times as much. ... The whole affair was a cozenage.'
88 Cranfield MSS., 8236, 1622, Selwood forest; *ibid* , 8328, 1622, Crown forests in general, parts of Whittlewood, Barnwood and Sherwood being specially mentioned; *S.P.D. Jas. I*, LXXXIV, No. 46, Norden's Survey of Kingswood Forest.
89 *Leviathan*, chap. xxiv.
90 The following figures, which I owe to the kindness of Mr. F. J. Fisher, are based on the lists of manors and their owners contained in the *V.C.H.* They relate to manors whose ownership is

known at all the four dates given below in the seven counties of Herts, Beds, Bucks, Surrey, Worcs, Hants and the North Riding of Yorks.

	1561	%	1601	%	1640	%	1680	%
Total	2547		2547		2547		2547	
Belonging to owners with 4 manors and under	1445	56.7	1457	57.2	1638	64.3	1684	66.1
Belonging to owners with 5 manors and under 10	490	19.2	544	21.3	488	19.1	556	21.8
Belonging to owners with 10 manors or more	612	24.0	546	21.4	421	16.5	347	13.6

91 H. J. Habakkuk, 'English Landownership, 1680–1740,' in *Econ. Hist. Review*, Vol. X, No. 1, Feb. 1940, p. 2.
92 *Chanc Petty Bag., Misc. Rolls*, No. 20, gives the names of persons fined for depopulation 1635–8. The five counties in question are Leicester, Northants, Notts, Hunts and Lincs, which accounted for 506 out of 589 individuals fined and for £39,208 out of £44,054 collected. The names of M.P.s are taken from the *Official Returns of Members of the House of Commons* (1878).
93 H. F. Russell Smith, *Harrington and his Oceana*, chap. III.
94 J. Wright *History and Antiquities of Rutland* (1684), p. 135; E. J. Benger, *Memoirs of Elizabeth Stuart, Queen of Bohemia* (1825), pp. 68, 285; Grove, *Alienated Tithes*, under Leicestershire, parishes of Bitteswell, Laund, Loddington, Melbourne, and Owston; Add. MS. 18795, pp. 2–22, which shows Sir William Harrington and a partner buying Crown lands between Dec. 1626 and Feb. 1627.
95 Several of the families concerned had acquired peerages under James or Charles.
96 *Oceana*, ed. S. B. Liljegren, pp. 49–50.
97 The figures in this paragraph relate to the counties of Herts, Beds, Bucks, Surrey, Hants, Worcs, N. Riding of Yorks, Glos, Warwick, Northants. For those of the first seven counties I am indebted, as before, to Mr. F. J. Fisher.
98 Sir Edward Walker, *Observations upon the Inconveniences*, etc. (1653), especially his remarks on the effect of granting monastic lands to 'mean families'; E. Ludlow, *Memoirs*, ed. C. H. Firth, Vol. II, p. 59; *Memoirs of the Life of Colonel Hutchinson* (Everyman ed.), pp. 59–60.
99 Thomas Wilson, *op. cit.*, p. 23.
100 *Court and Times of Charles I*, Vol. I, p. 331.
101 Burton's *Diary*, Vol. III, p. 408. See on the whole subject Firth, *The House of Lords during the Civil War*, pp. 21–32.
102 Dryden, *Absalom and Achitophel*, Pt. I, 777; H. Thorndike, *Theological Works*, Vol. V, pp. 440–2, 337–9, 371–3; Sir W. Temple, *Miscellaneous Writings*, Pt. III, p. 16; Burnet, *History of his own Times* (1815 ed.), Vol. I, p. 12; Algernon Sidney, *Discourses Concerning Government* (1750 ed.), pp. 311–13; *Somers Tracts*, Vol. XIII, p. 679, Richard Harley, 'Faults on both Sides'; C. Davenant, *A Discourse upon Grants and Resumptions*. See also P. Larkin, *Property in the Eighteenth Century* (1930) pp. 33–57.
103 *A Memorial Offered to Her Royal Highness the Princess Sophia (1815)*. Foxcroft (*Life of Gilbert Burnet*, II, App. II, p. 556) ascribes the work to George Smythe of North Nibley.

A POSTSCRIPT

The article on 'The Rise of the Gentry' published in *The Economic History Review* of 1941 (Vol. XI, no. 1) has, I understand, occasioned some discussion. The latest contribution to the debate is contained in Mr. Trevor-Roper's interesting *Supplement* of April 1953. Whether the scope and tenor of my essay are accurately indicated by his reference to 'Professor Tawney's searchlight seeking only to illuminate prosperity among the gentry and aristocratic decline' its readers are better qualified than its author to judge; nor does space permit me to pursue his speculations on the role of the Independents in the revolution and of the 'mere', 'lesser' or 'declining' gentry among the Independents. One of his criticisms, however, raises issues possibly of some interest to future workers in the same field, and sufficiently specific to be discussed at not excessive length. This note is confined to it.

I take seriously the not uncommon contemporary opinion, to which Mr. Trevor-Roper gives short shrift, that the two generations before the Civil War saw an advance in the fortunes of the class described as the gentry. The criticism in question relates to part of the statistical evidence adduced in my article as offering some corroboration of that view. The relevant figures are those contained in the Table in note 90 of my article, and those appearing in Section VI. The former shows the direction of the changes taking place in the relative importance of estates of different sizes in terms—a point touched on below—of manors owned. The latter illustrate the opinion expressed by Harrington and others as to the simultaneous alteration, which they believed to have occurred, in the distribution of land between different categories of owners.

It is unfortunate, I think, that Mr. Trevor-Roper, in his preoccupation with the fate of the aristocracy, concentrated his whole attention on the second set of figures, and, unless I have overlooked some passage, ignored the first. In reality, of course, it was precisely the growth, depicted in the first, of middle-sized estates as compared with large which prompted contemporary comments on the change in the 'balance' of property, and to which reference has recently been made from different angles by writers entitled to respect, including Professor Campbell, Dr. Hoskins and Mr. Stone. On a few of the causes of that movement I endeavoured, in touching on the effects of the Dissolution, of the sale of royal domains and of the progress, such as it was, of a more business-like agriculture, to throw a little light. The Table in note 90 shows it at work. It does so without raising the problems of definition and classification which, not unnaturally, perplex Mr. Trevor-Roper, and which cause him to dismiss as a mare's-nest, not only my own very inadequate contribution, but the conclusions of intelligent observers who knew the facts at first hand.

Obviously, as I emphasized in my article, the movement in question was accompanied by changes in the opposite direction. To call attention to its significance no more implies a denial of the existence of imposing fortunes, whether territorial or derived from commerce and finance, at the upper end of the scale than would a similar reference by a historian of Victorian England to the rising incomes and influence of manufacturers and mine-owners. But one cannot disprove the reality of a trend merely by producing a handful of specimens which do not reflect it; and, as a criticism on the argument of my article, Mr. Trevor-Roper's useful little catalogue of noble plutocrats is, it seems to me, beside the point. In order to refute my by no means novel thesis that, in the period concerned, economic and political tides were running in favour of medium-sized estates and the social groups based upon them, Mr. Trevor-Roper should have produced equally comprehensive figures showing that no discernible trend affecting the size of estates occurred, or that, if one did occur, its direction was contrary to that suggested in my Table. Such new evidence would have been a welcome addition to our knowledge of a difficult subject, of which, I should be the first to agree, I touched only the fringe. Unfortunately, apart from interesting individual instances, Mr. Trevor-Roper does not attempt to supply it.

A contribution which treats the central issue so lightly is necessarily something of an *ignoratio elenchi*; but it may, nevertheless, contain suggestive observations on other points. One such point rightly raised by Mr. Trevor-Roper is the question of the relative gains made and losses sustained, in respect of landed property, by the peers as compared with the gentry. On his strictures on my use, in that connexion, of the category, manor, I need not dwell. My comments on the ambiguities of the term were more emphatic than his own. The fact remains that, in employing manors as a rough index of property owned, I followed, as most students of agrarian documents and literature will, I think, agree, the prevalent practice of the day. To sweep aside, as a mere will-of-the-wisp, that whole mass of contemporary usage, on the ground that a manor was 'a definition of rights, not a unit of wealth',[1] is not—to speak with moderation—according to light. The main burden, however, of Mr. Trevor-Roper's censures on this part of my article rests, as I understand him, elsewhere. As I explained, I classified as manors owned by gentry in 1640 those owned by families so described in 1561, even if those families had in the interval been ennobled. The result, he remarks, is to compare the properties of a growing body of gentry with those of a stationary or diminishing group of peers. 'No wonder the gentry, thus calculated, appear to "rise" at the expense of the peerage.'

This objection to the classification used in my article did not escape my notice when, after some hesitation, I decided to adopt it. An obvious alternative to it, and one not open to the same criticism, would have been an arrangement which included in the manors owned in 1640 by peers, and excluded from the manors owned at that date by gentry, all those in the ownership of families ennobled since 1561. I considered that course and rejected it. I did so, I hope—though one never knows—not as one of the criminal crew of 'advocates of theories who have looked for the evidence which they want only in the field in which, if found, it would fit those theories', but for a more pedestrian reason. It seemed—and seems—to me unrealistic to credit to the peerage properties many or most of which had been acquired by gentry before they were ennobled, and the successful accumulation of which, as Mr. Godfrey Davies reminds us, had been among the attributes mentioned in 1629 by the Lords as qualifying their possessors to blossom into peers. Indeed, in view of the mass additions[2] to the peerage which, when allowance is made for peerages extinguished, more than doubled between 1603 and 1639 the lay membership of the House of Lords, and which, of course, converted by a stroke of the pen properties owned by gentry into properties owned by peers, the adjective 'unrealistic' strikes me, on second thoughts, as too weak a word. If only James and Charles had manufactured, not a miserable handful of ninety or so peers, but a full-blooded three hundred, how dizzy the heights to which, on the procedure which I am rebuked for rejecting, aristocratic landed fortunes would have been seen to soar, and how tragic the stagnation or decline of those of the gentry!

A classification, whether employed by Mr. Trevor-Roper or by myself, which permits a change in the nomenclature of property-owners to be confused with a shift in the ownership of property clearly will not do. I am not at all concerned, however, to defend as beyond reproach the basis of calculation adopted in my article. It had, in my opinion, the advantage of throwing light on the dynamic tendencies at work, but I should agree that it was more useful for that purpose than as a precise statement of the situation obtaining in the year 1640. The gravamen of Mr. Trevor-Roper's indictment is, I understand, that, in crediting to the gentry, instead of to the peers, the manors owned by families ennobled between 1561 and 1640, I artificially limited the aristocracy to 'a diminishing group of families which happened to be noble at the beginning and still noble at the end of the period'. If such was my sin, I am happy to earn an easy absolution by substituting, against my better judgement, the second for the first of the two methods of classification mentioned above. The change, needless to say, makes some difference to the figures in Section VI of my article. The important question is how great that difference is.

An attempt to offer a provisional answer to that question is made in the Table printed below. In the case of 2,547 manors in seven counties the number of manors owned in 1640 by families ennobled since 1561 is at my disposal.[3] The figure appears to have been approximately 186. Lines 2 (*a*) and 2 (*b*) of the Table set out the distribution of manors in 1640 between different categories of owners on two assumptions: (*a*) that the 186 manors concerned should be credited, as in my article, to the gentry, (*b*) that, as I understand Mr. Trevor-Roper to hold, they should be credited to the peers. Thus the reader has before him the results of two alternative methods of classifying the figures for 1640. Comparing them with each other, and both with the figures for 1561 which appear in line (1) of the Table, he can reach his own conclusions for himself. One further point should, perhaps, be mentioned. Mr. Trevor-Roper reproves me for failing to take account of 'the yeoman and merchants who throughout the period were buying manors', and whose property, he suggests, I improperly included in that of the gentry. Whatever significance that criticism may have possessed for the figures printed in my article (Section VI), it has no application to those in line 2 (*b*) of the Table given here. The latter assign to the gentry the manors of yeomen and merchants gentilized between 1561 and 1640 in precisely the same manner as they assign to the peers the manors of gentry ennobled between those dates. Thus the majestic goddess, Parity of Reasoning, to whom Mr. Trevor-Roper rightly makes his bow, has received her due.

The Ownership of 2,547 Manors in Seven Counties in 1561 and 1640

(1) 1561

Total	Crown	Peers	Gentry	Ecclesiastical	Colleges, Hospitals and Schools	Other
.2547	242	335	1709	185	67	9
	(9.5%)	(13.1%)	(67.1%)	(7.2%)	(2.6%)	

(2)1640

(*a*) *Assigning to gentry manors owned by families ennobled 1561–1640*

Total	Crown	Peers	Gentry	Ecclesiastical	Colleges, Hospitals and Schools	Others
2547	53	157	2051	179	76	31
	(2.0%)	(6.1%)	(80.5%)	(7.0%)	(3.0%)	

(*b*) *Assigning to peers manors owned by families ennobled 1561–1640*

Total	Crown	Peers	Gentry	Ecclesiastical	Colleges, Hospitals and Schools	Other
2547	53	343	1865	179	76	31
	(2.0%)	(13.4%)	(73.3%)	(7.0%)	(3.0%)	

The points in this Table which first deserve notice are, perhaps, two. In the first place, a comparison of 2 (*a*) and 2 (*b*) shows that, as would have been expected, the difference made by crediting to the peers, instead of to the gentry, the 186 manors owned by families ennobled between 1561 and 1640 is substantial. The effect is more than to double both the number and the percentage of the manors owned in 1640 by peers, and to reduce the proportion then owned by gentry from 80 to 73 per cent or by over one-eighth. On my original basis of calculation, which corresponded with that of 2 (*a*), peers owned in 1640 just over one-sixteenth, and gentry four-fifths, of the manors concerned: on that used in 2 (*b*) the former then owned something between one-seventh and one-eighth, and the latter slightly less than three-quarters. On the second method of classification, the gentry still owned more than five times as many manors as the peers, but the change produced by the substitution of it for the first, though not revolutionary, is evidently marked.

In the second place, it is necessary to return to the object with which the figures were originally compiled, and to compare the distribution of manors in 1561 and 1640. For the reasons stated above, I do not accept the view that the correct course is to assign to the peers all the manors owned at the second of those dates by families ennobled since the first. If, however, that issue be waived, and a comparison made between (1) and 2 (*b*), the following points emerge.

First, in spite of the transference of the 186 manors in question from gentry to peers, those owned by the latter have increased between 1561 and 1640 by only 8, or between 2 and 3 per cent. Their property, in short, has been virtually static. The manors owned by the former have increased, again in spite of the same transference, by 156, or by approximately one-tenth.

Second, the proportion of manors in the ownership of the peers is at both dates almost exactly the same, 13 per cent of the total. That in the ownership of the gentry has risen from slightly more than two-thirds to just under three-quarters.

In view of these facts, it cannot plausibly be argued, as far as the seven counties in question are concerned, either that the landed wealth of the nobility was on the ascent between 1561 and 1640, or that that of the gentry was stationary or in decline. The movement, in short, was in the opposite direction from that which, unless I misunderstand him, is suggested by Mr. Trevor-Roper.[4]

It is proper that emphasis should be laid on the differing results of the alternative bases of calculation in 2 (*a*) and 2 (*b*). I am grateful to Mr. Trevor-Roper for inciting me to ascertain the dimensions of the difference in question. It does not seem to me, however, that the employment of the second method greatly alters the picture of the upper strata of rural society suggested by the first. Whether the gentry owned in 1640 four-fifths of the manors or just under three-quarters is, no doubt, an interesting question, but it is not one of the first importance. In either case they remained, as owners of that species of property, overwhelmingly the predominant group, and one whose lead had in the two preceding generations increased. Partly because, in the ceaseless reshuffling of property between well-to-do landowners, they gained, in these counties, during the eighty years in question, more from the peers than the peers gained from them, but principally because it was the gentry, not the nobility, who acquired the lion's share of the estates sold by the Crown, their preponderance was more marked in 1640 than in 1561.[5]

An apology is due for inflicting on the reader this tedious re-examination of the figures contained in my article. If I have ventured to trespass on his patience, the reason has not been a proprietary attachment to a thesis which, when published, thirteen years ago, in *The Economic History Review*, had no pretensions to originality, and which since then, corrected, supplemented, elaborated, refuted, and on occasion, perhaps, partially confirmed, has floated upwards into intellectual spheres beyond its author's worm's-eye view. It has been merely a desire to review my admittedly crude conclusions in the light of the latest criticisms on them. Mr. Trevor-Roper's *Supplement* contains a variety of observations, some questionable, some instructive, on topics of interest not touched on in my article. While welcoming his strictures on the latter, I remain, save on points of detail, unconvinced by them. On some important subjects, which space forbids me to discuss, for example—to mention only one—the course of landed incomes—his comments do not seem to me to be confirmed by such additional evidence as recent work has brought to light; nor, though agreeing that grants by the Crown deserve a heavier emphasis than I gave them, do I regard them as possessing in this connexion the preponderant significance ascribed to them by Mr. Trevor-Roper. For the rest, apart from a faint distrust of his occasional orderly-room manner with those bold, bad men, the seventeenth century deviationists[6] who fail to keep in step, my principal grounds of dissent from those of his criticisms to which I have here confined myself are two.

The first, to which I have already referred, is his failure to rebut, or indeed, to examine, the evidence indicating a growth of what, for lack of a better phrase, I have called medium-sized estates, as compared with the relative decline of large. I regard that change, which has parallels in other departments of economic life, as among the most important movements of the day. The Table in note 90 of my article illustrating it is probably, on a broad view, of greater significance than the statistics relating to the distribution of manors between different categories of proprietor; but pointing, as they do, in the same direction, the two sets of figures reinforce each other. If the movement revealed by the first is a mere figment, it should surely have been possible for Mr. Trevor-Roper to produce some evidence to that effect. As far as I can see, apart from some interesting biographical matter, he produces none.

In the second place, he greatly exaggerates, it seems to me, the effect of my assignment to the gentry, instead of to the peers, of the manors owned in 1640 by families ennobled since 1561. The choice of statistical methods is partly a matter of judgement, and my judgement on the point in question remains what it was. Since, however, Mr. Trevor-Roper's opinion differs from mine, I have been happy to give a trial to a method of calculation which I understand him to regard as not open to the same objections as that used in my article. The results, as given above, do not, it seems to me, go far to confirm his suggestion that the rise of the gentry is an optical illusion which the procedure preferred by him would be sufficient to dispel. *E pur si muove.* Even when submitted to Doctor Trevor-Roper's lowering treatment, the incorrigible patient continues to swell.

An erring colleague is not an Amalakite to be smitten hip and thigh. My correction of some of Mr. Trevor-Roper's misconceptions has, I trust, been free from the needless and unpleasing asperity into which criticism, to the injury of its cause, is liable on occasion to lapse. Let me conclude by referring to a topic of, I hope, a non-controversial kind. A comment which I am disposed to make, not only on his contribution and my own, but on much other work in the same and adjacent fields, relates to the ambiguities of the terminology employed. 'Nobility' is, perhaps, an exception; but the groups described by the words 'aristocracy' and 'gentry' melt at their edges into each other, and the terms themselves contain an element of opinion as well as of fact. There are indications that 'yeoman' carried different shades of meaning in different regions. 'Merchant', as used by contemporaries, commonly embraced, not only the wholesale exporters who asserted in vain their exclusive title to the name, but financiers of several different types, as well as, in spite of protests, shopkeepers who might ship a parcel or two, but whose stand-by was retail trade. On the disastrous twilight shed by the worst offender of all, a very prince of darkness, 'the middle classes'—a phrase then, in a slightly different form, coming into use—it is needless to dwell.

Categories so general are not useless, and cannot be discarded. Apart from their serviceableness as missiles in the mutual bombardments of historians, they have the virtue of suggesting problems, if at times they increase the difficulty of solving them. It would obviously be an advantage, however, if the composite social entities described by these comprehensive terms could be broken up, and the crude classifications in vogue today supplemented by an analysis sufficiently refined to bring to light the variety of species, economic, regional and cultural, within the groups concerned, which our conventional phraseology tempts us to overlook. How such a more discriminating procedure can most hopefully be attempted, and what lines it should pursue, cannot here be discussed. It seems to me, however, that the problem is sufficiently important to deserve that part of the attention of economic and social historians should be devoted to it.

Notes

1 Mr. Trevor-Roper's description of a manor is correct enough, as far as it goes; but it omits too much to be of more than limited use. Since—to mention nothing else—the rights concerned derived their value from the actual and prospective income yielded by them, his sharp contrast between a 'definition of rights' and 'a unit of wealth' is a false antithesis. It can hardly be suggested that surveyors, in recording such rights, were uninterested in their economic aspects, or that, in stating the revenue from a manor and indicating methods by which it could be increased, they did not regard the property in question as a 'unit of wealth'. What possibly Mr. Trevor-Roper means is that a manor was not a uniform or standardized unit. If so, his statement is, not only true, but a truism.

2 The lay membership of the House of Lords appears to have been 59 at the death of Elizabeth. She had created in the course of her reign 8 new peers. Those created by James numbered about 60, and those created by Charles in the first fifteen years of his reign, exclusive of 8 eldest sons of peers called up, about 30. (G. Davies, *The Early Stuarts, 1603–1660*, p. 264.) The number of peerages extinguished between 1560 and 1640 is given by Mr. Trevor-Roper (*Supplement*, p. 5) as 20. The net addition to the peerage made between 1603 and 1639 would appear, therefore, to have been in the region of 70.

3 The seven counties in question are Hertfordshire, Bedfordshire, Buckinghamshire, Surrey, Worcestershire, Hampshire and the North Riding of Yorkshire. Those represented in the figures in Section VI of my article, but not included here, are Gloucestershire, Warwickshire and Northamptonshire, for which the number of families ennobled 1561–1640 is not at the moment to hand.

4 'The rise of the aristocracy under the Stuarts is far more significant than any decline they may have experienced under Elizabeth, and ... the decline of the declining gentry in the early seventeenth century is at least as significant as the rise of the rising gentry' (*Supplement*, p. 32). See also the reference to the 'decline of the gentry' in Mr. Trevor-Roper's article 'The Elizabethan Aristocracy: an Anatomy Anatomised', in *Econ. Hist. Rev.*, 2nd ser., III (1951), pp. 294–5, n. 5.

5 I note with interest that, on the point of the landed property of peers, Mr. Stone has arrived, by a much more thorough and comprehensive investigation than mine, at conclusions similar in kind to those suggested by me. In his admirable article, 'The Elizabethan Aristocracy—a Restatement' (*Econ. Hist. Rev.*, IV (1952), no. 3), he has shown that, between 1558 and 1602, the net sales of manors by peers created before 1602 amounted to 28 per cent of the manors owned, inherited and granted 1558–1602, and, between 1603 and 1642, to 16 per cent of those owned, inherited and granted 1603–42. In the twelve and a half years represented in his article, 'all the peerage, old and new taken together in 1642, held slightly fewer manors than did the Elizabethan peers in 1558. The peerage had more than doubled its numbers, but its landed property had failed to increase.' Mr. Stone's contrast between the rates at which noble disinvestment was taking place in the periods before and after 1603 is a great improvement on my treatment of the subject. He does not discuss the question of the purchasers of the 337 manors

(net) disposed by the peers over the whole period. If the properties in question went the same way as in the counties covered by my figures, a large proportion of them were absorbed by the gentry.

6 See, for example, *Supplement*, pp. 44–7. I must confess to finding the argument of these pages slightly obscure. Statements by Bacon, Raleigh and Selden are dismissed, partly, if I rightly understand Mr. Trevor-Roper, because they relate to a past too remote to be relevant, partly because they refer to political factors with which, he appears to imply, I have no concern. Statements by later writers and speakers are rejected, partly on the opposite ground that they relate, not to 'a historical process' of some length, but to 'the violent change of the last decade', partly because their evidence, 'being evidence of confiscation not voluntary sale, is quite irrelevant to Professor Tawney's thesis'

I stated in my article that, at the period in question, 'economic and political conditions combined to mobilise real property'. I am somewhat surprised, therefore, that Mr. Trevor-Roper should seem to suppose that I was concerned solely with the former, and that political factors were outside my purview. I also dwelt at some length on the gains accruing to the gentry as a result of the Dissolution, gains in which both confiscation and 'voluntary sale' played a part. I am not less surprised, therefore, to be told that my business was with the latter alone. If it was proper, as obviously it was, to refer to the changes in the distribution of property caused by the greatest confiscation of the sixteenth century, I find it difficult to grasp why it is 'quite irrelevant' to refer to the analogous changes produced by the greatest confiscation of the seventeenth, and to cite contemporary opinions on them.

I have not elsewhere thought it necessary to notice Mr. Trevor-Roper's minor misinterpretations of my views, such, for example, as his ascription to me of the opinion—which I expressly disclaimed—'that it was only the gentry who took trouble over their estates'; but one of them, since it relates to Harrington, ought, perhaps, to be corrected. After referring to a passage in which I correctly stated that Harrington's relatives had obtained ecclesiastical and royal property, and that the author of the *Oceana* had, therefore, an instance of such a transfer beneath his eyes, he continues, 'In other words [*sic*] the Harringtons themselves were'—according to me—'a family of "rising" gentry'. I made no such statement. To assert that many gentry found in the acquisition of such property a means of rising is not to suggest that all who acquired it were rising gentry. Mr. Trevor-Roper's admonitory disquisition on the history of the Harringtons, therefore, is off the mark.

4

The Abolition of Economic Controls, 1918-21 (1941)*

I INTRODUCTORY

The subject of the present Memorandum is the Abolition of Economic Controls in the period following the Armistice of 11th November, 1918. It may obviously be treated from several different points of view; but one reason for studying it is a practical one. It is to ascertain what light, if any, the experience then obtained throws on the problems which may be expected to arise at the conclusion of the present war. It is assumed in the following pages that it was primarily that motive which gave rise to the suggestion that the subject should be examined.

If it is approached from that angle, several questions suggest themselves, some of which may conveniently be mentioned at the start. What was the nature of the causes which led to the rapid demobilisation of the machinery of State intervention built up during the last war? Did the system in question leave any permanent legacy behind it, and, if so, of what kind? Were the consequences resulting from de-control in accordance with those anticipated by the advocates of that policy, and, in so far as they were not, what were the reasons for the discrepancy? Does the history of the post-war period, seen in the perspective now open to us, suggest that the Government acted wisely in making haste to divest itself of the greater part of the increased authority over economic life, which the war had conferred on it? Or are there grounds for thinking that it might with advantage have retained part of its new powers for a longer period? If the latter view be taken, is it possible to distinguish the particular departments of economic affairs in which the case for the continuance of some types of control was relatively strong from those in which it was weaker or non-existent? If it is held that the maintenance of some controls, which were abolished, would have been desirable, in what form should they have been maintained? Could the organs created, and methods employed, during the war have been applied without alterations to the purpose of peace? Or, even had the new power assumed by the Government survived, in whole or in part, the crisis which produced them, would the constitution and procedure of the bodies exercising those powers have required substantial modification, if they were to function effectively in circumstances different from those for which they had been designed?[1]

An examination of the policy of de-control must have as its background the system which that policy found in existence and wound up. No comprehensive study of the British war economy of 1914–18 has been made; but useful books[2] exist on different aspects of the subject, and it is neither necessary nor possible to discuss it here in detail. It is sufficient by way of introduction to refer briefly to two points, without a grasp of which the significance of the post-war developments can hardly be appreciated. The first is the dimensions of the economic activities of the Government at the date of the Armistice. The second is the general character of the process by which the machinery required to carry on those activities had been constructed.

(i) The Dimensions of the Control System

Down to 1914, the intervention of the State in economic affairs was important, but restricted. It was confined in the main to three well-defined spheres, (a) social policy, (b) finance, (c) commercial relations with foreign powers. From 1916 onwards, governmental activity had considerably increased; but its extension took the form of supplementing the provisions of the first two categories by measures similar in principle to those already contained in them, not of the assumption of responsibility for departments of economic life hitherto outside its scope. The policy generally accepted, with differences of detail, by most sections of opinion was a combination of cautious interference, on grounds of social expediency, at one end of the economic scale with a deliberate abstention from interference, except by way of taxation, at the other end. Minimum Wage Acts were added to Factory Acts; Old Age Pensions and Insurance to the Poor Law; the limitation of hours in mines to regulations as to safety; super-tax to income tax; but the Government, apart from the Post Office and a few naval and military establishments, did not own or administer business undertakings, did not concern itself with the organisation of industry or the marketing of its products, did not attempt directly to influence the course of trade, did not intervene, except as a borrower, in the money or capital markets. Thus, while barriers were erected against the downward thrust of economic pressure, the upper ranges of business enjoyed almost complete freedom. It was assumed that the unrestricted initiative of profit-making entrepreneurs would secure the most effective utilisation of national resources, and that the consumer would be protected against exploitation by competition.

This combination of free enterprises and State regulation did not survive the war. In the first two years of the struggle, it continued to receive lip-service; but it was at once qualified, or abandoned altogether, at some important points. In the last two years it was jettisoned wholesale. The distinctive characteristic of the policy which took its place was not merely the enlargement of the economic activities of the State, but a change in the purposes to which they were applied and in the ranges of economic life affected by them. The over-ruling fact was scarcity. The first problem was to secure that limited resources were mobilised for the purpose of winning the war, and applied to different objects conducive to that end in the order of their relative urgency; the second to ensure that the diversion of man-power and capital to military requirements, with the dislocation caused by it and the opportunities for profiteering given by a rising market, did not react so injuriously on the standard of life and *morale* of the civilian population as to cripple the military effort, instead of assisting it. The method employed for the solution of both problems was the same. It was the intervention of the State, not merely, as in peace, as a protective agency, but as an organising, directing, and sometimes managing authority. The Government commandeered property; requisitioned stocks; prescribed in accordance with priority schemes the objects for which labour, raw materials and plant were to be used; licensed some middlemen and cut out others; sometimes laid down the course to be followed in the transit of commodities from producer to consumer; regulated prices and profits, rationed the consumption of certain categories of goods, and was itself engaged in business on a large scale. The sequence and changes in intensity of economic strains at different points can be traced by observing the slow extension of control to successive spheres of economic life. By 1918, when the system[3] was at its height, few departments of economic activity escaped it altogether.

Through the Railway Executive, the Ministry of Shipping and the Canal Control Committee, the Government was by that time master of the whole field of land and sea transport, requisitioning all British shipping, deciding its cargoes, destinations, the routes to be followed by vessels and the dates of their sailing, fixing freight rates and limiting profits. Through the Ministries of Food and Agriculture it determined the utilisation of the land of the country, gave orders as to the crops to be grown, organised distribution, fixed prices, and entered the market itself on a large scale, as a buyer and seller of agricultural produce. Of the two chief extractive industries, coal-mining and iron-mining, the latter was under the command of the Ministry of Munitions; while the former and larger, with an annual output, at 1913 prices, in the region of £150,000,000, was under that of the Coal Controller, armed with extensive powers over the production, transport and distribution of coal at home and abroad, as well as over prices, profits and the financial side of the industry, and holding in the background, as a sanction, the right to take over, in whole or in part, the management of any or all the undertakings concerned. Judged by *personnel*, much the largest single industry which Great Britain had yet known was the production of Munitions of War. Through the Ministry of Munitions the Government, in addition to a greatly expanded Woolwich arsenal, owned, by 31st March, 1918, over 250[4] national factories, mines and quarries; superintended the operations of about 20,000 controlled establishments; employed directly in the first and indirectly in the second about 2,000,000[5] workers making munitions of war, over two and a half times the aggregate number engaged in 1913 in the coal industry, together with an office staff of over 65,000;[6] and spent, during the three and a half years of the Ministry's existence, an annual average of round about £570,000,000[7] a year, a sum not far short of one-third of the total national product or dividend on the eve of the war. Outside the purview of the Ministry was a large block of other industries concerned with munitions of war, including, in addition to much else, the vital industry of ship-building, which also were working under the orders of the Government.

Not only was the Government much the largest single manufacturer in the country, it was also the greatest and, for a time, indeed, almost the sole importer. A long list of raw materials, jute, flax, hemp, wool, hides and leather, oils, oil-seeds and fats, timber and many kinds of metals; and an equally impressive list of food-stuffs, sugar, wheat, meat, bacon, tea, butter, cheese and dried fruits, totalling in the aggregate over 90 per cent in value of the whole import trade of the country, together with home-produced supplies of wool, meat, margarine, condensed milk, tallow, and other commodities, were purchased on the Government's account, and distributed through machinery working under its direction. In the end over four-fifths[8] of all the food consumed by civilians was bought and sold by the Ministry of Food, and over nine-tenths was subject to maximum prices fixed by it; while the sales of raw materials by the War Office up to 31st March, 1919, amounted to £221,687,505, its profits to £38,720,525, and the value of its stocks on hand at the date in question to £111,414,458.[9] Holding these great supplies of raw materials and food-stuffs, the Government was in a position to ensure that they were used to the best advantage, with the result that control spread downwards from raw materials to the processes by which they were worked up. Having eliminated speculation, the Government could sell to the manufacturer at a stable price fixed for a reasonably long period; could allocate supplies on a scheme of priorities based on the relative urgency of different uses; could introduce a costings system to determine the costs of manufacture at different stages; could fix a price which would cover 'conversion costs', and would offer a reasonable, and no more than a reasonable, profit to a manufacturer of normal efficiency. Thus considerable bodies of producers and dealers became in effect agents of the Government, working either on a fixed commission or within profit limits fixed by it.[10]

What was done on these lines, with the co-operation of bodies representing the industries concerned, in the case of jute, flax, woollens and worsteds, hides, leather, the manufacture of boots and, by way of brief experiment, in that of civilian clothing, was also done in the case of food-stuffs. Possessing a monopoly of the purchase and import of sugar, the Royal Commission on Sugar Supplies was able from the start to control retail prices, and later virtually turned the retailers into Government employees, selling, at a fixed rate of profit, on public account. After the establishment of the Wheat Commission as the sole purchaser and importer, the former grain importers came to occupy the same position. When all flour mills with a capacity of five sacks or more were taken over by the Ministry of Food, they were administered by their former owners on behalf of the Government, with a guarantee from the latter of the pre-war rate of profits. Smithfield market, which supplied meat to about one-quarter of the population of Great Britain, virtually became in the last year of the war a non-profit-making Public Utility Company administered, under the Food Controller, by a Control Board composed of officers of the Ministry, of some former heads of private businesses acting as salaried officials, and of representatives of the other interests concerned. The description of the meat trade as a whole, with its total output bought by the Government, and distributed by auctioneers acting as Government agents, official grading committees, and some two thousand food committees, as a 'gigantic multiple shop',[11] is hardly an exaggeration. The activities of the Central Control Board (Liquor Traffic), established under the Defence of the Realm (Amendment) Act of 18th May, 1915, attracted less attention; but, in the narrower sphere assigned it, they were not unimpressive. The Board used with caution its power to acquire property and carry on itself the business of supplying liquor. It did so only in three areas; and in only one of these, Gretna and Carlisle, where it became owner of 368 out of 415 licensed premises, did it offer an example of nationalisation on a sufficient scale to be significant. As a regulating authority, empowered to inspect and close any licensed premises or clubs, to prohibit the sale of any particular liquor, and generally to supervise the conduct of the trade, it acted more boldly. By the end of 1916, the areas scheduled by the Board included a population of some 38,000,000. At the date of the Armistice, the whole country, with the exception of some purely agricultural areas, had been brought under its control.[12]

An even more novel departure, and one which, before the war, would have been pronounced wholly impracticable, was the creation, above these national controls, of certain great international organisations, entrusted with functions of much the same kind as those already mentioned, but discharging them on behalf of groups of states, not of particular countries. The reasons for this development were partly economic, partly political and strategic. On the one hand, unity of action, whether by way of joint purchasing programmes or of actual joint purchase, made it possible to buy on a predetermined plan, with the advantage that liabilities were known in advance; avoided the danger of driving up prices by competition; secured that different countries obtained their supplies from the nearest and cheapest sources; and, in some cases, lowered costs by substituting one buying agency for several. On the other hand, since the strength of the allied chain was that of its weakest link, the maintenance of the common military effort demanded that no allied country should suffer an economic breakdown, and that neutrals should not be thrown by intolerable economic strains into the arms of the enemy.

Both advantages were realised, in different degrees, by the inter-allied controls[13] which developed in the last year of the war. The first inter-allied economic organ to be established, the *Commission Internationale de Ravitaillement*, set up in August, 1914, and containing representatives of the allied purchasing departments, did useful work in pooling knowledge, distributing orders, and substituting orderly buying for the scramble for limited supplies which would otherwise have taken place; but it did not itself enter the market. Some of the international bodies later brought into existence did business on a world-wide scale. Thus the Wheat Executive, established in November, 1917, arranged for the co-operative buying of cereals through the British Wheat Commission on behalf, first, of Great Britain, France and Italy; then of those countries with the addition of Greece, Portugal and Belgium; then of nearly all the European neutrals; till, in 1918, some sixteen countries, exclusive of those included in the British Empire, were being supplied through it. The International Sugar Committee, formed in the autumn of 1917, bought the whole Cuban sugar crop of the following year for allocation among the allies, and in 1918 the United States Sugar Equalisation Board, which had taken over its functions, did the same. The Oil-seeds Executive and Meat and Fats Executive arranged joint programmes for the purchase of the articles concerned on behalf of Great Britain and France, while leaving the actual buying to the respective Governments. Inter-allied Programme Committees dealt in the same way with wool, hides and leather, jute, hemp and flax, as did the *Commission Internationale d'Achats de Bois* with timber. The establishment of the British Ministry of Shipping at the end of 1916 was followed in the next year by the creation of an Allied Maritime Transport Council and Executive. The primary function of the latter body was to treat allied shipping as a single fleet, which was to be employed to the best advantage of the common cause, irrespective of the country to which particular vessels belonged. In fact, however, once it got to work, its powers and functions became much more extensive than its title would suggest. Since shipping was at that time the limiting factor, the trade of different countries was dependent on the tonnage made available for their service. The Allied Maritime Transport Executive, which allocated the tonnage, in effect determined the amount and kind of imports which particular states should receive, and, therefore, the level of industrial activity both in the countries producing the goods shipped and in those to which they were sent.

It would be easy to elaborate the picture by adding to the instances already given further examples of the extension of the authority of the State over all, or nearly all, departments of economic life, some, such as cotton, timber and paper, of the first importance, others of minor, though genuine, significance, like road-stones, matches and hosiery-needles. It is probably not an exaggeration to state that not less than two-thirds[14] of the gainfully employed workers in the country were engaged in 1918, though many of them may not have known it, in industries subject to one form or another of war-time regulation. Enough has been said, however, to show that the machinery of economic intervention had attained, by the end of the war, considerable dimensions. What was the nature of the process by which it grew?

(ii) An Essay in Improvisation

It would be unprofitable to trace in detail the successive stages of the movement in different branches of trade and industry. There is one general feature of it, however, which can be briefly stated, and which, since it had some bearing on the post-war problem, it is important to grasp. The most obvious, and not the least significant, characteristic of the British system of war-controls is that, for all its magnitude and complexity, it was almost entirely an improvisation. It is clear to-day that, in the eight years before 1914, the possibility—or, as some thought, the probability—of war was constantly present to the minds of leading members of the Cabinet, and that steps to prepare for the contingency were unobtrusively taken. But the war of 1914–18 was the first in which most, if not all, of the nations concerned had passed through an Industrial Revolution, had at their disposal the technique of power-driven machinery and mass production, could summon modern science and technology to intensify their efforts, and were knit together in a web of economic interdependence. Few statesmen in any country, when the war began, and not many when it ended, appear to have realised the significance of that fact. Hence military and naval preparations, especially in this country, were not accompanied by equally systematic economic preparations. When hostilities began, the former required to be enormously expanded to meet the emergency; but their *cadre*, at least, existed before 1914. The latter had to be built, from foundations to roof, while the war was proceeding.

That statement requires, it is true, some slight qualification. Arrangements had been made in advance, under the Regulation of the Forces Act of 1871, for placing the railways, in return for a guarantee of pre-war profits, at the disposal of the State, their management being entrusted to a Railway Executive taking its orders from the Government, with the President of the Board of Trade as Chairman. With the congestion and dislocation anticipated as a result of the movement of troops and munitions, retail prices, it had been feared, would rise, and Employment Exchange managers had been instructed to furnish the Board of Trade, on forms previously issued, with weekly returns of retail prices. The promptitude with which, on 20th August, the Government appointed a Sugar Commission to handle an article previously obtained, to the extent of two-thirds, from Austria and Germany, and the gradual formation between November and February of a wheat reserve of some 3,000,000 qrs, by means of secret purchases made by a private firm on behalf of the Government, may point to decisions on these matters taken while peace was still in the balance. On the whole, however, the absence of economic plans worked out in advance, and ready to be brought into immediate operation when the necessity arose, is among the most striking features of the first phase of the war.

Apart from the special case of the railways, the British war-book appears to have contained little or nothing on the subject of economic policy. The decision taken in the first week of the war to guarantee the solvency of the banks and discount houses was of fundamental importance; but the account subsequently given by the then Chancellor of the Exchequer lays more emphasis on the unexpectedness of the crisis than on plans prepared in advance to meet it.[15] The Army Contracts Department of the War Office, which was the Department first and most immediately concerned with supplies, began by assuming that its traditional methods—competitive tenders, centralised buying, the restriction of orders to firms on a list compiled in time of peace—would with minor modifications be adequate to the emergency. In the matter of munitions, 'the doctrine implicitly acted on', writes a civil servant then employed in the War Office, 'was that, the higher the price and the greater the freedom allowed to the private contractor, the greater would be the increase in the supply; it followed that, if only the Government paid high enough prices and left private firms to their own devices, munitions would be forthcoming in abundance'.[16]

That such was the course to which the Government began by intending to adhere, and that nothing was further from its thoughts than the formidable apparatus which later came into existence, is proved even more convincingly by the rudimentary, and, indeed, precarious character of the legal powers which it had thought sufficient for its purpose. The Defence of the Realm Act empowered it to make regulations for ensuring 'the public safety and the defence of the realm'; but neither the earlier regulations made under the Act, nor, in the view of the legal advisers of the Government, the Act itself, gave authority to any Department completely to control a trade, to determine the basis of payment for goods requisitioned, or to fix maximum prices. Equally important, they made no provision for settling the question of compensation. One of the first cases of large-scale requisitioning, therefore—that of sand-bags—took place under a clause in the annual Army Act, originally intended to authorise the requisitioning of horses and vehicles, provided that one of His Majesty's principal secretaries of state, a General Officer Commanding, a Justice of the Peace, a Chief Constable and his subordinates all co-operated in the adventure. The question of compensation was handled by invoking the theory, which had caused annoyance under Charles I, that the Crown, in virtue of the Royal Prerogative, can take possession of such private property as it pleases, without being under any legal obligation to indemnify the subject, and can then settle the matter by making, if it thinks fit, an *ex gratia* payment.[17]

The utterances of Ministers reveal the same unconsciousness of the economic repercussions to which the war would give rise, of the necessity of any novel organisation to meet the shock, and of the results which, once established, such an organisation would produce. 'Our desire', remarked the Home Secretary in the House in the early days of August, 1914, at the moment when the Chancellor of the Exchequer was mobilising the credit of the State for the rescue of the City, 'has been not to interfere with ordinary trade at all, but to leave the traders to conduct their own business.' The cases in which action by the Government succeeded in reducing prices below the level which they would otherwise have reached, were destined to be not few; but in the autumn of the same year, the Financial Secretary of the War Office defended his Department in the House of Commons by stating it to be axiomatic that the Government would always pay more for its purchases than private individuals, and the same statement was repeated, a few months later, by the President of the Board of Trade. More than a year after the outbreak of war, when the Sugar Commission had been established for twelve months, and important controls had already been organised under the War Office, Mr. Runciman was still insisting that the consumer was protected by competition between producers, and strenuously opposing the appointment of a Food Controller. The maintenance of adequate supplies of food-stuffs at reasonably stable prices was obviously vital; but in 1916 it was still possible for a Departmental Committee to dismiss a plan for regulating exports by means of licences with the remark that 'methods of private trade were better adapted than the Government scheme to avoid financial loss'.[18]

Nor, finally, can it be said that the professional economists showed much greater foresight. Some of them probably thought that the war, for economic reasons, must necessarily be short; few, if any, of them appear to have understood that, under modern conditions, the nature of a war economy is such as to compel the intervention of the State on an unprecedented scale. Laymen, naturally, understood it even less. For twelve months or more after 1914, the mottoes, 'Business as usual', and 'Everything for the War', which were the contribution of the Press to victory, lived in happy incompatibility side by side. Political Labour pressed in October, 1914, for the control of food and shipping; but, in negotiations between trade unions and employers' associations, wages were being fixed in 1915 for 'the duration of the war'. During the next three years the public became increasingly aware of restrictions on the liberty of producers and consumers; but it thought of them in terms of particular commodities and individual trades, not of a new war economy affecting all sides of life. It was unprepared for the assumption by the State of the direction of economic life, and to the end hardly realised that such a change had taken place.

How then, it may be asked, did the impressive fabric of State control, which was the most striking of the immediate economic fruits of the war, come to be constructed? The answer is that it was not deliberately constructed at all. Looking back to-day, one can discern, no doubt, certain dominant trends affecting, in different degrees, all sides of the policy. The discovery that the regulation of all stages in the production and sale of a commodity is not more difficult, but easier, than the regulation of one stage; the consequent disposition to push control back from the final product to its manufacture, and from manufacture to raw materials; the gradual substitution for a welter of *ad hoc* committees, each appointed to deal with some particular problem, such as retail prices or the licensing of exports, of large organisations with comprehensive powers—these tendencies recur with sufficient frequency to be regarded as the reflection of some general and constant characteristics of the problem to be solved. To suppose, however, that they were present, except at a later stage, to the minds of those who organised controls is to under-estimate the difficulties of the situation confronting them and to over-rationalise their response to it. In reality, the system, if such it can be called, was only to a small extent the result of design, and, even at its zenith, in the latter part of 1918, was rarely, if ever, envisaged as a whole. The different parts composing it had the common feature of being a reaction to scarcity, actual or threatening, and of being jolted forward by successive changes which made scarcity more acute. But, though all were the result of external stresses, they met those stresses in different ways. Each had an independent origin. Each was an individual response to an unforeseen crisis. Each grew by a logic of its own, and developed the special technique appropriate to the material which it handled. Like factory and public health legislation in the last century, each justified every additional advance as an exceptional concession to some specific emergency, which, because it was exceptional, raised no question of principle. Thus a collectivism was established which was entirely doctrineless. The most extensive and intricate scheme of State intervention in economic life which the country had seen was brought into existence, without the merits or demerits of State intervention being even discussed.

The character of the system is well illustrated by the economic activities carried on by a Department not usually regarded as one of the giants of Big Business. The majority of the war-time transactions of the War Office owed their existence to powers—at first far from adequate powers—conferred by the Defence of the Realm Act; remained to the end without further statutory sanction; were rarely discussed in Parliament or the Press; and had not originally been planned by the Civil Servants who were their authors on anything approaching the scale which they ultimately attained. The story of all of them is of a slow growth from stage to stage, as the solution of one problem revealed another behind it, and that a third in the offing.

One example must suffice. With the rush to enlist which followed Lord Kitchener's appeal for men, almost the first industry to feel the strain of the new war demand was woollen and worsteds. The War Office system of buying went to pieces in an orgy of speculation; prices rose to fantastic heights without affecting the supply, since the sources required to provide it were not in existence. The action first taken by the Government was to prohibit in October, 1914, the export of raw wool, and to substitute, towards the end of the same year, collective agreements with associations of manufacturers for the competitive tenders from individuals which had hitherto been the practice. Prices, were, as a consequence, somewhat reduced, but they still remained excessive; and these initial steps were followed, rather more than a year later, by further measures. The whole output of the mills was requisitioned; the costings system, already introduced into the jute industry, was applied to the manufacture of woollens and worsteds; prices were fixed on the basis of cost of production in the normal firm, *plus* a fair profit. The market for raw wool, however, was highly unstable. The third stage, therefore, was reached in the summer and autumn of 1916, when, a shortage of raw materials being anticipated, the Government prohibited all private dealings in wool, and then purchased, first, the whole British clip and, next, the unsold balance of the Australian and New Zealand clips. The State, being in control of the raw material, was now in a strong position; and in 1917 a fourth step was taken. The Government fixed selling prices of raw wool and tops, both for civilian and military purposes; required top-makers to comb for it on commission; issued tops to spinners who spun them at a rate fixed on conversion costs; delivered the yarn to manufacturers, who were paid on the same basis; and built up a reserve of wool to meet the shortage expected in the following year. Finally, when, as a result of the restrictions on manufacture, prices of civilian clothing rose, the Control Board established in 1917 to allocate wool and yarn launched a scheme for the production of standard clothing to be sold to civilians at a maximum price fixed by itself.[19]

The story of the other War Office controls, such as jute, flax and linen, hemp, hides and leather, was *mutatis mutandis* similar, and reinforces the same conclusions. In no case was the type and scale of regulation which ultimately emerged envisaged from the start. In each case control grew from stage to stage over a period varying from six months to nearly four years. In each it pushed back to the acquisition of the raw materials, and was carried forward by a more rigorous regulation of the later stages of manufacture. Nor was the history of the controls administered by Departments specially created for the purpose so different as might at first be supposed.

The nearest approach to a new Department springing fully armed into existence was the Ministry of Munitions. Its powers were novel and formidable; its establishment, by the Act of 9th June, 1915, was the climax of an agitation which had lasted since the end of the preceding year. It was at once the first, the greatest, and the most controversial example of a new war economy which the crisis was to produce. Even the Ministry of Munitions, however, was the heir of organisations which had preceded it, such as the Cabinet Committee on Munitions, the Armaments Output Committee of the War Office, the branch of the War Office which dealt with contracts for war stores, and the Committee for the production of high explosives. In spite of its apparent novelty, and of the stature which it ultimately attained, it grew by a process of gradual accretion. New functions were being transferred to it from other Departments two years after its establishment in 1917. Even at the end of that year, it was still far from being the Leviathan which it was to become by the Armistice.

In the case of the three other controls which ultimately became Departments, the slide into regulation was slower and more circuitous. A Cabinet Committee on food had been appointed in the first week of the war; but two years and four months elapsed between the decision, in August, 1914, to make the purchase of sugar a State monopoly and the establishment in December, 1916, of the Ministry of Food. The latter, when first created, was only one agency among many dealing with food questions. It was not till the latter part of 1917 that it devoured its rivals, and achieved unquestioned supremacy as the national housekeeper, though even then the Sugar and Wheat Commissions retained a formal dependence, and the importation of refrigerated meat from South America and the British Dominions remained in the hands of the Board of Trade. The Coal Industry was obviously crucial to the successful prosecution of the war. Not only British industry and the British navy but coal-less Italy, and France, whose chief coalfields lay in the occupied departments of the *Nord* and *Pas de Calais*, were dependent on supplies of British coal. There is no sign, however, that the Government devoted any consideration to the reactions on it of the war, till its attention was first drawn to the subject in February 1915, by a rise in retail coal prices. As a consequence, a succession of committees was appointed—a Departmental Committee on the rise in coal prices, a Coal Mining Organisation Committee to maintain output, and a Coal Exports Committee to control exports; in May, 1915, coal exports were prohibited under licence; and in July of the same year a Price of Coal Limitation Act was passed. January, 1916, brought another committee, the Central Coal and Coke Supplies Committee, with eleven district committees, to regulate the distribution of coal at home; and September, 1916, saw a Supervisor of Committees appointed to co-ordinate their work. It was not, however, till

December, 1916, after the threat of a stoppage in South Wales, that the collieries of that district were brought, by regulations made under D.O.R.A., into the possession of the Board of Trade, and not till March, 1917, that the same system was extended to the industry as a whole. The growth of control in the shipping industry had a history equally long drawn-out. The regulation of different aspects of the industry was entrusted, during the first two and a half years of the war, to a still larger group of separate committees. It was only in December, 1916, that they were finally brought together in a Ministry of Shipping responsible for dealing with the problem as a whole, and only a year later, in December, 1917, that the Ministry became the parent of the Inter-allied Maritime Council.

The piece-meal, empirical, process by which war-controls developed had consequences of some importance. While the war continued, it facilitated their growth. The economic break-waters which, if seen as a whole, would have caused cries of alarm, grew, like coral islands, through the unseen activities of the industrious, but silent, insects composing the Civil Service. Each addition to the structure was related to some immediate necessity of incontestable urgency. Opportunities for a frontal collision of principles were reduced to a *minimum*, for there was no obvious point at which a stand could be made. Once the war was over, what had been a source of strength became a weakness. War collectivism had not been accompanied by any intellectual conversion on the subject of the proper relations between the State and economic life; while it did not last long enough to change social habits. With the passing, therefore, of the crisis that occasioned it, it was exposed to the attack of the same interests and ideas as, but for the war, would have prevented its establishment.

II THE MOVEMENT TO DE-CONTROL

The system whose extent and development has been thus summarily indicated, reached its zenith in the autumn of 1918. At the date of the Armistice, the greater part of British agriculture, mining and manufactures; transport by land and water; and trade, both foreign and domestic, was carried on in accordance with regulations normally made, it is true, with the approval of representatives of the interests concerned, but administered for the most part either by Civil Servants or by business men acting in conjunction with them, under the authority of the Government, with Acts of Parliament as their ultimate sanction. Controls had grown up, if not in response to a popular demand, at least with a large measure of general consent. Partly owing to the strains arising from the submarine campaign, partly as a result of the entry into the war of the United States, they had received notable extensions in the preceding twelve months, particularly in the international sphere. Proposals for their further elaboration were under consideration at the moment when the allied armies were approaching the German frontier.

Less than three years later this whole structure had vanished. The control organisations functioning under the Board of Trade and the War Office had been among the earliest to be established, and were among the first to fall.[20] A few of them ceased to exist early in 1919, the majority later in the same year, and one or two in 1920, some, though not many, being extinguished at a stroke, others losing their powers one by one, others again receiving a brief and illusory extension of life by their transformation into committees to advise the government during what was then known as the period of Reconstruction. The departments established under special Acts of Parliament had a somewhat more complicated history and a slightly longer life. The Ministry of Munitions, the Ministry of Food, and the Coal Control Department shed some of their multifarious functions, as they had acquired them, piece-meal. These three departments were finally wound up on 31st March, 1921. The Railway Executive followed them on 14th August of the same year. The great international transport organisation, of which the British Ministry of Shipping was the parent, had already, after a period in which it was shorn of many of its powers, gone the way of all flesh; the Allied Maritime Transport Council on 7th April, 1919, the Allied Maritime Transport Executive, which had combined its work for another ten months under the Supreme Economic Council, on 9th February, 1920, when, with the coming into force of the Peace Treaty in January of that year, the transference of German vessels to the Reparation Commission deprived it of such work as still remained to it. The Sugar Commission ended with the Ministry of Food. The Wheat Commission died by inches a few months later. At the date of its second Report, in 1925, some outstanding accounts still remained to be settled; but the proportion of the miller's requirements which it provided had been tapered down month by month since April, 1921, and the Commission ceased to supply wheat from August of that year. The last of the war-controls to be abolished was that concerned with the sale of alcoholic liquor. The restrictions imposed by it had been gradually relaxed between February, 1919, and June, 1921. The Licensing Act of 17th August, 1921, completed the process. It abolished the Liquor Control Board; made statutory and uniform certain conditions, such as those relating to hours of sale, which the Board had imposed; and transferred any property vested in it to the Home Secretary or the Secretary for Scotland.

The dismantling of a great apparatus of social intervention is necessarily less impressive than the spectacle of its creation; but the problem which it raises may be equally important. The period of war economy accelerated the demise of the individualist, competitive phase of British capitalism. It stimulated organisation and combination among manufacturers; advertised rationalisation; strengthened the demand for tariffs; and encouraged, in another sphere, the settlement of wages and working conditions by national rather than local agreements. These consequences, however, did not at once become apparent, and, in the field of public policy, the legacy which the war-controls left to the immediate future was a meagre one. The Mining Industry Act of August, 1920, created the Mines Department of the Board of Trade; transferred to the latter powers under enactments relating to mines and quarries previously exercised by the Home Office; gave it the functions of the Coal Controller for one year after 31st August, 1921; empowered it to make schemes with regard to the drainage of mines; and established a welfare fund by a levy of a penny a ton on coal produced. It is improbable that, had no Coal Control Department existed, the Act would have been passed. The Railways Act of August, 1921, which amalgamated the railways of the country into four large groups, was even more clearly the child of war experience, and was timed to come into operation within a week of the date at which the Railway Executive laid down its task. The skeleton organisation for maintaining food supplies during strikes can be traced to the preparations made by the Ministry of Food for dealing with the railway stoppage of September to October, 1919. The establishment, seven years after the Armistice, of a Food Council was the last faint ripple from the storms which that Department had been created to ride.

All this, however, was somewhat small beer. The work of demolition was done thoroughly, as well as in haste. What should be the verdict on it? The direction of economic activity by authority, which was the most general aspect of the arrangements discarded, had come into existence, as has already been pointed out, not by the deliberate substitution of a regulated for a free economy, but by way of improvised adjustments, some large, but many small, to the series of unforeseen and changing emergencies produced by the war. It is a commonplace, however, that institutions created under one set of conditions tend to be employed, and successfully employed, to meet the requirements of another. The question of the expediency of summary de-control cannot be settled merely by reference to the cessation of the particular crisis which caused controls to be established. Even when full allowance is made for the economic watershed represented by the transition from war to peace, the merits of the course followed still remains to be considered. What causes produced the policy of the clean sweep? Did the whole utility of the machinery at work in the early autumn of 1918 automatically disappear with the negotiation of the Armistice, or, if not then, with the coming into operation of the Peace Treaty in January, 1920? Or is there reason to think, in the light of the experience of the following decade, that some part of it, at any rate, might with advantage have been retained?

It may be noted, in the first place, that rapid and complete decontrol was not the foregone conclusion which it is apt to seem today. Its victory was ultimately so decisive that it is natural to regard it as the result of a policy deliberately adopted and systematically carried through. Such a policy undoubtedly later came into existence; but, in the last year of the war, the situation was still too fluid, and other issues too absorbing, to allow it to take shape. To think of it as exercising before the Armistice the power which subsequently it acquired is to telescope different phases of opinion and to over-rationalise the attitude of the Government.

Post-war problems had been under consideration by a standing committee of the Cabinet as early, at any rate, as 1916. They naturally included economic and social subjects; and when Mr. Lloyd George's Government established, first—in March, 1917—a new Committee, and then—in July—a Ministry of Reconstruction, such subjects formed the major part of the agenda of both. It might have been expected that the machinery of economic regulation set up during the war, its merits and defects, and the possible future utility either of it or some modification of it, would have been included in the long list of topics on which the Ministry was instructed to report. To make the necessary investigation would possibly, in the circumstances of the time, have been somewhat difficult; but other inquiries were, in fact, carried out, and such a report would have been of the greatest value. It would have enabled the public and the Government to reach an informed opinion on important and controversial issues, which were later to be drowned in a stream of clap-trap. The failure to insist on its production was a serious misfortune. It is to be hoped that a similar error will not be repeated.

That failure, however, was not due to the fact that the question of policy had already been decided. In 1917 and 1918 the apparatus of war-controls was being rapidly extended. The account of their organisation and achievements contained in the Reports of the War Cabinet does not leave on the reader the impression that they were regarded by the Government merely as one of the regrettable necessities of war, to be swept into oblivion at the earliest date possible. It is recognised that certain of the measures in force will lose their relevance on the return of peace; but it is also pointed out that steps taken to meet the crisis have revealed possibilities of more than transient significance. It is stated, for example, that the zoning system enforced in the case of the transport of coal has produced 'an immense resultant saving to the railways of labour, engine-power, and wagon capacity'; that the general application of the costings system to industry has given industrialists a knowledge of their position which previously they did not possess, and which 'will have ... very beneficial effects upon methods of production after the war'; that the Wool Control Board has secured 'what has never been ensured before—even employment throughout the trade'; that the purchase and supply of raw materials by the Government has not only put an end to 'the undue profits previously resulting from private speculation', but has 'enabled the Government to control the costs of production at every stage', and has 'for the first time brought within the sphere of practical politics the possibility of fixing relatively stable world prices for fundamental staples'. It is not implied in the Reports that controls should be continued indefinitely in their existing form; on the contrary, frequent reference is made to the changes which will accompany the transition from war to peace. It is emphasised, however, that their too abrupt abandonment is a danger to be avoided, that the economic experience obtained during the war has been of far-reaching importance, and that future policy must incorporate the lessons which it has taught. 'Reconstruction', it is insisted, 'is not so much a question of rebuilding society as it was before the war, but of moulding a better world out of the social and economic conditions which have come into being during the war. ... The war has brought a transformation of the social and administrative structure of the State much of which is bound to be permanent.'[21]

Such utterances were partly due, no doubt, to a natural desire to present in an attractive light the increased stringency of regulation necessitated by the strains of the last two years of the war. It would be an error, therefore, to take them too seriously. But, whatever the reasons which prompted them, the sentiments expressed in them were sufficiently powerful to cause proposals, which would later have been frowned on, to meet, down to the latter part of 1918, with a not unsympathetic reception in high places. It was quite in accordance with the mood of the moment that the Government should give its blessing to the action taken by the Wool and Leather Control Boards to arrange for the manufacture and sale at officially fixed prices of clothing and boots for civilian consumption; should accord a respectful hearing to the recommendation of the Central Control Board (Liquor Traffic) for the nationalisation of the supply of Alcoholic Liquor and appoint committees to report on the financial aspects of State purchase; and should consider favourably beating swords into plough-shares by sanctioning the drafting of a bill for the conversion of the demobilised Ministry of Munitions into a Ministry of Supply.[22] The proposal of the Astor Committee that the Government, having bought out the wholesale milk firms, should entrust the supply of milk to a Public Utility Company, and the advocacy by Mr. Churchill of the nationalisation of the railways, reflected the same general attitude. While the war continued, opinion in the Cabinet on post-war policy was, it seems, still undecided. When on 31st July, 1918, a deputation from the National Union of Manufacturers waited on the Prime Minister and the Chancellor of the Exchequer to demand emancipation from war-time restriction, Mr. Bonar Law comforted them with the assurance that there was nothing that the Government desired more; but Mr. Lloyd George, who was not the man to close doors before he need, was more discreet. He repeated the formula as to the desirability of freeing industry from Government, but he accompanied it by an eloquent admonition not to forget the lessons taught by the war as to the value of 'State action, State help, State encouragement, and State promotion'.[23] How precisely his audience interpreted his remarks remains a matter for speculation; but it is clear, at any rate, that the Cabinet continued, even after the Armistice, to encourage the view that large plans of reconstruction had a place in its programme. Its spokesman announced, in the course of 1919, when opinion had already hardened against serious reforms, that it intended to carry through the nationalisation of mineral royalties and compulsory amalgamation of collieries; the unification of all internal transport, including roads and canals; and the reorganisation of the building industry.[24] In domestic, as well as in international affairs, the war, it was felt, marked the end of an epoch. The aspirations suggested by phrases such as 'a new social order' might, no doubt, be discounted; but the fact that the war had greatly strengthened the hold of authority on the economic system was too obvious to be challenged. It was natural to consider whether, instead of returning to the uncovenanted mercies of pre-war individualism, the new relation between the State and industry, which had developed in the intervening years, could not be used, if not as a lever by which to set in motion, without undue disturbance, the large schemes of economic organisation expected in some quarters, at any rate as a buffer by which to break the shock of the transition from war to peace.

Even had that phase of opinion lasted longer and exercised more influence than in fact it did, to act on it would not have been so easy as at first sight appeared. Merely to refrain from abolishing machinery already in existence sounded a simple matter; but the truth was that the Government had not a cleaner slate on which to write. The cessation, within a fixed period after the termination of the war, of the novel types of economic intervention practised during it had been expressly provided for by Parliament in the legislation under which they had been established. The majority of controls owed their existence to regulations made under the Defence of the Realm Acts,[25] and, in the absence of some new enactment prolonging them, necessarily ended when it lapsed. The decease of the Departments set up by special legislation was similarly predetermined, in the sense that the Acts concerned provided, not only for their creation, but also for their extinction. The Ministry of Munitions, for example, had been established for the period of the war and not more than twelve months after its conclusion. So also had been the Ministry of Food and Shipping. The Coal Mines Agreement Confirmation Act, from which the most important of the powers exercised by the Coal Control Department were derived, had provided that the Agreement, if not previously determined by the Coal Controller, should cease to have effect on the expiration of six months after the termination of the war; and the subsequent Mining Industry Act, which transferred the powers of the Coal Controller to the newly created Mines Department of the Board of Trade, did so only for the space of one year after 31st August, 1920. In all these cases, in the absence of special measures to prolong it, control would automatically lapse in a specified period. De-control, in short, which required only inaction, was the line of least resistance. Though it dissolved an imposing fabric of organised activity, it was the continuance of an accepted policy, not the reversal of it.

That fact, though of minor significance, was not wholly unimportant. It meant that the burden of proof was thrown, not on the advocates of de-control, but on its opponents, and that the Government, if it desired to perpetuate beyond the statutory limit any part of the machinery of economic regulation existing at the Armistice, would be obliged for that purpose to seek fresh authority from Parliament. It was improbable that the Parliament which emerged from the election of 1918, unless convinced that immediate de-control menaced social stability, would greet with enthusiasm proposals for legislation which went beyond the indispensable minimum.[26] A Government armed with strong convictions and a well thought out policy, might have succeeded, no doubt, in getting its own way; but, though some members of the Cabinet may have thought that there was more to be said for the maintenance of controls than found public expression, their belief in the advantage of that course stopped short of militancy. At the time of the Armistice, the strength of the armed forces was approximately 4,725,000; while the workers in munition factories was not far short of 3,000,000. The first concern of the Government was to carry through the task of facilitating the movement into peace-time industry of this formidable host, without a dangerous interval of unemployment. If that task was to be successfully accomplished, the rapid revival of business was essential, and other considerations must take second place. The future of certain great controls on the cessation of hostilities had been the subject of departmental investigations long before the Armistice. Plans had been prepared by the officials concerned for effecting the transition from a war to a peace economy with the minimum of dislocation, or in the case of those parts of the former which might be thought worth preserving, for adapting them, with the necessary modifications, to the new conditions.[27] What was lacking was, not competent technical advice, but a considered policy on matters of principle. The Government appears to have made no attempt to survey the problem as a whole, to inform itself and the public as to the merits and defects of different war-controls, or to discriminate between those whose utility had ceased and those which could with advantage be retained. Being without any general view, it was ready to be pushed. The pressure of business interests, the clamour of its supporters, the noise made by the Press, the advice of the Treasury, the economic situation, and, still more, prevalent illusions about the economic situation, all pushed in one direction.

Individual business men, and particular trade associations, had co-operated, with admirable public spirit, in the administration of the war economy. Some of them realised, as the prospects of peace rose above the horizon, that the benefits of control had not been all on one side; while others, even if they disliked it in principle, were conscious that a too abrupt emancipation from unwelcome restrictions might possibly prove a dubious blessing. Shipping and raw materials, it was pointed out, were both likely to be short; that being so, the Government, it was argued, should continue temporarily to control the allocation of tonnage, to maintain schemes for the joint purchase of indispensable supplies, and to ration manufacturers.[28] Wages in some industries stood at a level which could not be maintained if control were withdrawn. The Government, it was said, had put employers concerned in a fix; before repudiating its responsibilities, it must first get them out of it. But caution, compromise, discrimination were not, at the end of 1918, among the virtues most in fashion. Warnings to wait, before taking irreversible decisions, till the curtain had lifted on the post-war scene, fell, as a rule, on deaf ears.

The hard-headed leaders of business were not troubled by the reflection that to step into the same stream twice is not given to man. They appear, with some exceptions, to have expected, once the last shell was fired, to skip happily back into a pre-war world, whose only significant change since it shot Niagara would consist, by a happy dispensation, in its more ravenous voracity for British goods. 'This country', declared Lord Inchcape, in an onslaught on 'the irritating and wasteful interference' of the Government, 'will have an uphill task to get back to the position which it occupied in 1914.'[29] Lord Inchcape was a prince in Israel, and 'Back to 1914' became a common cry. The one remaining barrier between industry and that Elysium was offered, it seemed, by the barbed wire entanglements erected by the mischievous ingenuity of officials, and maintained in defiance of common sense by their interested ambition. To make short work of these abominations became almost a crusade. The great staple industries[30] of the past, shipping, iron and steel, engineering, textiles and coal—though the last had later some reservations to make—were emphatic as to the blessings to be anticipated, once the nation had ceased, in the words of *The Economist*, 'to pay people for putting difficulties in the way of private enterprise'.[31] Their spokesmen had been accustomed for two generations to give orders to Governments. Control was odious to them, not merely because it contracted the scope for remunerative business, but as the expression of an antithetic creed, which challenged their power, as well as their profits. It was 'alien to the British genius', tended 'to paralyse individual effort', and 'was bound to extinguish private enterprise and lead to state ownership'.[32] Among these industries were some, it may be remarked in passing, which were to fill the country with their lamentations during the following decade.

The demand for a return to unrestricted freedom had found expression, before the war ended, in the Reports of the Departmental Committees appointed by the Board of Trade to consider the post-war prospects of different industries. In the boom and depression of the three ensuing years, impatience became a passion. The fall in prices and rise in unemployment, which seems to have begun shortly before the Armistice, did not continue much beyond the following March. For approximately a year, from May, 1919, to April, 1920, though for a longer period in some industries and a shorter in others, the economic climate was tropical. The demand for most kinds of consumer's goods was expanding. Capital expenditure, postponed during the war except in war industries, required to be undertaken; while shipping and railways had heavy losses to make up. Thanks to these factors, to Government borrowing to meet a deficit, and to the busy manufacture of bank credit and paper money, prices were rising at the rate of 2 to 4 per cent a month. That the future will necessarily resemble the immediate past; that trees, if let alone, will grow into the sky; and that upward movements, once started, will continue for ever, seems to be, if not the first article of the practical man's faith, at least a superstition on which, given the opportunity, he is not averse from acting. To these believers in perpetual motion it appeared to be sound sense to buy with borrowed money, provided that the interest did not exceed the rate at which prices were thought certain to continue to rise for the cogent reason that they were already rising. So they bought, borrowed, and drove them still further up, with shrill cries of excitement, as of children on a merry-go-round. Then the incredible happened. The Government betrayed uneasiness. Bank-rate was raised—too late—to 6 per cent in November, 1919, and to 7 per cent in April, 1920.[33] It was evident that an attempt was about to be made to recover control of the monetary situation. The change of policy was a pin-prick, not an earth-quake; but, coming when it did, it let the gas out of the balloon. The index number of prices had been 192 in 1918 and 206 in 1919. It reached its peak in April, 1920, when it was 266.1, and for the first six months of that year averaged 258.2. In 1921, it was 155 and in 1922 131. The unemployment percentage averaged 3.1 in the last half of 1920, when the boom had already passed its height, 13.5 in 1921, and 13.8 in 1922. In April, 1920, all was right with the world. In April, 1921, all was wrong.

The fall in the economic barometer had sensational consequences. Every side of public policy was affected by it. Reconstruction, when not dropped into the dust-bin, was put on the shelf. Education, housing, factory legislation, minimum wage legislation, the improvement of agriculture, the reorganisation of the coal industry, of building, and, except for the grouping of railways, of transport, were all suddenly discovered to be a danger to the State. Most of the few reforms actually carried into law before the end of the war survived, though some did not; but all were attacked, and several were whittled down. On further reforms, including those most advertised, the veto was absolute. The government appeared determined to prove that post-war reconstruction is a contradiction in terms, and found that task, at least, not beyond its powers. Labour was thrown on the defensive. For two years after the election of November, 1918, its temper and policy reflected a combination of industrial strength and political weakness not unusual in itself, but unusual on that scale. Trade union membership[34] stood in 1920, when the Labour members in the House numbered only sixty-three, at 8,024,000, out of an employed population of about 14,000,000. But it is of the nature of industrial organisations to be at the mercy of the state of trade; and, once the depression set in in earnest, trade unionism crumbled. It fought resounding battles, but they were all rear-guard actions.

The last chapter in the story of war-controls must be read against that hectic background. The boom and slump affected them in different ways, but both were equally fatal to them. The former, with the opportunities which it offered for easy money, stirred starved appetites to new and clamorous life. The cheerless winter of conversion costs and fixed commissions suddenly melted into the spring of a profit-makers' paradise. The gambling instinct, balked or dormant during the war, reawoke all the keener for its temporary hibernation. It reached its climax of happy recklessness in the orgy of speculative reflotations that ran riot in Lancashire, but other ranges of business, such as iron and steel, engineering and shipping were not unaffected by it. The depression completed what the boom had begun. It forced businesses to struggle fiercely for a precarious foothold in markets slipping away from them, and made competitive ruthlessness a condition of survival. Both turned every firm's hand against its neighbours, destroyed the rudimentary solidarity which the war had fostered, and caused restrictions, which had been previously borne with resigned grumbles, to become the target of a fury of virtuous indignation. Business interests were not under-represented in Parliament. From the first day after the Armistice, when the Government was told that 'every trade and industry that they have touched they have hampered and injured',[35] a roar of continuance of war-time restrictions; and the denunciations of the 'vague megalomania', which perpetuated 'huge and acquisitive departments',[36] were echoed to the Press. The Cabinet scanned the sky, trimmed its sails, and ran before the storm.

It had taken quite early a short way with the 85 national factories (out of the 245 or so in the possession of the Ministry of Munitions at the time of the Armistice) which had been stated by the Demobilisation and Reconstruction Committee to be suitable either for use or for disposal as industrial concerns.[37] In January, 1919, it had decided that State establishments could be employed to manufacture only those articles of which the Government was the sole buyer, and in the production of which did not compete with private enterprise. Discovering that such articles either did not exist or were too few to permit of economical manufacture, it gave instructions that the factories in question should be sold, and threw in, in addition, some of the 20 factories which the Committee had expressly advised it to retain.[38] On the question of converting the Ministry of Munitions into a Ministry of Supply, in order to centralise Government buying, it was somewhat slower in reaching a decision. A bill for the establishment of a Ministry of Supply was actually drafted; but, when the subject was last discussed by the Cabinet in March, 1920, the subject was shelved for fear of parliamentary hostility to the creation of a new department, and even before the final extinction, a year later, of the Ministry of Munitions, it had been silently dropped.[39] The Government's attitude to the rest of the war-time apparatus of economic regulation showed equal pliability. At the time of the Armistice the continuance of the control of industry by the State had been described by a Minister in a speech to a business audience, as a policy which, though the Government intended to wind it up, would remain 'necessary for some time to come'.[40] Just over a year later, another Minister advised the Cabinet that his own control department ought to remain in existence for a further five years.[41] A year after that, a third Minister was explaining to an applauding House of Commons that the control of industry by the Government was 'a thoroughly abominable thing'.[42] The Cabinet found itself compelled temporarily to adopt special measures with regard to food and coal. With those two exceptions, it threw the reins on the neck of the dominant forces of the day, and allowed events to take their course.

That negative attitude was not peculiar to one country. It is encountered on the Continent, as well as in England. It was as powerful in the United States as it was in Europe. In France[43] some attempt was made to apply war-machinery to civilian purposes. Almost immediately after the Armistice, on 26th November, 1918, the *Ministère de l'Armement et des Fabrications de Guerre* was converted into a *Ministère de Reconstruction Industrielle*, which, while continuing to supply manufacturers with fuel and raw materials, also produced articles, such as doors and windows, needed for the reconstruction of the devastated areas. The general policy of the Government, however, as laid down in the *Journal Officiel* of 25th December, 1918, was to 're-establish freedom of business transactions with the utmost possible rapidity', and that policy was acted on. The railways were handed back to the companies on 2nd January, 1919, though later, in France, as in England, reorganisation proved necessary, and a decree of 29th October, 1921, created a common board of management acting under a Supreme Railway Council. A decree of 1st July, 1919, dissolved the departments concerned with requisitioning and price-fixing, with the exception of the Wheat Supply Service, which survived down to 1st August, 1921. The re-opening of the ports to foreign imports automatically ended most of the so-called 'consortiums'.[44] The few survivors, such as those handling coal, mineral oil, and industrial alcohol, were abolished by a decree of 24th February, 1921.

The American reaction against the continuance of war-controls was equally decided. The organisations principally affected by it were the great international bodies handling food, raw materials and shipping. British business was still hypnotised by memories of a vanished age of 'industrial supremacy'. The United States had not yet discovered what it means to be a creditor and an exporting nation; and the views of American business were hardly more realistic. Thinking in terms of nineteenth century self-sufficiency, it regarded its late allies as an unsound proposition, which it could drop, at any moment, without injury to itself; and the edge of its economic distrust was sharpened by political suspicions. Europe, it thought, was not only bankrupt; it was also incorrigible. If America was to preserve either its prosperity or its virtue, it must shun contamination by the mystery of iniquity which brooded over a continent plainly destined to damnation.

That combination of commercial caution with a tranquil consciousness of moral superiority had found one of its earliest and most truculent expressions in a letter from Mr. Hoover. 'This Government', he wrote, in crushing a proposal for concerted international action to supply food and other essentials to starving and exhausted peoples, 'will not agree to any programme that even looks like Inter-allied control of our resources during peace; our only hope of securing justice in distribution, proper appreciation abroad of the effort we make to assist foreign nations, and proper return for the services we will perform, revolves around complete independence of commitment to joint action on our part.'[45] The practical conclusion to which such sentiments led was an attitude by no means peculiar to the United States, but which, whether adopted in America or in Europe, was a grave misfortune. Looking back from the vantage-ground of 1941, we can see that the sharp antithesis between the economic conditions of war and those of peace was an illusion; that a world racked by four years of misery could not suddenly go forth, like a giant, to renew its strength; and that the way to make certain that the patient's break-down would outlast the shock that had caused it was to cut off the provision which might have nursed him back to health. Those truths, which seem truisms today, were concealed from contemporaries. Largely under the influence of the United States, the inter-allied economic organisations were quickly dissolved. The American delegate on the Inter-allied Munitions Council, which handled not only armaments, but wool, cotton, timber, petroleum, flax, hemp, coal and numerous other articles, took the view that he had no mandate to deal with peace problems, and the Council was wound up. The Leather and Hides Executive, after producing a storm of protest in the United States, went the same way. So did the Nitrates Executive. So, finally, did the most important of all the inter-allied controls, the Allied Maritime Transport Council, whose proposals had occasioned Mr. Hoover's outburst.[46] One is tempted to say that some of these organisations were condemned to death at the moment when not the least useful passage in their lives was about to begin.

It will be seen, therefore, that, if the British Government erred in yielding to the demand for rapid de-control, it was not alone in its mistake. The movement of opinion before which it retreated was a general one, carrying with it the propertied classes of most industrialised nations. It was the last spasm of nineteenth century individualism, striving to recapture on its deathbed the crude energies of its vanished youth. Nor, again, was the final rush of Great Britain into de-control a mere headlong flight before business interests on the ramp. There were two other considerations which pointed in the same direction. In the first place, as has already been remarked, the most urgent of the domestic problems confronting the Government in the six months following the Armistice, was to ensure the speedy transfer of ex-soldiers, and of workers previously employed in war-industries, into civil employment. The possibility of their rapid absorption depended on the revival of industry; and the revival of industry, the Government was assured by most of those who spoke for industry, depended partly on the removal of war-controls. In the second place, several of the most important controls had a financial, as well as an industrial and commercial, face. During the war it had worn a veil, which dropped on the return of peace. In 1919, it was not frightening, for the world looked the other way. By the end of 1920, it was unmistakably all frowns.

In spite of the well-staged hysterics of the Press, the administrative expenses of the machinery of control had been in relation to the business handled so minute as to be negligible. But the State, in a few cases, thought it expedient to use it to subsidise the consumer, and the costs thus incurred were not a trifle. The Sugar Commission paid no subsidies during the war, but in 1919 and 1920, it deliberately kept prices below the commercial level, and made a loss on the two years of £22,000,000. The Wheat Commission sold imported cereals to millers at the Food Controller's price for the British article; and the millers, who themselves were controlled, sold flour to the bakers at a price below their own expenses. From September, 1917, to December, 1920, the so-called 'bread subsidy' averaged, in round figures, £50,000,000 a year. For a time the Central Live Stock Fund had sold American meat at less than cost price, and the adverse balance to be met by subsidies had amounted by September, 1918, to approximately £2,000,000. While food, not unnaturally, was the principal liability, it had not been the only one. The Ministry of Munitions had fixed prices for steel, and having entered on that basis into a multitude of contracts, found it expedient, when costs rose, not to scrap the agreements, but to pay increasing subsidies, some direct, some indirect, which made the real cost of steel an impenetrable mystery. The coal industry, as usual, was in a fog of its own. It was not subsidised; but it was governed by a highly complicated agreement between the Coal Controller and mine-owners, negotiated in July, 1917, and subsequently confirmed by the

Coal Mines Agreement, (Confirmation) Act of February, 1918, under which the State guaranteed to concerns producing 'a standard output' a 'profit standard', based on the profits of any one of the three abnormally good years immediately preceding the war; took, via the Inland Revenue Department, 80 per cent of the profits above that standard; left 15 per cent with the Coal Controller as a pool to meet the guarantee; and allowed 5 per cent to mine-owners as 'coal-mines excess profits'. When prices were high, the Government was on velvet. But what would happen if they broke?[47]

For five years the Treasury had led a forlorn life. Now it crept from its corner, making mournful noises. It seems unfortunate to-day that it did not do so sooner. It was partly influenced, it is to be presumed, by the desire to do nothing which might check an industrial revival at a moment when it was of vital importance that ex-service men and war-workers should move quickly to new jobs; but the price paid was somewhat heavy. The cause of much subsequent trouble was the delightful debauch of 1919–20, and the chief cause of that was inflation. A bucket of cold water then, before the hot fit became a fever, would have been worth an ocean later. The Treasury, whose speciality was cold water, was somewhat slow to turn the tap. More than two years before, in November 1917, Lord Rhondda, the then Minister of Food, had told the Peers that, not he, but the Chancellor of the Exchequer, was 'the real controller of prices'. If so, the controller had temporarily abdicated control. He did not reverse the financial engines till the spring of 1920, when they were racing at a speed which turned any jolt into a crash. In the matter of war-controls, the expenses of the most expensive of which, compared with inflation, were a bagatelle, the Treasury's influence was in two cases of importance. In the first, its attitude was a cautious hostility, in the second a reckless one. It waged, from the last half of 1919, a war of attrition against the Ministry of Food, demanding to be consulted before the price of any article was reduced, and then suggesting that the Ministry should cease its purchases of food after March, 1920.[48] Political forces—whether fortunately or not need not here be discussed—defeated its offensive. The Ministry had been sentenced to death in May, 1919, and reprieved in June. It was again pulled back from the grave, when all but in it, in January, 1920, to be interred for good in March, 1921. The Treasury's frontal attack on the Coal Control Department was more successful. It was also more disastrous.

The episode, like much of the history of coal in these singular years, was at once odd and tragic. It was not to be expected that, at a moment when de-control was being hailed as a formula of salvation, and when coal, in the eyes of all respectable persons, had suddenly turned from black to red, the complicated system of coal-control should survive intact; nor, in its existing form, was it desirable that it should. Much depended, however, on the date and manner of its decease. It might be gradually demobilised, or it might fall with a crash, in which case a good deal else was likely to fall with it. Some of the outworks of the edifice had already been removed. The export restrictions had gone in May 1919, the Coal Transport Re-organisation Scheme and the limitation of coal prices in August of the same year. The kernel of the system, however, remained in the shape of the arrangements already mentioned, under which standard profits were guaranteed to the mine-owners and surplus profits—less an additional payment also made to the mine-owners—accrued to the State. Legislation passed in 1920 provided that this part of control should continue till 31st August, 1921. On this central arch rested the wage arrangements of the industry.

The coal industry, for all the difficulties confronting it, had served the public well during the war, and had done not too badly for itself. In spite of a rush to enlist which, in the first twelve months of the war—long before conscription was heard of—swept over a quarter of a million miners into the army, output had been creditable. For the four years 1915–18 it averaged between 9 and 10 per cent below that of the years 1910–13; while a comparison of profits (inclusive of royalties) for the same periods shows an increase of 108 per cent. Since the Inland Revenue, as has been explained, took 80 per cent of the profits above a standard fixed for each colliery, while the Controller retained 15 per cent, the profitableness of the industry had not been a matter of indifference to the State. The capital fact after the Armistice was the demand for British coal abroad, especially from France, the great part of whose coal fields were still out of action, and from Italy, to whom coal had become almost a luxury import. As a consequence, export prices of coal rose to unprecedented heights.[49] In 1918, 34,173,915 tons were exported, realising £52,416,330. In 1919 the corresponding figures were 38,466,593 tons and £92,297,685. In 1920, they were 28,862,895 tons and £120,319,241. Thus the tonnage exported was in 1920 actually less than in 1918, but its value was more than twice as high.[50]

The Government was anxious, for financial reasons, to make the most of that gold-mine. After withdrawing certain restrictions on export, it had substituted, by an order of 28th May, 1919, minimum prices for fixed prices in the case of shipments to France, Italy, Belgium and Portugal, as well as to British possessions and protectorates. Prices continued to rise during that year, and the greater part of 1920. The revenue which the Exchequer derived from the industry rose with them. In June, 1918, apprehensions had been expressed in the House of

Commons that the control of coal might involve the State in heavy liabilities. In November, 1919, the President of the Board of Trade announced that the possible deficit had been converted, by the end of the financial year, into a profit of £170,000,000. Such wind-falls were intoxicating. There was much talk at the time of the wickedness of the miners in producing less coal than their critics thought desirable. The Government believed it, or thought it good business to affect to believe it. By way of demonstrating its conviction that any tonnage raised could be sold at a profit, it actually insisted that the agreement which followed the stoppage of October, 1920, should contain a provision relating wage-movements to changes in the total output of the industry.

Unfortunately, in its eagerness to make hay while the sun shone, it appears not to have reflected that the sale of hay might possibly be affected by its price. The allies of Great Britain—in particular France and Italy—were not unnaturally furious at what they regarded as a shameless attempt to exploit their post-war embarrassments. The latter was helpless till she developed her water-power, which in the next decade she did. The former also speeded up the development of water-power in the south; but her own mines were slowly coming back into action, and she was beginning to receive reparations coal from Germany. Hence she was not altogether a passive victim. She retaliated by fixing, through the *Bureau des Charbons*, maximum prices for British coal at a figure well below current values. Still less does it appear to have occurred to Ministers that the rise in prices was unlikely to continue for ever, or that, by continuing to maintain a highly remunerative financial partnership with the coal industry when trade was good, they incurred an obligation not to terminate control abruptly the moment that happy condition ceased. The wage system of the industry—to mention nothing else—had been profoundly affected since 1917, by the action of the State. If a break-down was to be avoided, it was essential that sufficient notice of de-control should be given to permit of a planned and orderly transition to a new régime.

That truism was self-evident. In fixing 31st August, 1921, as the date at which control would cease, the Government had taken some account, at least, of it. Both mine-owners and miners had agreed to the Government's decision, and had based their plans upon it. Now it was suddenly reversed. In December, 1920, there were signs that the golden age was drawing to a close. By the beginning of the next year the tide had unmistakably turned. In January, 1921, the expenses of the industry exceeded its returns by £4,800,000; in February by £4,500,000 odd. The Cabinet—not for the last time where coal was concerned—was seized with panic. It decided, in spite of its undertaking and of protests from mine-owners and miners alike, to cut its losses and leave its partners in the lurch. In the latter part of February it announced that de-control would take place at just over a month's notice—five months sooner than it had promised—on 31st March. The consequences of its breach of faith were those to be expected, and it is needless here to dwell on them. The movement to wind up the war economy, as has already been remarked, was a more complex process than is sometimes suggested; but, in the case of the coal industry, the last chapter of the story is simplicity itself. It is the classical example of de-control from fright.

The continuance of control in the coal industry would have involved a considerable, if temporary, burden on the public, though probably a lighter one, than, all things considered, resulted from its summary abolition. In the case of liquor[51] control, nothing of the kind was to be anticipated. In the three years 1st April, 1918, to 31st March, 1921, the Control Board had made a profit of $12^1/_2$ per cent on a capital of approximately £1,270,000; and, when the Board was abolished by the Licensing Act, 17th August, 1921, its business at Carlisle and Cromarty Firth, though not at Enfield, had continued, as explained above, to be carried on by the Home Office on the same lines as before. The danger, however, of an undertaking of the kind being conducted at a profit appears to have been regarded in some circles with only less alarm—if, indeed, it was less—than that of its making a loss. The Geddes Economy Committee of 1922 was equal to the emergency. It drew attention, as, in view of the facts, it could hardly avoid doing, to the substantial profits made, but it saw in them a ground, not for hope, but for fear. It condemned the 'experiment in the direct administration of the Liquor Traffic' on the grounds, not that it was unprofitable, but that it might not, in future years, be so profitable as it had been.[52] A verdict so incapable of refutation carried instant conviction, and the objectionable 'State undertaking' was shortly afterwards wound up.

III THE POLICY OF DE-CONTROL: COMMENTS AND CRITICISMS

What conclusions, if any, of significance for the future are suggested by the history epitomised in these pages? The economic order, both international and domestic, has undergone, in the last twenty years, considerable changes. Partly as the result of a deliberate attempt to learn from, and improve on, the methods of the past, the technique of mobilising British resources for military purposes at present in use, is, in some respects, markedly different from that previously employed. While, however, the problems confronting Great Britain and the world when the present war concludes will not be identical with those which faced them at the end of the last, they will be a different species of the same genus. It would be an error to seek their solution by a mere appeal to past experience, but to ignore that experience would be even more short-sighted. The last period of war-controls was not barren of suggestions for similar emergencies. The last period of de-control may also yield some lessons. What are the most important of them?

The first issue which arises can be simply stated. It is concerned with the principle of de-control itself. It is of the nature of modern war to cause a sensational increase, both of range and of intensity, in the authority exercised by the State over economic life. When the crisis ends, three alternative courses are possible. In the first place, a prompt return to pre-war conditions may be the objective chosen, and the machinery of economic controls may be rapidly demobilised, in order to attain it. The completion of the de-control is likely, even so, to be spread over some years; but de-control is the goal sought, and delays in achieving it are acquiesced in with reluctance, as an unavoidable evil, not prescribed in advance as successive stages in a process which will be dangerous, if accelerated, and which, if a break-down is to be avoided, it is expedient to retard. It may be held, in the second place, that the transition from war to peace is necessarily, under modern conditions, a somewhat lengthy voyage, with reefs on either hand; that, while restrictions imposed in the crisis should in due course be abolished, their maintenance during that intervening period is only less necessary—if it is less necessary—than during war itself; and that their removal must take place by carefully regulated degrees, as normal economic conditions are slowly re-established. The third view which may be taken is different from both. The shock given by war to the conventional economic routine is not, it may be argued, an unqualified evil. It is appalling in its destructiveness; but some of the counter-measures evoked by it, though the children of a passing crisis, contain possibilities of more than temporary significance, of which the most should be made. The course of wisdom, on that view, is not to consign war-controls wholesale to indiscriminate oblivion. It is to sort out from the welter of emergency expedients those containing a promise of permanent utility, and to incorporate the latter in the post-war economic order. In practice, no doubt, these alternative policies, and especially the two last, overlap at their edges; but the difference of principle between them is none the less important. At the close of the last war, the Government, after a brief flirtation with the second, jumped head-over-heels into the arms of the first. The question to be answered is whether subsequent events confirmed the wisdom of its choice.

The case for immediate de-control can be briefly stated. During the greater part of history, the normal condition of the world has been one of scarcity. In all scarcity economies, given an effective central government, the control of economic life by authority is not the exception, but the rule. The shortage of essential supplies is, in such conditions, a recurrent catastrophe, which everyone has experienced more than once in his life, and is at all times a danger. The State intervenes to prevent it by compulsorily mobilising economic resources and economising their use. As a result of the modernisation of production and transport, first in Great Britain, then on the Continent of Europe, and in North America, then in parts of the Far East, their scarcity ceased, after the middle of the nineteenth century, to be the haunting terror which till recently it had been. With the retreat of the spectre, the devices employed to exorcise or appease it were discarded as obsolete. War brought both back. Labour, consumption goods and capital all become deficient. It was necessary, if the war was to be won, to cope with that shortage.

The expedients adopted, though immensely more elaborate and more efficient than those used in the past, differed little from them in principle. Since victory was generally accepted as the over-ruling end to which all others must be subordinated, the commodities to be made, and the allocation of the resources required to make them, could no longer be settled by the effective demand of consumers, or cake would be produced instead of bread, high-heeled shoes in place of army boots, and motor-cars in place of shells. They must be determined by the Government in accordance with a scheme of priorities based on a decision as to the order of relative urgency in which victory required different needs to be satisfied. Since the hundreds of thousands of articles, from forage caps to heavy guns, covered by the elastic term munitions had to be created from resources, in the shape of skilled workers and plant, which did not yet exist, the only limit to the rise in prices was the depth of the State's pocket and its readiness to be swindled; while however preposterous the increase, it would not increase the supply in the time required, or correct itself by doing so. It was necessary, therefore, to resort to a régime of fixed prices, and to do so not only for military supplies but for many commodities in civilian use, since the latter, as well as the former, were deficient. The necessity of controlling prices had two further consequences. In the first place, it could rarely be effective unless all stages of production were brought under control. Hence the great purchases by the Government of food-stuffs, such as sugar, wheat and meat, and raw materials, like flax and wool; the application of a costings system to manufacturers; and their remuneration on the basis of fixed conversion costs, *plus* a reasonable profit. In the second place, once prices were fixed, the distribution of goods, whether steel, ships or food, ceased to depend on the varying abilities of would-be purchasers to pay for them. It became necessary, therefore, to allocate them on a predetermined plan, so that recourse to some system of rationing became indispensable. Finally, the demand for a greatly increased output from a diminished civilian population led to novel restrictions on the *personnel* of industry. It was deemed essential, not merely to protect certain categories of workers against the claims of the fighting services, and periodically to 'comb out' the army itself, but to economise labour by down-grading certain jobs, by insisting on the transfer of workers from non-essential to essential occupations, and by checking the movement of workers from the latter by instituting a system of leaving certificates.

The capital fact which stamped on the economy of 1914–18 its peculiar character was therefore simple. It was the abrupt termination of an age of relative abundance, which, novel though it was, everyone assumed to be permanent, and the sudden return of an age of scarcity, which, though the normal conditions of mankind, no one remembered. A host of prophets, from the compilers of the official war-book to the authors of imaginative romances, had attempted to forecast the effects of a world-conflict; but none had foreseen its economic consequences. It is not surprising therefore, that the most obvious of those consequences should have been slow to be grasped, and that most of the measures required to grapple with them should have been introduced tardily and piece-meal. It is equally natural that the demand for the abolition of restrictions on economic enterprise should have been vocal before the Armistice, and insistent after it.

The arguments used to defend State control in time of war had only to be reversed, to appear, once the crisis was over, convincing arguments against it. The intervention of authority in every detail of economic life had been prompted by the necessities of an extraordinary situation. Now normal conditions were about to return; normal methods of doing business should be encouraged to return with them. Government priority schemes became, if not actually impracticable, at any rate unnecessary, with the attainment of the one agreed objective by reference to which priorities had been fixed, and, becoming useless, became mischievous, since they thwarted the free exercise of preferences by consumers. When materials and labour were no longer deficient, and supplies, as a consequence, could be rapidly increased, price-controls, rationing, the licensing of dealers, the State Purchase of wool and wheat, the fixing of the costs of the different processes of manufacture, the limitation of profits, similarly lost their virtue. With producers eager and able to increase their output, exorbitant charges would correct themselves, and the public would be protected by free competition more swiftly and more effectively than by the chill fingers of bureaucracy. Government occupation, with or without actual ownership, of railways, canals, mines, shipyards, shipping and munition factories had not less clearly had its day. Not only did it create a sense of insecurity prejudicial to prosperity, but these assets, if transferred to private individuals alert for profitable business, would be used to supply a hungry world with an energy and efficiency beyond the competence of the State. Thus the logic which had justified controls in November, 1918, condemned them in December. Unfettered individual enterprise had served the nation well in the past; it was reasonable to suppose that once released from its chains, it would serve it in the future with equal success. It would maximise production, adjust payments to services, and provide the surplus required to ensure its own growth, with the automatic regularity of a self-adjusting mechanism.

How far such a picture gives a valid account of the normal operations of the pre-war economic system need not here be discussed. Given the acceptance of its premises, the demand for immediate de-control was not without cogency. It is obvious, however, that the case thus presented rested on certain assumptions, which it was important to submit to critical analysis, since they would, if invalidated, gravely discredit the proposals based on them. Of those assumptions the most important were two. The first was that the interlude between war and peace would be short; the second that, when it was over, the environment in which enterprise must function would not differ materially from that existing before the war. For certain departments of economic life, both assumptions were justified. For others, including some of the most important, both were fallacious.

It is easy for the majority of business men to appreciate, and allow for, the ordinary uncertainties of their profession. The course is staked out; the nasty corners and bad hedges are well known; to bear the risks incidental to business is part of their trade, and, if profits are the payment for risks, a not unremunerative one. It is more difficult for them to realise, especially in a continent accustomed by nearly half a century to take an ordered routine of existence for granted, that the very possibility of continuous economic activity depends on the maintenance of an elaborate frame-work of economic habits, social conventions, rules of law, and political organisation, which is a highly artificial product, and with the crumbling of which the operations of business are arrested or stultified. Such, however, is the fact. It might have been expected, in view of the unprecedented destructiveness of military operations, of the shattering blows which the economic systems of all countries encountered, and of the political upheavals which overturned Governments in some of the greatest of them, that the significance of that truism would have sunk home before the war concluded. In fact, it seems not to have done so, at any rate so generally as was necessary if grave errors were to be avoided. The Economic Conference held in Paris in 1916 had much to say on the subject of international commercial rivalries, of the importance of submitting the enemy powers, when peace returned, to special disabilities, of the necessity for prohibitions, tariffs and other restrictions. The Departmental Committees, composed mainly of business men, which reported two years later on post-war economic prospects, embroidered the same themes, and added to them numerous, and sometimes useful, suggestions on matters of detail. Both thought principally in terms of the competitive advantages to be secured by particular industries and by individual countries or groups of countries. Neither they, nor the House of Commons, nor indeed the Cabinet, appear to have understood that the kind of world—a highly novel kind—to meet whose demands the industries had been organised, and on whose continuance the prosperity of the countries depended, had ceased to exist. The patient required to be nursed through a long period of convalescence, and could not expect, even at the end of it, to lead the same life as before the operation. They thought it sufficient, having removed his bandages, to exhort him to take up his bed and walk.

It was the existence of this wide-spread dislocation which was the crucial feature of the post-armistice period. It was the failure to appreciate its full significance which vitiated the prevalent treatment of economic policy in general, and of the problem of Government controls in particular. Under the pre-war economic system, equilibrium, when disturbed, had been re-established by a multitude of minute, but ceaseless, readjustments, carried out, under the promptings of economic self-interest, by countless individuals. The system functioned after a fashion, though with a shocking mass of needless waste, brutality and suffering; but it could function at all because of the presence of three conditions. The first was that the readjustments required were small; the second that they were made against the background of a system which itself was relatively stable; the third—a corollary of the two former—that the time available in which to make them, though often too short for individuals, was long enough not to involve large masses of men in a sudden revolution in their manner of life. A market might be contracting, but it was not halved at a stroke. A trade might be injured by a tariff; but it did not wake up to find half a dozen new frontiers, each with its own line of custom houses, established overnight. Some currencies might make awkward jumps, though in practice few did; but one did not order goods in the morning, and find their price doubled when they were delivered in the afternoon. A craft, or a whole industry, might decline; but, though individuals suffered cruelly, the shift from agriculture to mining, or from textiles to machine-making, normally took place, not by the displacement of masses of adult workers, but by a change in the occupations entered by the rising generations.

In the post-war period these three conditions had ceased to exist. The changes required were not small, but large. When 'readjustment' is prescribed, the first question to which the doctor must reply is 'Readjustment to what?' In the economic and political conditions of the five years between the German revolution and the withdrawal of France from the Ruhr, it was a bold man who would attempt an answer. It was a bolder one who, with large populations threatened with unemployment, and some not far from starvation, would venture to invoke the healing influence of time. To expect the problems which such a situation presented to be solved by the normal operations of the competitive economic system was hardly more reasonable than to rely on it to meet a break-down in China caused by flood or drought. The truth is that war conditions did not end with the war, and that collective disorganisation, whether in a single industry, or on the larger scale of a country, required a collective effort to cope with it. It is difficult, no doubt, to fix a precise date by which normal economic life can be said to have been re-established but Germany did not restore her currency till 1924, and Great Britain did not return to the gold standard till 1925. It was only in the latter year—between six and seven years after the cessation of hostilities—that, according to the League's figures, the output in Europe reached its 1913 level; while certain particularly unfortunate industries, both in Great Britain and on the Continent, continued to bear the scars of the conflict for long after that. Special machinery had been required to carry the country through the war. Except on the childish assumption that peace had been re-established when the last shot was fired, or when the treaties were signed, special machinery was also needed to carry it over the difficult passage from war to peace.

Of such war-machinery the various controls had only [been] one part, but a not unimportant one. Given the view that they had no permanent contribution to make, and that a return to the pre-war economy was the objective to be aimed at, there were, doubtless, some of them whose retention merely as an interim measure was hardly worthwhile. With the world sliding as it was, precipitation was the last thing to be desired; and it is probable on a long view, that less harm would have been done by the needless continuance in existence of types of intervention which had played their part than actually resulted from a too hasty plunge into general de-control. Nevertheless, it is true that there were various aspects of the system of economic regulation in force at the Armistice, whose case for a further lease of life was not a strong one.

Some of the price-fixing activities of the Ministry of Food are an instance in point. During the war, when the shortage of supplies facilitated the operations of speculators and rings, those activities had been fully justified, and had succeeded, on more than one occasion, in teaching these vermin manners. After the war, however, the situation, as far as most food-stuffs were concerned, was different. The most important factor in the continuous and general rise of prices, which began in April, 1919, was inflation, and profiteering was less its cause than its consequence. It may have been expedient to maintain in existence the Wheat and Sugar Commissions, on the ground that the articles that they handled presented special problems; but the wisdom of continuing the control of other food-stuffs over the autumn of 1919 seems, at best, somewhat questionable. It was probably due as much to the wish to be armed to meet a possible railway strike as to considerations suggested by the general food situation. The Profiteering Act of the same year was merely eye-wash. It was on a par with witch-baiting, except that it was not the supposed friends of Satan, but the Government, with its reluctance to strike at the root of the trouble by checking inflation, which had the evil eye.

It did not follow, however, that because some controls had had their day, others had no useful part to play in the post-war world. Whether they had or had not depended on the circumstances of particular departments of economic life. Those parts of it which had been so little disturbed by the war and post-war conditions as to be able at once to resume their pre-war activities on the former scale, needed no nursing. Those in which distortion or dislocation had gone so far that they could hardly function till the havoc was repaired were in a different position. They were the victims of a blow affecting, not merely individuals, but the whole system of organisation on which economic health depended, and something more than individual effort was needed to set them on their feet. Such cases were not unimportant. The most striking of them arose from the break-down of the international economic system. Others occurred in connection with the domestic economy of particular countries. In both cases the continuance—or, if necessary, the creation—of bodies exercising the powers of a Control Board, which could steer an industry or a region through a period of crisis, would have been an advantage.

As a foil to the example of the price fixing side of the Ministry of Food, three examples may be given. The Cotton Control Board, composed of employers, workers, merchants and representatives of the Government, had been appointed by the Board of Trade in June, 1917. The occasion of its creation had been a reduction of the supplies of raw cotton, caused by shortage of tonnage, which threatened a scramble, with rocketing prices. Its primary function was to regulate the consumption of cotton, which it did by fixing the proportion of machinery to be run. Since, however, the reduction in the output of mills involved the playing off of workers, the Board also imposed a compulsory levy on firms, the proceeds of which were administered by the unions, and used to make payments to workers who, under the rota system adopted, were temporarily idle. The limitation on the percentage of machinery to be run was continued for about three months after the Armistice; but, as supplies of raw cotton were no longer short, the orders of the Board of Trade, from which the Control Board derived its powers, were of doubtful legality. The Board of Trade revoked them in February, 1919, and the Cotton Control Board died. It was buried under the name of the Cotton Reconstruction Committee.

The Board was abolished at the moment when the most critical period in the recent history of the cotton industry was about to begin. In the latter part of 1919 and the opening months of 1920, Lancashire fell a victim to the speculative ramp which has already been mentioned. Partly through the intervention of London racketeers who did not know a mule from a loom, over 260[53] mills changed hands in eighteen months. Values were driven up to fantastic figures.[54] The industry was loaded with a mass of watered capital representing little except greed and credulity, which hung round its neck for the next ten years, and which did not—to mention only one point—make wage negotiations easier. Then the weather changed.

In 1920 imports of raw cotton, home consumption of yarn and piece-goods and exports of both, had been, as was to be expected, well below the pre-war figure. From 1923 onwards, instead of recovering, they all tumbled down. The causes of that long decline have been endlessly discussed. The most important of them are obvious, and it is needless to examine them here. The consequences, especially on the manufacturing side, were the redundant machinery and the under-employed workers which remained the chief problems of the industry down to the beginning of the present war.

Whether a Cotton Control Board, not necessarily composed in the same way or with the same limited powers as that of the last war, could have checked the speculative re-financing of 1919, it is not easy to say. If it had merely told the truth and called things by their right names, it would have done some good. In fact, however, if it had kept its head, it need not have been wholly helpless. Intervention by the Government to check unsound capitalisation by controlling capital issues and pressing caution on the banks was clearly desirable. It would have been difficult for it, however, to impose that policy on Lancashire, unless supported by the approval of the cotton industry itself. A responsible authority, concerned with the long-run interests of the trade, was required, in order to give a lead. Had the Cotton Control Board continued to exist, it would have been the natural body to take the initiative. Machinery of the kind was certainly needed in order to cope with the ensuing depression. To suppose that an industry composed, on the manufacturing side, of a multitude of firms, mostly small firms, could set its house in order by uncoordinated individual efforts was as reasonable as to expect several thousand motorists to drive safely through Cheapside without a rule of the road. If the cotton industry was to adapt its pre-war organisation, with tolerable speed, to the harsh realities of the post-war world, a central authority was clearly indispensable. The Cotton Control Board, remodelled and armed with larger powers of compulsion, could have supplied it. It is significant, indeed, that every subsequent scheme put forward, whether by employers or by the unions, for setting the industry on its feet, has had the re-establishment of some kind of Control Board[55] as its essential feature, and that the demand has been partially conceded, eighteen years after the abolition of the first Cotton Trade Control Board, by the Cotton Trade Enabling Act.

Coal-mining offers a second example of an industry in which the continuance of control would have been desirable. It had grown with extraordinary rapidity in the two decades before the war. Its output for the five years 1909–13 was 20 per cent above the level of 1899–1903; its personnel 35 per cent. In 1913 tonnage raised, exports, profits and workers employed were all at their peak. The ease with which it found wealth washed to its shores had not been an unmixed blessing. The coal industry of the Ruhr was organised in a small number of large undertakings; and after the war, that of the north of France moved in the same direction. The British coal industry resembled a pampered youth who refuses to grow up. Its structure had been crystallised in the days before serious competition became a reality. With its 1,500 odd companies working some 3,300 pits, and selling to a mixed multitude of not far short of 30,000 factors, distributing merchants and dealers, the industry carried into the post-war period an organisation, or lack of organisation, and still more, a psychology, which had served it well enough in the past, but which was singularly unsuited to stand severe shocks.

With the conclusion of the post-war boom the shocks came. On the one hand, the number of persons employed in 1919 was only slightly lower than the figure for 1913, 1,025,604 as against 1,110,884, and in 1923, the year of the French occupation of the Ruhr, actually stood above it, with a total of 1,203,000. On the other hand, the export market, which had absorbed in 1913 one-third in value of the total raised, sharply contracted; and exports, once the spurt of 1923 was over, continued to fall till they reached a level just over one-half of the pre-war figure. Their decline was the result of causes which were not temporary, but permanent. As a consequence of the development of the domestic coal industries of different countries, of the increasing use of hydro-electric energy, and of the substitution of oil for coal, less coal of any kind was passing in international trade than before, and Great Britain had a diminished share of a diminished total. The truth was that, while the first phase of the Industrial Revolution on the Continent had been a benefit to the British coal industry, the second phase hit it hard.

A discussion of the larger problems of policy would not here be in place; but one chapter of the story is strictly relevant to the subject of controls. In the wintry world confronting it, it was necessary for the *personnel* of the industry to be deflated. The question was how deflation should take place. When an industry is faced by the certainty, not merely of temporary, but of prolonged, unemployment, the right course is simple, probably—since the great ones of this world do not love to bathe in Jordan—too simple to be followed. To men in the prime of life, between 20 and 50, unemployment, whatever provision is made for it, must always be a tragedy. Not only is it such men who have the heaviest family responsibilities, but prolonged unemployment destroys the meaning of existence for them. The same is not equally true of the young and the old. In such a situation, therefore, the sensible course, both on economic and social grounds, is to concentrate employment on workers of the age of optimum employability; to hold recruits back from entry into the industry by continuing their education for twelve months or two years longer; and to speed up the exit of older workers from it, by making suitable financial provision for them if they retire. If that course is followed, several age-groups are removed, and employment is concentrated on the remainder. Since the age at which boys are allowed to go down the pit in England is lower than in most other civilised countries, and coal is an industry in which, owing to its exacting nature, the average age-level is unusually low, it is one to which those measures are specially appropriate.

With the contraction of the demand for coal, and—though at a later date—the progress of mechanisation and nationalisation, such a policy was clearly needed. To make it effective, however, an authority was required which could plan and carry it out. The Coal Controller's Department, or, after its extinction, the Mines Department of the Board of Trade, would have been the proper organ to apply it. But the Act which established the latter did not confer on it the necessary powers; while the industry possessed no machinery by means of which it could take action itself. As a consequence, though deflation took place, it took place in the slowest, least economical, and most cruel manner. The *personnel* of the industry was reduced by 20.7 per cent between 1923 and 1929, and by another 17.3 per cent between 1929 and 1937; but the cost fell almost wholly on the miners. They were not formally sentenced to economic death by inches, but they incurred it as though they had been. Nor was that all. The coal industry was littered with a number of small, half obsolete concerns which led, in normal times, a miserable life, but which hung on in the hope that a chance rise in prices would bring them back into activity. An authority armed with the powers possessed, during the war, by the Coal Controller, could have accelerated the movement to concentrate production in the more efficient areas and concerns which everyone including leading mine-owners knew to be desirable. Ultimately, such a movement got under way, but, again, at a snail's pace. In the meantime, the unhappy industry, and the human beings dependent on it—a population about three times that of New Zealand—staggered from crisis to crisis, while mine-owners and governments vied with each other in protesting that there was nothing whatever which required to be done, and that, even if there was something, there was no means of doing it. Given the absence of a controlling authority, the last statement was correct. But why, when it was evident that the industry was entering stormy seas, was the authority abolished? The official answer in 1921 was economy. Five and a half years later, in the autumn of 1926, it appeared less convincing.

It would be easy to add further examples of industries—consider only the long tragedy of ship-building and marine engineering on Tyne-side—in which the continuance of control in some form would have been an advantage. What actually occurred, in the case of a good many of them, was that individual enterprise, for a return to which their spokesmen were clamouring in 1919 and 1920, was found in the course of the next decade to be a polite name for suicide, and that industrialists proceeded to suppress it by organising combines. It became evident, in fact, that the real object of the business world's idolatry was, not the free competition to which lip-service still continued to be paid, but a free hand either to compete or to combine as it thought most profitable, and that it had no objection to the principle of control, provided that business men, not the State, were the controllers. That chapter of the story is likely to raise some serious problems at the end of the present war, when the question may well be, not whether controls should be continued, but whether they can safely be continued without a change of the *personnel* in charge. Twenty years ago, however, that question had hardly arisen. Instead of discussing it, it is worthwhile to consider briefly one more specimen from the past, of a different kind from those hitherto considered.

The most remarkable feature of the economic history of the last two years of the war was unquestionably the growth of inter-allied organisation. By the time of the Armistice, the greater part of the imports of France, Italy and Great Britain were handled under schemes made and carried out, not by individual countries, but by inter-allied bodies, acting, whether by way of joint programmes or of actual purchase, on behalf of the principal allies as a whole. Not only the great staples, such as sugar, wheat, wool, jute, hemp, petrol and timber—to mention no more—but Spanish lead, tin, tobacco, and even quinine, were subject to inter-allied control. The individual commodities concerned ran into thousands, and their aggregate value into hundreds of millions. The whole immense business, however, depended on shipping. Even in Great Britain, which in 1914 owned half the world's tonnage, shipping was a comparatively small industry, employing only some 450,000 persons, but it was the key-stone of the economic arch. If that collapsed, everything else collapsed with it. Hence, of all the inter-allied organisations, none, not even the Wheat Executive, approached in importance the Inter-allied Shipping Control.

Into the earlier developments of shipping control in the principal allied countries it is needless to enter. In Great Britain it passed in the first two years of the war through the usual introductory phase, in which a collection of separate *ad hoc* committees dealt separately with a variety of inter-dependent problems. That stage ended in December, 1916, with the establishment of the Ministry of Shipping, some six weeks before the opening of the intensified submarine campaign. Early in 1917, the Government, which, in spite of the extension of requisitioning, had left some tramps and the majority of liners free to accept charters in the open market, made requisitioning universal, and a new chapter began. In France, Italy and the United States, control, as in Great Britain, developed gradually; but by the end of 1917, it was reasonably complete. It was on the shipping controls of these four countries, and particularly on the British, that the Inter-allied Control system was erected.

The turning-point was the Paris Conference of 29th November, 1917, at which all the allied powers were represented. As the result of a decision then taken to adjust the import programmes of the allies to the tonnage available, and to allot tonnage between the different countries in the way best calculated to promote the common effort, an allied Maritime Transport Council and Executive were created, which started work in January of the following year. From that time onwards to the Armistice, they, and the eleven or so programme committees established by them, handled the enormous business of harmonising the competing claims of different countries, commodities and services—food, munitions, coal, timber—the transport of the American armies, the relief of distress in Belgium, and a score of other requirements all urgent, but not all capable of being met—and of seeing that shipping was made available to meet different needs in the order of their relative urgency. Tonnage, during the last two years of the war, was the limiting factor; and the allocation of tonnage determined not only what quantity, but what kind of imports, for civilian as well as for military needs, different countries could receive. The authority which rationed tonnage, therefore, had a decisive influence, not only on the military effort, but on the whole economic life of the allied countries, and of most neutrals as well. It did not exercise its power in a dictatorial manner; but it became, almost in spite of itself, through the mere logic of facts, an economic dictator.

That position did not survive the cessation of hostilities. Munitions shipments, sinkings, the transport of American troops to France, all suddenly ceased. The stringency of the shipping situation was, therefore, diminished, and the power of the Allied Maritime Transport Council diminished with it. Two factors, however, continued to make its work of great importance. In the first place, though war strains were relaxed, peace brought its own requirements, in the shape of demands for shipping to repatriate troops, and to move wares required to make good the shortage which was the legacy of the war; while, at the same time, port-congestion, delays in discharging and, later, the cessation—probably the premature cessation—of Government requisitioning, reduced the effective supply of tonnage. In the second place, there was a larger issue. Shipping control, though originally established in order to keep the rise of freights within reasonable limits, had acquired, for the reasons explained, more comprehensive functions. The Allied Maritime Transport Council had become, in effect, an authority rationing all kinds of supplies which required to be moved by sea. The condition of Europe at the Armistice, and, indeed, for several years after it, made the continued existence of some international economic authority, to carry on work of the same kind, indispensable. In November 1918, the greater part of the Continent was short of food-stuffs, raw materials and coal; both then and later, there were devastated regions requiring the means of physical reconstruction. Parts of it, again, were not far removed from actual starvation, but had not the means to pay for food. If a break-down was to be avoided, it was necessary that concerted action should be taken to acquire and distribute essential commodities of which the supply was deficient. Moreover, such action, though its continuance might be required for several years, must begin immediately. Though, in short, the limiting factor had become, with the cessation of hostilities, finance rather than shipping, international machinery to carry Europe over the perilous passage from war to peace was the sole alternative to chaos.

As the one going concern, which could act at once, and which possessed the necessary experience and *personnel*, the Allied Maritime Transport Council was the natural body to come to the rescue. It did its best to ensure that the opportunity was not missed. A fortnight before the Armistice, on 28th October, it urged that a provision for the transference of German and Austrian vessels, and for their operation by itself, should be included in the allied terms. A little later, it proposed that it should itself be converted, with certain modifications, into a General Economic Council, through which the work of the various programme committees could be co-ordinated. The plan was circulated by the British Government to the Governments of France, Italy and the United States; but, largely through the refusal of the last to co-operate, it was rejected. Three months later, in February, 1919, another body, the Supreme Economic Council, assumed some of the functions proposed, including the management of the German and Austrian ships, which were put at its disposal in March; but an opportunity had been missed, and it did not return. For one thing, there was all the difference between entrusting the work required to an existing authority, staffed by a *personnel* which had been dealing during the war with similar problems, and assigning it to a new and hastily improvised organisation. For another thing, short though the delay now seems, it was in the conditions then obtaining, which almost everywhere were grave and in some countries desperate, a serious matter. Part, at least, of the economic and political chaos of parts of Central Europe in the critical years following the Armistice must be ascribed to the failure of the allied governments to appreciate the extent of the economic disintegration which had taken place, and to realise that the maintenance of economic controls during the slow and painful process of reconstruction was as necessary as it had been during the war.

It is submitted that, in the three instances examined, the continuance of controls armed with compulsory powers, though not necessarily in the form in which they existed at the Armistice, would have been to the general advantage. It would not be difficult to adduce other examples of which the same statement is true; timber and other building materials are a case in point. The post-war histories of different industries were, however, not the same, and the problems which different controls, had they continued, would have been called upon to handle, differed widely in urgency. It may well be the case, therefore, that the examples given above would prove, on further investigation, to be exceptional. Further, the desirability of maintaining, after the termination of hostilities, the machinery of regulation established during the war cannot be determined without reference to the other issues which faced the Government at the Armistice, and which are likely to arise at the end of the present war. It must be weighed in relation to the necessity of facilitating the absorption into peace-time employment of ex-soldiers and munition-workers, and to the measures to revive economic activity which may be necessary for that purpose.

Nevertheless, one general conclusion with regard to the future of war-controls appears, in the light of past experience, to be reasonably certain. It is that the view prevalent in 1919 and 1920, and accepted, after some hesitation, by the Government, and that there is a strong presumption in favour of prompt and general de-control is unquestionably erroneous. If that view still exists, it ought to be discarded altogether and at once. Modern war is an exhausting operation, from which some parts of the economic organism recover more easily than others, but which involves for many a somewhat lengthy convalescence. In certain cases early de-control may have been the wisest course, though, even so, it should not have been hurried through, but should have been carefully timed with reference to the circumstances of the industries concerned and to the general economic situation. In other cases, it was a grave blunder. Discrimination was essential, but no serious attempt at discrimination was made. To repeat that mistake would be unpardonable.

If that view be accepted, to what conclusions does it point? It is expedient to distinguish between the short-run and long-run aspects of the problem, between the policies appropriate to the period of post-war convalescence, and those which should be part of a permanent regimen. These categories are not mutually exclusive, but it is convenient, nevertheless, to consider them separately. The measures suggested below, with the exception of No. I, are concerned primarily with the period of transition from war to peace.

I. An intelligent post-war policy on the subject of war-controls cannot be formulated or carried out, unless full information as to their organisation and functions is easily available, not only to the Government, but also to the public. In the absence of such information, the public is at the mercy of misleading press campaigns, and the Government finds it difficult not to be swept off its feet. It is necessary, therefore, that, before the end of the war, a Report should be published containing a survey of the different controls brought into existence during the war, the reasons which caused them to be established, their organisation, the work which they have done, and the effects of the war on the industries concerned.

It is important that this information should be made available in a single Report, dealing with the subject as a whole, and thus enabling its magnitude to be grasped, and different types of war-control to be compared with each other. No such comprehensive Report was produced either before or after the end of the last war. The trading accounts of different control organisations were published, with the auditor general's comments; and references to war-controls were contained in other official documents, such as the Reports of the Departmental Committees set up by the Board of Trade to consider the post-war position of different industries. The former were instructive as far as they went, but were necessarily confined to the financial aspects of the subject. The references to it contained in the latter were merely incidental. They were always superficial, and sometimes *ex parte*. Neither provided the thorough and comprehensive survey which is the first condition of a sensible policy. Neither was read, or could be read with profit, by more than a minute fraction of the public.

II. It is essential that adequate time should be allowed in order to prepare the policies appropriate to different industries or problems, and to bring them into action. With that object in view, the following steps should be taken:

(1) A committee to consider post-war policy with regard to the future of war-controls should at once be established, with instructions to complete its work well before the end of the war. The subject is a large one. Not only are many different departments of economic life now controlled by the Government, but the methods of control employed are of many different kinds. What is required, therefore, is not one policy for general application, but several—perhaps many—different policies. The Report, whose compilation has been recommended in I above, would be the natural starting-point for the Committee's work. Even so, its task would be long and arduous. Unless the Government and the country are again to be caught unprepared, it is essential that it should be completed before the conclusion of the war.

(2) It is important that the transition from a war to a peace economy should take place as smoothly as possible. If, that is to say, some controls are to be wound up, they must be wound up at what, in view of economic conditions, is the right moment. If some controls are to be continued, but in a modified form, there must be no break between existing arrangements and those which are to succeed them. There ought, for that reason, to be 'a stand-still period', during which existing controls are continued without alteration, till the moment has come either to end them or put something better in their place.

The corollary of that policy is that there must be no automatic de-control, in the sense of de-control which takes place either because the

Act conferring the necessary powers has lapsed or been repeated, or because the continuance of control was limited by Parliament to a specific period after the end of the war. Neither the economic conditions of the post-war period, nor the manner in which different controls would function in practice, could be foreseen when such legislation was passed. Its results may, therefore, be extremely mischievous. The Government should have power to deal with the subject of war-controls in the light of such circumstances as exist at the end of the war, and of the best forecast which it can make of future conditions. If it does not possess that power under existing legislation, it should seek the necessary authority from Parliament. The obvious course would seem to be the passage of an Act continuing controls in the existing form for a further specified period, which the Government can extend, but not shorten, by order in Council.

(3) In the case of controls which it is decided to wind up, it is of the greatest importance that adequate notice, e.g. not less than one year, should be given. The wage arrangements of an industry, the scale of operations of different firms, and the provisions of raw materials, may all be affected by the transition from a controlled to a free economy. There may be a strong temptation to move the date of de-control forward for financial or other reasons, as was done in 1921 in the case of the coal industry. That temptation should be resisted.

(4) For the same reason, when it is decided to terminate a control, the possibility should be considered of doing so by a series of steps fixed in advance. That course was followed, after the last war, in the case of the arrangements between the Wheat Commission and the millers, the proportion of grain supplied to the latter below the market price of British grain being gradually tapered off by monthly percentages. It seems a reasonable one.

III. The most important facts in the economic history of the years immediately following the last war were the post-war boom and depression. The prevention or control of similar movements at the end of the present war will be among the most important tasks then confronting the Government. It is assumed that the steps to be taken with that object are dealt with in other memoranda, and nothing, therefore, is said on that subject here. There is one point, however, which should be borne in mind in considering the future of the various controls. It is concerned with the date at which de-control, if thought desirable, should take place. Even in those cases in which de-control is the policy decided on, it should not be brought into operation till a sufficient period has elapsed to allow for the boom and depression, if they are not—as it is to be hoped they will be—prevented from running their course. The chief reasons are two. In the first place, the larger the area of economic life which the Government controls, the stronger its position in dealing with a threatened or actual depression. Through its financial controls, it can check speculative re-financing, and can influence the amount of capital expenditure undertaken in a given period. As a large purchaser, it affects the demand for consumer's goods. Through its industrial controls, it can help to determine the measures adopted by industry to meet a depression, when such occurs. To surrender these powers at a time when a depression may be expected would be extremely short-sighted. In the second place, it is desirable that the transition to de-control, when that is the policy adopted, should take place at a time when general economic conditions are relatively stable.

IV. The expediency, or otherwise, of continuing control; the form which, if its continuance is decided on, its machinery should take; and, if de-control is the alternative approved, the date of de-control, are matters of vital importance to all engaged in the industries in question. Before any decision on the policy is taken, it is essential that representatives of all the interests concerned should be consulted. The rapid and complete de-control which took place after the last war was predominantly a business man's policy, and there is little evidence that the Government troubled to ascertain the views of the workers. Such a procedure is obviously inequitable. It will be necessary that before any policy on the subject is formulated on the present occasion, the trade unions, the co-operative societies and other working-class organisations should have the fullest opportunity to state their views.

V. The machinery of economic regulation cannot be improvised. Its success depends largely on the experience of those working it, and on the existence of a habit of co-operation among them. It is important, therefore, that, as long as controls are maintained, there should be the maximum possible continuity between their war-time and peace-time personnel.

VI. The functions of many control bodies will in some respects be different after the war from those performed by them during it. One of the most obvious effects of the last war was an unnatural distortion of the industrial system. Some industries were atrophied; others were hypertrophied. The result was a stagnant pool of unemployment or partial employment on the north-east coast, on the Clyde, in South Wales and several other colliery districts, which twenty years later, in 1939, had not yet been drained. It must be expected that the present war will tend to produce the same result, though on what scale it is as yet impossible to say. Some of the measures to deal with it are of general application and require direct action by the Government; others, given adequate machinery, can be introduced industry by industry. Some of the necessary steps, in particular the regulation of entrance into industry of new recruits and the acceleration of the exit of veterans, have already been mentioned. To work out in detail such measures and to supervise their operation will be not the least important of the post-war duties of control authorities.

Arrangements to bridge the transition from war to peace are not the only measures which require to be considered. It is a common experience that reforms which, but for the jolt given by an emergency, would not have been introduced, become, once adopted, contributions to civilisation which are valued for their own sake, and which continue to be extended long after their origin in a crisis has been forgotten. The impetus given to public health legislation by epidemics of cholera; the debt owed by the School Medical Service to revelations of physical defects among recruits; the heavier taxation of wealth caused by the exigencies of the last war, are cases in point. The better utilisation of economic resources for the general benefit, and the more effective organisation of economic effort for the service of the public, are clearly among the major problems of our day. It is conceivable that expedients adopted at a moment when the supremacy of public over private interests was generally admitted may have some light, at least, to throw on their solution.

The subject does not lend itself to summary treatment, nor is a Memorandum on the relaxation of controls at the end of the last war the proper place to discuss it. Few, however, can meditate on the turbid history of the twenty-one years between 1918 and 1939 without feeling some sympathy with the sentiment expressed by the Cabinet, when it wrote, before peace brought disillusionment, that the problem is 'not so much one of re-building society as it was before the war as of moulding a better world out of the social and economic conditions which have come into existence during the war'.[56] Few can reflect on the part played by economic factors in heightening the tension between nations and classes without asking themselves whether the post-war world would not have avoided some, at least, of its disasters, if the institutions created in the course of the conflict, instead of being hastily jettisoned, had been encouraged to make such contribution as they could to the tasks of peace. It has been remarked by one of their chief architects, Sir Arthur Salter, that at a time when 'between half and two-thirds of the productive capacity of the country was with-drawn into combatant and other war-service ... Great Britain sustained the whole of the military effort, and maintained her civilian population at a standard of life which was never intolerably low, and for some periods, and some classes, was perhaps as comfortable as in time of peace'.[57] Numerous factors—a greater intensity of labour, the work of persons previously unemployed in industry, the concentration of production in the most efficient plants, the sale of foreign securities, the deterioration of equipment to a value exceeding the new assets created, and other devices for living on capital—played their part in making possible that achievement. It remains, nevertheless, the single most surprising feature of the economic history of the period. It can hardly be doubted that the more ruthless elimination of waste, and the deliberate organisation of productive resources to meet requirements in the order of their relative urgency, contributed their share to it. The medicine of the constitution cannot be its daily food; but it is as important to observe a healthy regimen of life in normal times as in emergencies, and it should be easier to do so. The lessons of experience ought not to be summarily rejected merely because war was the stern schoolmaster who taught them.

Such a statement does not ignore the difference between the economic conditions of war and those of peace. It merely points out that, when the former bring to light possibilities which may also be important for the latter, it is foolish not to profit by them. The practical conclusion to which it leads is not the enumeration of a catalogue of specifics, but an attitude of discriminating and open-minded inquiry, which selects from the wealth of experiments made those of permanent significance. Three types of intervention practised during the war deserve to be considered, as possible claimants for inclusion in that category.

The great international organisations created for the purpose of pooling the purchase and allocation of essential food-stuffs, materials and shipping, may fairly be regarded as one case in point. They offered a practical demonstration of two neglected truths. They proved, in the first place, the reality and magnitude of the movement of the last half-century towards economic unification, but for which they would hardly have been conceived and certainly could not have been launched. They established, in the second place, the possibility of turning that movement to account for the benefit, not of this nation or that, but of large groups of nations, by collective action to make common provision, on an equitable basis, for needs common to all. Is it extravagant to suggest that, had those organisations been preserved, and the spirit informing the more enlightened of them diffused, they might have become the nuclei of a rational economic order transcending national boundaries, and thus have served as centres of stability counteracting by the influence of their example and the weight of their authority the slide into a welter of economic nationalisms which has been not the least fatal of the curses of our day? What was needed was not exhortation, or resolutions on the blessings of free trade, but a practical counterpoise to anarchy in the shape of international machinery doing better for all countries what each did badly for itself, and ruinously for its neighbours. Such machinery was created under the spur of necessity. It seems unfortunate today that it was not permitted to survive, when, if no longer a necessity, it remained an advantage.

The pre-war economic system—to cite a second instance—had made effective demand the arbiter of production; and since, in societies characterised, like Great Britain, by violent inequalities of income, effective demand is not an index of real needs, it had necessarily devoted some considerable part of its limited resources to producing the wrong things for the gratification of the wrong people. Priority schemes, determining the order in which different requirements should be met, and the rationing of supplies, had been the most important of the war-time correctives. If waste is injurious in war, what precisely are the grounds for thinking it a matter of indifference in peace? There may be reasons for holding it to be economically advantageous that labour and machinery employed during hostilities to make lorries or railway wagons should turn over, as soon as they cease, to the manufacture of expensive motor-cars, and that part of the tonnage engaged in carrying articles of common necessity should be hastily diverted to the import of luxuries. But the burden of proof rests on the supporters of that paradox, and it is prudent to wait till they have made out their case before basing national policy on so slippery a foundation. The State, while the emergency lasted, controlled the allocation of capital and raw materials in order to ensure that they were applied first to the production of guns, shells and ships, and, only after these pre-requisites of victory had been provided, to objects, however laudable, of secondary significance. Is it not equally practicable, and but little less important, to control them for the purpose of ensuring that economic resources such as land, minerals and timber, are skilfully husbanded and intelligently developed; that the population is well housed; and that the young grow up, both at home and in school, in a healthful and stimulating environment?

Nor—to give a third example—was the experience of particular industrial Controls irrelevant to the consideration of a long-run peace policy. It is difficult to believe that nothing of more than ephemeral significance was to be learned from the unification of railways, and later of canals, under the direction of bodies responsible to the Government; from the check on exorbitant prices which was made possible by the existence of national factories; from the results of systematic costing both in saving public money and in levelling up standards of management; from the elimination of speculation in the purchase of raw materials, the reduction in the number of middle-men, the pooling of trade secrets, and the virtual conversion of some industrialists and merchants into agents working on commission for the State; from the Coal Transport Re-organisation Scheme, and the effect of the power, conferred on the Board of Trade, to cause minerals adjacent to an open mine to be worked in derogation of the rights of the owner of the area in question, both of which the chief technical adviser to the Coal Controller, himself a strong advocate of de-control, desired to be retained[58] when all else should have gone. Investigation would, doubtless, have shown that some of these war-time expedients were needless or impracticable once the transition period was over, and that others, before being perpetuated, required modification. The fact remains, however, that the slack which the State could take up was found, once its search-light was turned upon industry, to be surprisingly large, and that the assumption, implicit in not a few of the subsequent onslaughts on Controls, that competition kept production keyed up to a standard which admitted of no improvement, was revealed, when the pinch came, to be a mere superstition. A considerable part of the productive effort of the country was organised for a time on lines not wholly dissimilar to those of a public utility undertaking, and efficiency, so far from losing, appears actually to have gained. The truth is that, for reasons not difficult to state, the British economic system which went into the crisis had some of the defects of a fair-weather vessel. It is a question whether it would not have faced with better fortune the bleak post-war world if it had retained more of the discipline which saw it through the storm.

As far, therefore, as the teaching of experience is concerned, the case for believing that it would have been prudent, when the last war concluded, to sort out those features of the War-Control system which could with advantage be perpetuated, is unquestionably strong. Neither general de-control, nor—except as an interim measure to secure a breathing-space—the general continuance of control was a sensible formula. The merits of different Controls were not the same; while even those among them, for the continuance of which convincing arguments could be adduced, required amendments if they were to work well in peace. What was needed, in short, was discrimination; and to demand discrimination in the atmosphere of the years following the Armistice was to cry for the moon. The course of wisdom, as has already been suggested, would have been to anticipate events, instead of waiting on them. It would have been for the Government to obtain, while the war still continued, a full Report on the facts of the control system, together with recommendations relating both to transitional measures and to those aspects of it which deserved to be given, with suitable alterations, a permanent place in post-war economic policy, and thus to be armed in advance with a well-thought-out plan.

The need for a Report and a plan is not less urgent to-day. Whatever view may be taken of the history of the last twenty years, two, at least, of the lessons to be learned from it are not likely to be disputed. The first is that a stable international system is a mirage, as long as the policies of the states on whose support it must rest are a struggle to avoid economic domination by their neighbours or to impose it upon them. The second is that the qualified economic autocracy, which descends from the last century, has had its day, and that industrial organisation, in order to be recognised as equitable and to be reasonably efficient, must rest on consent. The machinery of economic Controls is needed, in one form or another, for an attack on both problems. Established during war, it was swept away wholesale on the return of peace, instead of being reconstructed. It would be unpardonable if a similar error were made a second time.

The problems arising, however, at the end of the present war, if similar in kind to those left by the last, will not be identical with them, and will in some respects be more difficult. As a result—to mention only one point—of the growth of combinations, the cry for prompt and general de-control is likely to be less loud; the attempt to use State control as a buttress for monopoly will probably be more determined. The question whether particular Controls should be continued, or not, may well be less important than it was twenty years ago. The question, which then had hardly emerged, of the constitution of the authorities by which control, if continued, shall be exercised, and of the methods by which the public interest shall be protected, may well be more acute. But such issues belong to a study of the contemporary situation, and cannot properly be discussed in the present Memorandum.

Notes

* Public Record Office, Cabinet Papers, 117.40. An abridged version may be found in *Economic History Review*, xiii (1941), pp. 1–30.

1 Attention has been confined in the present Memorandum to British experience. Certain kinds of intervention by the British Government, however, prepared the way for the creation of international bodies, and could hardly, indeed, have been effective in the absence of them. In the case of some of such bodies, the problem of the transition from a war to a peace economy arose in an acute form. Reference is made to such cases in the proper place.

2 No official Report has been published on the war-control system as a whole, nor does a complete use of controls appear to exist; but valuable matter is contained in Cd. 8447 *Memorandum on War Office Accounts*), Cmd. 788 (*Ministry of Munitions Trading Accounts*), the Reports of the War Cabinet for 1917 and 1918, and the Report of the Public Accounts Committee. Much the most elaborate study of war-controls, which has a semi-official character, is the privately printed *History of the Ministry of Munitions*. It deals with a number of topics besides munitions in the narrower sense of the term, and it is regrettable that it has not been made more generally accessible. Next to that, the most instructive works are the volumes published by the Carnegie Endowment for International Peace in The Economic and Social History of the World

War, British Series, in particular E. M. H. Lloyd, *Experiments in State Control*; J. A. Salter, *Allied Shipping Control*; W. H. Beveridge, *British Food Control*; R. A. S. Redmayne, *The British Coal-mining Industry during the War*; H. D. Henderson, *The Cotton Control Board*; N. B. Dearle, *Dictionary of Official War-time Organisations*. All the above, except the last, are by authors who themselves administered controls, and who had access to official sources. The Reports of the various Departmental Committees appointed by the Board of Trade to consider the post-war prospects of different industries, the *Labour Gazette*, the *Board of Trade Journal, The Economist*, and volumes of Hansard, 1918–21, should also be consulted. Interesting side-lights are supplied by Winston S. Churchill, *The World Crisis and the Aftermath*; D. Lloyd George, *War Memoirs*; and L. Chiozza Money, *The Triumph of Nationalisation*.

3 The object of the pages which follow is merely to give an impression of the dimensions of the system of control which was brought into existence during the war, and which de-control subsequently abolished. No attempt, therefore, is made to offer a systematic classification of different types of control. Further, certain controls, in particular those concerned with finance, with wages, and with rents, are not discussed in the present Memorandum.

4 *History of Ministry of Munitions*, vol. II, pt I, pp. 47–8. The figure does not include, of course, the mines under the Coal Control Department.

5 *Ibid.*, vol. VI, pt III, pp. 48–9. The figure relates to munition workers in the narrower sense of persons employed in the metal and chemical trades. If miscellaneous workers are included, the figure in January, 1918, was 3,416,439 (*loc. cit.*, p. 54), Churchill's *The Aftermath*, p. 32, puts the persons 'directly under the orders of the Ministry of Munitions' at 'nearly 5,000,000', but it is not clear how that figure is obtained.

6 E. M. H. Lloyd, *op. cit.*, p. 24.

7 *Ibid.*

8 W. H. Beveridge, *op. cit.*, pp. 56–7.

9 Cmd. 788 (*Ministry of Munitions Trading Accounts*, 1920).

10 The best account of these arrangements is given by E. M. H. Lloyd, *op. cit.*

11 E. M. H. Lloyd, *op. cit.*, p. 177.

12 A full account of the work of the Liquor Control Board has been given by A. Shadwell, *Drink in 1914–22, a Lesson in Control*, from which the above facts are taken.

13 A brief account of some of the principal inter-allied organisations is given in the Reports of the War Cabinet for 1917 and 1918, and by J. A. Salter, *op. cit.*, pt III, ch. I. For more detailed information as to wheat and sugar, see W. H. Beveridge, *op. cit., passim*, and, for flax, jute, wool, hides and leather, oil-seeds, etc., E. M. H. Lloyd, *op. cit.*, chs VI–XII, XVI and XVIII.

14 The War Cabinet stated that, by the end of 1917, 'the vast majority of the people are now working directly or indirectly on public service' (*Report for 1917*). J. A. Salter (*op. cit.*, p. 19) estimates that 'between half and two-thirds of the productive capacity of the country was drawn into combatant or other war-service'. It is not clear whether his estimate includes occupations, such as agriculture and the distributive trades, which, while subject to war-controls, were working primarily for the civilian public.

15 D. Lloyd George, *War Memoirs*, vol. I, pp. 100–16.

16 E. M. H. Lloyd, *op. cit.*, p. 23.

17 *Ibid.*, chs IV and V.

18 For the views expressed by Ministers see E. M. H. Lloyd, *op. cit.*, p. 28, and W. H. Beveridge, *op. cit.*, pp. 6, 15, 22–3.

19 E. M. H. Lloyd, *op. cit.*, chs X–XII. For food, coal and shipping see the above-mentioned works of Beveridge, Redmayne and Salter.

20 In some cases, a specific date can be assigned for the termination of control. Thus the control of tobacco (though not of matches, which had been combined with it under one board) appears to have ceased on 11th January, 1919; that of paper on 3rd April, 1919; and that of road-stone quarries on 17th May, 1919. Such cases, however, are exceptional. All but the very simplest controls, even when they related to a single article such as wool, involved regulations of several different kinds (e.g., to mention only the simplest, as to purchase, sale, prices, import and export); while the more important controls, in particular the Ministry of Munitions and the Ministry of Food, were concerned with many hundred different articles. In most cases, therefore, different regulations, and regulations relating to different articles, were withdrawn at different dates. Further control might cease as far as future transactions were concerned, while being maintained as regards

stocks already in the possession of the Government. Hence, while it is usually possible to state the date at which a particular control finally ceased to function, it is not possible to trace the successive preliminary stages preceding complete de-control without giving lists of regulations, articles and dates running in some cases into several pages. The non-technical reader would learn little from such lists, and it has not been thought worthwhile to include them.

21 *Report of War Cabinet for 1917*, Introduction, pp. xv-xvi and xx. For the other quotations, see *ibid*, pp. 133–5, 143–4, 211–12, and *Report of War Cabinet for 1918*, pp. 214–15.

22 *Report of War Cabinet for 1918*, pp. 212–13, 217; E. M. H. Lloyd, *op. cit.*, pp. 247–53 and 449–50; *Report of War Cabinet of 1917*, and A. Shadwell, *Drink in 1914–22, a Lesson in Control*; *History of Ministry of Munitions*, vol. II, pt I (Supplement), pp. 8–15.

23 Quoted L. Chiozza Money, *op cit.*, p. 139.

24 Hansard, H. C. iii, 1780; *ibid.*, 110.2606.

25 The D.O.R. Act, 1914 (4 & 5 Geo. V, c. 29), 8th August, 1914, provides that H.M. in Council has power 'during the continuance of the present war' to issue regulations, etc. The various amending Acts (4 & 5 Geo. V, c. 63; 5 Geo. V, c. 8; 5 Geo. V, c. 34 & 37; 506 Geo. V, c. 42; 6 & 7 Geo. V, c. 63; 10 & 11 Geo. V, c. 79) extend the provisions, but say nothing as to the period of continuance. The Termination of the Present War (Definition) Act of 21st November, 1918, provided that 'H.M. in Council may declare what date is to be treated as the termination of the present war'. The war with Germany ended on 10th January, 1920, and with our enemy powers at subsequent dates, the last (Turkey) being 6th August, 1924. All the controls, however, had been wound up (except for certain outstanding accounts of the Wheat Commission) before the end of August 1921.

26 The War Emergency Laws (Continuance) Act, of 31st March, provided that 'whereas the D.O.R.A. regulations will expire at the termination of the present war; and it is expedient that certain of them shall continue in force thereafter ... the regulations mentioned in schedule 2 shall, subject to certain limitations, continue in force till 31st August, 1920, subject to the power of the Government to revoke them by Order in Council'. Schedule 2 contained a list of regulations, including 2B (power to regulate war materials, stores, etc.); 2F to 2J (powers of Food Controller); 2JJ (power to regulate articles of commerce other than food, coal, gas, electricity, etc.); 9G (power to control coal-mines); 39BBB (powers of Shipping Controller). In explaining the bill, Mr. Bonar Law stated that the necessity for the bill 'depends ... upon the time when the Peace Treaty with Turkey, which will be the last, is ratified' (Hansard, 123, p. 1291). In fact the Treaty with Turkey was not ratified till 6th August, 1924, three years after war-controls had ceased to exist.

27 In November, 1917, the Minister of Munitions had appointed a Committee to consider the question of the liquidation of war-contracts and the transition to peace production, the report of which was received in October, 1918. The measures taken to meet the danger of mass unemployment included the completion of work already more than 60 per cent advanced, the abolition of over-time, suspension of payment by results systems, a reduction of hours to half the normal week, and the lavish granting of holidays (Churchill, *The Aftermath*, pp. 32–5). For the stages of de-control in the munitions industry, including the gradual withdrawal of subsidies, see also the *Report of the Cabinet Committee for 1918*, pp. 124–30. The Ministry of Food had ready a scheme for its dissolution (W. H. Beveridge, *op. cit.*, p. 268), the Coal Control Department was also prepared with plans (R. A. S. Redmayne, *op. cit.*, pp. 208–12).

28 E.g. *Final Report of Committee on Commercial and Industrial Policy After the War* (Cd. 9035), 1918.

29 *The Economist*, 28th December, 1918.

30 See the Reports of the Departmental Committees appointed by the Board of Trade to consider the position of various industries after the war, 1918, Cd. 9070 (Textiles), 9071 (Iron and Steel), 9072 (Engineering Trades), 9092 (Shipping and Ship-building), 9093 (Coal).

31 *The Economist*, 21st December, 1918.

32 *Report of Departmental Committee appointed ... to consider the position of the Shipping and Ship-building Industries after the War* (Cd. 9092), 1918.

33 R. G. Hawtrey, *A Century of Bank-rate*, pp. 212–13; H. Clay, *Post-war Unemployment*, p. 63.

34 W. A. Orton, *Labour in Transition*, p. 272.

35 Hansard, vol. 110, p. 2635, 12th November, 1918, speech of Sir J. Walton.

36 *The Times*, 14th April, 1919.

37 *History of Ministry of Munitions*, vol. II, pt I (Supplement), p. 38. The Demobilisation and Reconstruction Committee (June, 1918) had classified the national factories as follows:- (a) about twenty factories, apart from Royal Ordnance Factories, were recommended for permanent retention as munition factories, (b) about eighty-five were stated to be suitable for eventual disposal or use as industrial concerns, (c) about twenty-five were stated not to be suitable for industrial purposes, but might be used temporarily as stores, (d) about 115 would revert to their original owners and to pre-war uses.

38 *Ibid.*, vol. IX, pt I (Supplement), pp. 35–40, and vol. VII, pt I, pp. 79–80. Some criticisms on the policy followed will be found in L. Chiozza Money, *op. cit.*, pp. 65–6, 71, 143–4.

39 *History of the Ministry of Munitions*, vol. II, pt I (Supplement), pp. 8–15.

40 Churchill to meeting of employers, four days before Armistice, quoted W. A. Orton, *Labour in Transition*, pp. 172–3.

41 W. H. Beveridge, *op cit* , p. 306.

42 R. A. S. Redmayne, *op cit* , p. 246.

43 G. O. Galliard, *Histoire économique et financière de la Guerre*; P. Renouvin, *The Forms of War Government in France* (abridged from his *Du gouvernement de guerre*).

44 A 'Consortium' was an association of dealers or manufacturers interested in one class of goods, which centralised demands, purchased raw materials and sold them to its members under State supervision.

45 The letter is quoted by A. E. Zimmern, *The League of Nations and the Rule of Law*, pp. 157–8. It appears to have been addressed to Mr. Joseph Cotton, the representative of the U.S.A. Food Administration in Europe, and to have been received by him on 8th November, 1918. An invitation to co-operate in post-war economic reconstruction had been addressed by the British Embassy in Washington to the U.S.A. State Department on 15th October (*ibid.*, pp. 155–6); and, on 13th November, the British Government sent a communication to the United States, France, and Italy suggesting the conversion of the Allied Maritime Transport Council into a General Economic Council. This proposal, which originated with the A.M.T.C., was rejected by the U.S.A. (J. A. Salter, *op. cit.*, pp. 220–1).

46 *History of the Ministry of Munitions*, vol. VII, pt I, p. 72; J. A. Salter, *op cit.*, pp. 220–1.

47 W. H. Beveridge, *op. cit.*, p. 361 (sugar and wheat, and for a short period after the war cheese and bacon); E. M. H. Lloyd, *op. cit.*, p. 197 (meat); J. A. Salter, *op cit.*, p. 94 (steel); R.A.S. Redmayne, *op. cit.*, pp. 94–9 (coal).

48 W. H. Beveridge, *op. cit.*, pp. 304–5.

49 R. A. S. Redmayne, *op. cit.*, p. 228. Here are a few examples:

	Per Ton *3rd Jan., 1919*					Per Ton *24th Dec., 1919*				
	s.	d.		s.	d.	s.	d.		s.	d.
Best Northumbrian Steam Coals, f.o.b., Tyne	37	0	to	80	0	100	0	to	105	0
Foundry Coke, f.o.b., Tyne	49	6	to	65	0	100	0	to	110	0
Best Welsh Steam Coals, f.o.b., Cardiff.	40	0	to	50	0	95	0	to	105	0

50 *Ibid.*, p. 235.

51 A. Shadwell, *Drink in 1914–22, a Lesson in Control.*

52 'In view of the results so far obtained and of the risk of loss in future years, its continuance as a state undertaking would not appear to afford any special financial advantage to the tax-payer.' (*Ibid.*, p. 127).

53 The figure is taken from the *Oldham Chronicle Textile Trades Review*, 21st December, 1920.

54 *Ibid.* Here are the figures for 109 concerns:

No. of Companies	Spindles	Former Amount	Capital per Spindle	Amount	Sale per Spindle
109	10,511,792	£4,765,260	£0.9.1	£31,711,958	£3.0.3

55 E.g. *Report of Committee of Inquiry into the Cotton Industry*, 1929 (Précis of Evidence submitted by the United Textile Factory Workers Association and Draft Scheme for Cotton Control Board and Licensing system); P. E. P., *Report on the British Cotton Industry*, 1934;

Lancashire's Remedy, 1937 (Proposals for improving the position of the Cotton Industry, submitted by the joint Committee of Cotton Trade Organisations).

56 *Report of War Cabinet for 1918*, Introduction, p. 20.

57 J. A. Salter, *op. cit.*, p. 19.

58 R. A. S. Redmayne, *op. cit.*, pp. 211 and 212.

Part II
Reviews and Revaluations

5

Max Weber and the Spirit of Capitalism (1930)*

Max Weber was a scholar whose intellectual range was unusually wide, and whose personality made an even deeper impression than his learning on those privileged to know him. He had been trained as a jurist, and, in addition to teaching as a professor at Freiburg, Heidelberg, and Munich, he wrote on subjects so various as ancient agrarian history, the conditions of the rural population of Prussia, the methodology of the social sciences, and the sociology of religion. Nor were his activities exclusively those of the teacher and the student. He travelled widely, was keenly interested in contemporary political and social movements, played a vigorous and disinterested part in the crisis which confronted Germany at the close of the War, and accompanied the German delegation to Versailles in May 1919. He died in Munich in the following year, at the age of fifty-six. Partly as a result of prolonged ill-health, which compelled him for several years to lead the life of an invalid, partly because of his premature death, partly, perhaps, because of the very grandeur of the scale on which he worked, he was unable to give the final revision to many of his writings. His collected works have been published posthumously. The last of them, based on notes taken by his students from lectures given at Munich, has appeared in English under the title of *General Economic History*.[1]

The Protestant Ethic and the Spirit of Capitalism was published in the form of two articles in the *Archiv für Sozialwissenschaft und Sozialpolitik* in 1904 and 1905. Together with a subsequent article, which appeared in 1906, on *The Protestant Sects and the Spirit of Capitalism*, they form the first of the studies contained in Weber's *Gesammelte Aufsätze zur Religionssoziologie*. On their first appearance they aroused an interest which extended beyond the ranks of historical specialists, and which caused the numbers of the *Archiv* in which they were published to be sold out with a rapidity not very usual in the case of learned publications. The discussion which they provoked has continued since then with undiminished vigour. For the questions raised by Weber possess a universal significance, and the method of his essay was as important as its conclusions. It not only threw a brilliant light on the particular field which it explored, but suggested a new avenue of approach to a range of problems of permanent interest, which concern, not merely the historian and the economist, but all who reflect on the deeper issues of modern society.

The question which Weber attempts to answer is simple and fundamental. It is that of the psychological conditions which made possible the development of capitalist civilization. Capitalism, in the sense of great individual undertakings, involving the control of large financial resources, and yielding riches to their masters as a result of speculation, money-lending, commercial enterprise, buccaneering and war, is as old as history. Capitalism, as an economic system, resting on the organization of legally free wage-earners, for the purpose of pecuniary profit, by the owner of capital or his agents, and setting its stamp on every aspect of society, is a modern phenomenon.

All revolutions are declared to be natural and inevitable, once they are successful, and capitalism, as the type of economic system prevailing in Western Europe and America, is clothed to-day with the unquestioned respectability of the triumphant fact. But in its youth it was a pretender, and it was only after centuries of struggle that its title was established. For it involved a code of economic conduct and a system of human relations which were sharply at variance with venerable conventions, with the accepted scheme of social ethics, and with the law, both of the church and of most European states. So questionable an innovation demanded of the pioneers who first experimented with it as much originality, self-confidence, and tenacity of purpose as is required to-day of those who would break from the net that it has woven. What influence nerved them to defy tradition? From what source did they derive the principles to replace it?

The conventional answer to these questions is to deny their premises. The rise of new forms of economic enterprise was the result, it is argued, of changes in the character of the economic environment. It was due to the influx of the precious metals from America in the sixteenth century, to capital accumulated in extra-European commerce, to the reaction of expanding markets on industrial organization, to the growth of population, to technological improvements made possible by the progress of natural science. Weber's reply, which is developed at greater length in his *General Economic History* than in the present essay, is that such explanations confuse causes and occasions. Granted that the economic conditions of the sixteenth and seventeenth centuries were, in some respects, though by no means in all, unusually favourable to an advance in economic technique, such conditions had existed from time to time in the past without giving birth to the development of capitalist industry. In many of the regions affected by them no such development took place, nor were those which enjoyed the highest economic civilization necessarily those in which the new order found its most congenial environment. The France of Louis XIV commanded resources which, judged by the standards of the age, were immense, but they were largely dissipated in luxury and war. The America of the eighteenth century was economically primitive, but it is in the maxims of Franklin that the spirit of *bourgeois* capitalism, which, rather than the grandiose schemes of mercantilist statesmen, was to dominate the future, finds, Weber argues, its naïvest and most lucid expression.

To appeal, as an explanation, to the acquisitive instincts, is even less pertinent, for there is little reason to suppose that they have been more powerful during the last few centuries than in earlier ages. 'The notion that our rationalistic and capitalistic age is characterised by a stronger economic interest than other periods is childish. The moving spirits of modern capitalism are not possessed of a stronger economic impulse than, for example, an Oriental trader. The unchaining of the economic interest, merely as such, has produced only irrational results: such men as Cortes and Pizarro, who were, perhaps, its strongest embodiment, were far from having an idea of a rationalistic economic life.'[2] The word 'rationalism' is used by Weber as a term of art, to describe an economic system based, not on custom or tradition, but on the deliberate and systematic adjustment of economic means to the attainment of the objective of pecuniary profit. The question is why this temper triumphed over the conventional attitude which had regarded the *appetitus divitiarum infinitus*—the unlimited lust for gain—as anti-social and immoral. His answer is that it was the result of movements which had their source in the religious revolution of the sixteenth century.

Weber wrote as a scholar, not as a propagandist, and there is no trace in his work of the historical animosities which still warp discussions of the effects of the Reformation. Professor Pirenne,[3] in an illuminating essay, has argued that social progress springs from below, and that each new phase of economic development is the creation, not of strata long in possession of wealth and power, but of classes which rise from humble origins to build a new structure on obscure foundations. The thesis of Weber is somewhat similar. The pioneers of the modern economic order were, he argues, *parvenus*, who elbowed their way to success in the teeth of the established aristocracy of land and commerce. The tonic that braced them for the conflict was a new conception of religion, which taught them to regard the pursuit of wealth as, not merely an advantage, but a duty. This conception welded into a disciplined force the still feeble *bourgeoisie*, heightened its energies, and cast a halo of sanctification round its convenient vices. What is significant, in short, is not the strength of the motive of economic self-interest, which is the commonplace of all ages and demands no explanation. It is the change of moral standards which converted a natural frailty into an ornament of the spirit, and canonized as the economic virtues habits which in earlier ages had been denounced as vices. The force which produced it was the creed associated with the name of Calvin. Capitalism was the social counterpart of Calvinist theology.

The central idea to which Weber appeals in confirmation of his theory is expressed in the characteristic phrase 'a calling.' For Luther, as for most mediæval theologians, it had normally meant the state of life in which the individual had been set by Heaven, and against which it was impious to rebel. To the Calvinist, Weber argues, the calling is not a condition in which the individual is born, but a strenuous and exacting enterprise to be chosen by himself, and to be pursued with a sense of religious responsibility. Baptized in the bracing, if icy, waters of Calvinist theology, the life of business, once regarded as perilous to the soul—*summe periculosa est emptionis et venditionis negotiatio*—acquires a new sanctity. Labour is not merely an economic means: it is a spiritual end. Covetousness, if a danger to the soul, is a less formidable menace than sloth. So far from poverty being meritorious, it is a duty to choose the more profitable occupation. So far from there being an inevitable conflict between money-making and piety, they are natural allies, for the virtues incumbent on the elect—diligence, thrift, sobriety, prudence—are the most reliable passport to commercial prosperity. Thus the pursuit of riches, which once had been feared as the enemy of religion, was now welcomed as its ally. The habits and institutions in which that philosophy found expression survived long after the creed which was their parent had expired, or had withdrawn from Europe to more congenial climes. If capitalism begins as the practical idealism of the aspiring *bourgeoisie*, it ends, Weber suggests in his concluding pages, as an orgy of materialism.

In England the great industry grew by gradual increments over a period of centuries, and, since the English class system had long been based on differences of wealth, not of juristic status, there was no violent contrast between the legal foundations of the old order and the new. Hence in England the conception of capitalism as a distinct and peculiar phase of social development has not readily been accepted. It is still possible for writers, who in their youth have borne with equanimity instruction on the meaning of feudalism, to dismiss capitalism as an abstraction of theorists or a catchword of politicians.

The economic history of the Continent has moved by different stages from that of England and the categories employed by Continental thinkers have accordingly been different. In France, where the site on which the modern economic system was to be erected was levelled by a cataclysm, and in Germany, which passed in the fifty years between 1850 and 1900 through a development that in England had occupied two hundred, there has been little temptation to question that capitalist civilization is a phenomenon differing, not merely in degree, but in kind, from the social order preceding it. It is not surprising, therefore, that its causes and characteristics should have been one of the central themes of historical study in both. The discussion began with the epoch-making work of Marx, who was greater as a sociologist than as an economic theorist, and continues unabated. Its most elaborate monument is Sombart's *Der Moderne Kapitalismus*.

The first edition of Sombart's book appeared in 1902. Weber's articles, of which the first was published two years later, were a study of a single aspect of the same problem. A whole literature[4] has arisen on the subject discussed in them. How does Weber's thesis stand to-day, after a quarter of a century of research and criticism?

The interpretation of religious beliefs and social institutions as different expressions of a common psychological attitude, which Weber elaborated in his *Aufsätze zur Religionssoziologie*, is no longer so novel as when he advanced it. Once stated, indeed, it has the air of a platitude. The capacity of human beings to departmentalize themselves is surprising, but it is not unlimited. It is obvious that, in so far as doctrines as to man's place in the universe are held with conviction, they will be reflected in the opinions formed of the nature of the social order most conducive to well-being, and that the habits moulded by the pressure of the economic environment will in turn set their stamp on religion. Nor can Weber's contention be disputed that Calvinism, at least in certain phases of its history, was associated with an attitude to questions of social ethics which contemporaries regarded as peculiarly its own. Its critics attacked it as the sanctimonious ally of commercial sharp practice. Its admirers applauded it as the school of the economic virtues. By the middle of the seventeenth century the contrast between the social conservatism of Catholic Europe and the strenuous enterprise of Calvinist communities had become a commonplace. 'There is a kind of natural inaptness,' wrote a pamphleteer in 1671, 'in the Popish religion to business, whereas, on the contrary, among the Reformed, the greater their zeal, the greater their inclination to trade and industry, as holding idleness unlawful.' The influence of Calvinism was frequently adduced as one explanation of the economic prosperity of Holland. The fact that in England the stronghold of Nonconformity was the commercial classes was an argument repeatedly advanced for tolerating Nonconformists.

In emphasizing, therefore, the connection between religious radicalism and economic progress, Weber called attention to an interesting phenomenon, at which previous writers had hinted, but which none had yet examined with the same wealth of learning and philosophical insight. The significance to be ascribed to it, and, in particular, the relation of Calvinist influences to the other forces making for economic innovation, is a different and more difficult question. His essay was confined to the part played by religious movements in creating conditions favourable to the growth of a new type of economic civilization, and he is careful to guard himself against the criticism that he under-estimates the importance of the parallel developments in the world of commerce, finance, and industry. It is obvious, however, that, until the latter have been examined, it is not possible to determine the weight to be assigned to the former. It is arguable, at least, that, instead of Calvinism producing the spirit of Capitalism, both would with equal plausibility be regarded as different effects of changes in economic organization and social structure.

It is the temptation of one who expounds a new and fruitful idea to use it as a key to unlock all doors, and to explain by reference to a single principle phenomena which are, in reality, the result of several converging causes. Weber's essay is not altogether free, perhaps, from the defects of its qualities. It appears occasionally to be somewhat over-subtle in ascribing to intellectual and moral influences developments which were the result of more prosaic and mundane forces, and which appeared, irrespective of the character of religious creeds, wherever external conditions offered them a congenial environment. 'Capitalism' itself is an ambiguous, if indispensable, word, and Weber's interpretation of it seems sometimes to be open to the criticism of Professor Sée,[5] that he simplifies and limits its meaning to suit the exigencies of his argument. There was no lack of the 'capitalist spirit' in the Venice and Florence of the fourteenth century, or in the Antwerp of the fifteenth. Its development in Holland and England, it might not unreasonably be argued, had less to do with the fact that they, or certain social strata in them, accepted the Calvinist version of the Reformation, than with large economic movements and the social changes produced by them. 'Ce que MM. Weber et Troeltsch,' writes Professor Pirenne,[6] 'prennent pour l'esprit Calviniste, c'est précisément l'esprit des hommes nouveaux que la révolution économique du temps introduit dans la vie des affaires, et qui s'y opposent aux traditionalistes auxquels ils se substituent.' Why insist that causation can work in only one direction? Is it not a little artificial to suggest that capitalist enterprise had to wait, as Weber appears to imply, till religious changes had produced a capitalist spirit? Would it not be equally plausible, and equally one-sided, to argue that the religious changes were themselves merely the result of economic movements?

If Weber, as was natural in view of his approach to the problem, seems to lay in the present essay somewhat too exclusive an emphasis upon intellectual and ethical forces, his analysis of those forces themselves requires, perhaps, to be supplemented. Brentano's criticism, that the political thought of the Renaissance was as powerful a solvent of conventional restraints as the teaching of Calvin, is not without weight. In England, at any rate, the speculations of business men and economists as to money, prices, and the foreign exchanges, which were occasioned by the recurrent financial crises of the sixteenth century and by the change in the price level, were equally effective in undermining the attitude which Weber called traditionalism. Recent studies of the development of economic thought suggest that the change of opinion on economic ethics ascribed to Calvinism was by no means confined to it, but was part of a general intellectual movement, which was reflected in the outlook of Catholic, as well as of Protestant, writers. Nor was the influence of Calvinist teaching itself so uniform in character, or so undeviating in tendency, as might be inferred by the reader of Weber's essay. On the contrary, it varied widely from period to period and country to country, with differences of economic conditions, social tradition, and political environment. It looked to the past as well as to the future. If in some of its phases it was on the side of change, in others it was conservative.

Most of Weber's illustrations of his thesis are drawn from the writings of English Puritans of the latter part of the seventeenth century. It is their teaching which supplies him with the materials for his picture of the pious *bourgeois* conducting his business as a calling to which Providence has summoned the elect. Whether the idea conveyed by the word 'calling' is so peculiar to Calvinism as Weber implies is a question for theologians; but the problem, it may be suggested, is considerably more complex than his treatment of it suggests. For three generations of economic development and political agitation lay between these writers and the author of the *Institutes*. The Calvinism which fought the English Civil War, still more the Calvinism which won an uneasy toleration at the Revolution, was not that of its founder.

Calvin's own ideal of social organization is revealed by the system which he erected at Geneva. It had been a theocracy administered by a dictatorship of ministers. In 'the most perfect school of Christ ever seen on earth since the day of the Apostles,' the rule of life had been an iron collectivism. A godly discipline had been the aim of Knox, of the Reformed Churches in France, and of the fathers of the English Presbyterian Movement; while a strict control of economic enterprise had been the policy first pursued by the saints in New England. The Calvinism, both of England and Holland, in the seventeenth century, had found its way to a different position. It had discovered a compromise in which a juster balance was struck between prosperity and salvation, and, while retaining the theology of the master, it repudiated his scheme of social ethics. Persuaded that 'godliness hath the promise of this life, as well as of the life to come,' it resisted, with sober intransigence, the interference in matters of business both of the state and of divines. It is this second, individualistic phase of Calvinism, rather than the remorseless rigours of Calvin himself, which may plausibly be held to have affinities with the temper called by Weber 'the spirit of Capitalism.' The question which needs investigation is that of the causes which produced a change of attitude so convenient to its votaries and so embarrassing to their pastors.

It is a question which raises issues that are not discussed at length in Weber's essay, though, doubtless, he was aware of them. Taking as his theme, not the conduct of Puritan capitalists, but the doctrines of Puritan divines, he pursues a single line of inquiry with masterly ingenuity. His conclusions are illuminating; but they are susceptible, it may perhaps be held, of more than one interpretation. There was action and reaction, and, while Puritanism helped to mould the social order, it was, in its turn, moulded by it. It is instructive to trace, with Weber, the influence of religious ideas on economic development. It is not less important to grasp the effect of the economic arrangements accepted by an age on the opinion which it holds of the province of religion.

Notes

* Foreword to Max Weber, *The Protestant Ethic and the Spirit of Capitalism*, trans. by T. Parsons (1930), pp. 1–11.

1 Max Weber, *General Economic History*, trans. Frank H. Knight, Ph.D. (George Allen & Unwin). A bibliography of Weber's writings is printed at the end of the charming and instructive account of him by his widow, *Max Weber, Ein Lebensbild*, von Marianna Weber (J. C. B. Mohr, Tübingen, 1926). See also 'Économistes et Historiens: Max Weber, un homme, une œuvre', par Maurice Halbwachs, in *Annales d'Histoire Économique et Sociale*, No. 1, January, 1929.

2 Weber, *General Economic History*, trans. Frank H. Knight, pp. 355–6.

3 Henri Pirenne, *Les Périodes de l'Histoire Sociale du Capitalisme* (Hayez, Brussels, 1914).

4 See, in particular, the following: E. Troeltsch, *Die Sozialen Lehren der christlichen Kirchen und Gruppen* (1912); F. Rachfahl, *Kalvinismus und Kapitalismus* (*Internationale Wochenschrift*, 1909, i. III); L. Brentano, *Die Anfange des modernen Kapitalismus* (1916) and *Der*

Wirtschaftende Mensch in der Geschichte (1911); W. Sombart, *Die Juden und das Wirtschaftsleben* (1911. Eng. trans. *The Jews and Modern Capitalism*, 1913), and *Der Bourgeois* (1913. Eng. trans. *The Quintessence of Modern Capitalism*, 1915); G. v. Schulze-Gaevernitz, 'Die Geistesgeschichtlichen Grundlagen der Anglo-Amerikanischen Weltsuprematie. III. Die Wirtschaftsethik des Kapitalismus' (*Archiv fur Sozialwissenschaft und Sozialpolitik*, Bd. 61, Heft 2); H. Sée, 'Dans quelle mesure Puritains et Juifs ont-ils contribué au Progrès du Capitalisme Moderne?' (*Revue Historique*, t. CLV, 1927) and *Les Origines du Capitalisme Moderne* (1926); M. Halbwachs, 'Les Origines Puritaines du Capitalisme Moderne' (*Revue d'Histoire et Philosophie Religieuses*, March–April, 1925) and 'Economistes et Historiens: Max Weber, une vie, une œuvre' (*Annales d'Histoire Economique et Sociale*, No. 1, 1929); H. Hauser, *Les Débuts du Capitalisme Moderne* (1927); H. G. Wood, 'The Influence of the Reformation on ideas concerning Wealth and Property,' in *Property, its Rights and Duties* (1913); Talcott Parsons, 'Capitalism in Recent German Literature' (*Journal of Political Economy*, December, 1928, and February, 1929); Frank H. Knight, 'Historical and Theoretical Issues in the Problem of Modern Capitalism' (*Journal of Economic and Business History*, November 1928); Kemper Fulberton, 'Calvinism and Capitalism' (*Harvard Theological Review*, July, 1928).

5 H. Sée, 'Dans quelle mesure Puritains et Juifs ont-ils contribué au Progrès Capitalisme Moderne?' (*Revue Historique*, t. CLV, 1927).

6 H. Pirenne, *Les Périodes de l'Histoire Sociale du Capitalisme* (1914).

6

A Berkshire Farmer in the Reign of James I (1937)*

Robert Loder's Farm Accounts, 1610–1620 is an unusually good specimen of a class of records of which many examples exist, but few have been printed. Its backbone consists of the receipts and expenditure of a Berkshire farmer in the reign of James I. It belongs, therefore, to the same genus as the account of the farming of Henry Best, published by the Surtees Society, and Professor Lodge's recent volume *The Account Book of a Kentish Estate, 1616–1704*; but though the period which it covers is only about a decade, Robert Loder is more illuminating than John Toke. In the first place, his accounts are better done. He gives full particulars of his takings as well as his outgoings, shows the yields, costs and value of his principal crops, and either states his net profits on the year, or provides data sufficient for a plausible estimate of them. In the second place, his accounts are not merely accounts: they are accompanied by a running commentary, in which he weighs the merits of alternative policies, notes the failure or success of what actually followed, and draws from the experience of each year conclusions to guide his course in the next. The relative advantages of growing wheat and barley, of buying ewes or keeping a breeding flock, of time-work and piece work, are balanced against each other. We get an insight, therefore, not merely into the management of a farm, but—what is less easy to come by—into its manager's view of the problems to be solved and the difficulties to be overcome. The reader is saved much labour in summarising scattered data, and provided with an interpretation which puts the enterprise concerned in its proper setting, by the valuable introduction contributed by Mr. Fussell.

Robert Loder's farm, at Harwell, without being in the same class as the great agricultural undertakings of the age, was on the large size. It contained roughly 300 acres, of which about 150 were arable in the open fields, 100 were enclosed down, and the remainder were orchards and small enclosures, together with rights of common. He was engaged in what would now be called mixed farming. In addition to growing cereals, he ran a flock of 400 to 500 sheep and kept a dairy herd. His main interest, however, was clearly in the former, and, possibly for that reason, information as to the details of his animal husbandry is less full and precise. His range of crops was not large, even for his own period. No mention is made of rye, oats or buckwheat. Wheat and barley were the cash-crops; peas, beans and vetches the fodder-crops. The hay, the value of which was considerable—one year with another between one-sixth and one-seventh of the total—was presumably consumed on the farm, as was the bulk of the milk and milk products. The ordinary rotation appears to have been wheat, fallow, wheat or barley, fallow, with the legumes thrown in from time to time as a catch-crop.

The commercial results of Loder's sheep-farming are not clear, but on the cereals he did well. Judging by the proportion of the crop to the seed sown, of which full particulars are given, the yield of barley was lower than would be expected to-day, but that of wheat was surprisingly high. It averaged over nine years just over 30 bushels per acre, and in the last, 1620, reached the remarkable figure of 46.2, a return of between eleven and twelve fold. This side of his business was clearly a success. Assuming, as Loder appears to have thought, that the sheep about paid for themselves, and that he did not lose, at any rate, on his cattle, the results were not unsatisfactory. His receipts averaged from 1612 to 1620 £376.4s.10$^1/_4$d., of which rents accounted for 3.8 per cent, and the remainder came from farming operations, while his costs averaged £138 odd. His average net return, therefore, including the small items of rents, was in the region of £238. The figure was not large, when compared with the profits of specialist sheep-farmers, like the Treshams, or cattle-breeders, like the Wynnes, but it was not to be sneezed at. It is a pity that the accounts end just when they do. In the last year, there are hints of the depression which spoiled the tempers of the country gentry in the momentous Parliament of 1621. Loder decided in 1620 that it was 'good husbandrie, when corne is so cheape, not to sell any, except I can lay out my money at that rate for corne againe'. Though his wheat and barley crops in that year were well above the level of 1618, the cash return from them was down by nearly one-fifth.

The value of a work such as that edited by Mr. Fussell is not impaired by the fact that generalisations cannot be based on single instances. By revealing the economy of a seventeenth-century farm in its concrete detail, it suggests trains of thought which, if followed up, may lead to the revision of some conventional ideas as to the agriculture of the past. The business side of farming has been curiously neglected by historians, with the result that certain superstitions linger on. The common belief in the uncommercial character of pre-eighteenth-century agriculture is among them. In reality, if 'subsistence farming', in any strict sense of that ambiguous expression, ever had outside the books the importance which it has in them, the days of its primacy were by the reign of James I long over. Even small men had to market a substantial part of their output; they had cash outgoings to meet. The more substantial farmers, whatever their speciality, were not in agriculture for their health; they had their eyes on the market all the time. The figures of the consumption of wheat and malt by Loder's household show that it formed, except in the opening years, when he had little land under the former, only a small proportion of the total output. He appears to have sent his malt to London, via Henley and the Thames, and to have sold his wheat in local markets. Hence his careful attention to prices and costs. The whole tone of his notes proves that, as Mr. Fussell remarks, 'before all things he was a business man'. The pious ejaculations which enliven his accountancy are normally expressions of gratitude to Providence, not for bread in due season, but for rising profits.

Loder was not only a man of business; he was also in a small way, an 'improver'. Nor does his enterprise appear to have been much impeded by the social frame-work in which he worked. The technical deficiencies of his economy are obvious enough. The neglect of grass was in his case, as in others, the weakest link in the chain: insufficient and inferior winter fodder, low quality stock, and a shortage of manure, were among its consequences. On the other hand, his jottings suggest that the difficulty of making new departures on scattered parcels in open fields, and the restrictions imposed by the common course of cultivation, were less important than is usually implied. Harwell was a two-field parish, and Loder's arable lay in both fields. He appears, nevertheless, to have had considerable choice as to the crops which he grew. He did not keep all his strips in one field under one crop. In one year, for example, he grew in West Field, wheat, peas, vetches and pulse, while he let some of his strips 'lay laye', *i.e.* in grass; in another he had in the same field, land under barley, vetches and pulse, as well as under wheat; while from time to time he 'hitched' the fallow—*i.e.* reserved, and probably temporarily fenced, part of it—for leguminous crops. His procedure could be paralleled from other sources: grass 'lays', for example, were common in the arable fields of Northamptonshire, where the shortage of pasture was always a problem, and the methods of the Norfolk farmer described in Professor

Gray's *English Field Systems* show the same tentative flexibility as do those of Loder.

The truth is that the conventional picture which still lingers in the textbooks—the picture of open-field agriculture as a perverse miracle of organised torpor performed by village idiots—has no relation to realities. It probably descends from a careless reading of Arthur Young, whose dogmatic ghost continues to ride through agrarian history, unperturbed by the evidence discovered since the precocious rationaliser himself rode in flesh and blood. If so, it is a part of the Arthurian legend which ought to be discarded. The note of the agriculture of the past was not so indisputably petrifaction as some of its earlier students suggested. Even the Mouldys and Bull Calfs—not to mention Loder—behaved on occasion quite like human beings.

Notes

* Review of G. E. Fussell (ed.), *Robert Loder's Farm Accounts, 1610–1620* (1936), in *History*, XXII (1937), pp. 270–2.

7
A History of Capitalism (1950)*

That, in a country once regarded as the classic land of capitalism, the reception accorded the word should till yesterday have been more frigid than in nations for long with less experience of the fact is, at first sight, surprising. The reason was partly, no doubt, an intellectual tradition which viewed with repugnance the use of one of the timeless categories of theory to describe a particular chapter of historical development; but it was partly also the three centuries of piecemeal adaptation through which, in England, that phase has unfolded. France, though her traditional economy was slow to change, had seen its institutional framework demolished in five years; Germany, a society predominantly composed of peasants and small masters grow, in little more than a generation, into an industrial Leviathan. In both, a single lifetime had sufficed to reveal one régime in decline and another in the ascendant. In neither, whatever the language employed, was it plausible to deny that the second belonged to a different *genus* from the first. In England, modernization had its obstacles to surmount; but, in her case, contrasts of legal principle and economic organization leapt less readily to the eye. It was easier, therefore, for a terminology which underlined, not the continuity of social growth, but the novelty of its latest stage, to be dismissed in good faith by reputable thinkers as political claptrap or a mare's-nest of doctrinaires. Capitalism had had its modest place in the vocabulary of Chartist intellectuals; but it was only in the 1880's that the word acquired a wide currency in popular usage. It was not till 1894 that an important work by an English author accorded the suspected intruder a position in its title.

Mr. J. A. Hobson's *Evolution of Modern Capitalism* included in its second edition (1906) an introductory chapter which drew heavily on

Sombart; but, apart from that, it did not deal in long perspectives. The work of a gifted economist, who challenged conventional orthodoxies at more than one point, it was primarily, in spite of its title, less a history of capitalism than a penetrating examination of tendencies revealed by recent changes in industrial organization in Great Britain and the United States. In England the serious study of economic history started late, and still has leeway to make up; but its progress in the last half-century has not been slow. Mr. Dobb's *Studies in the Development of Capitalism* illustrates some of the influences which have left their mark on it. The author modestly disclaims the intention of attempting more than to select for investigation 'certain aspects of economic development' and 'to answer certain specific questions', nor can his book be said to tread unbeaten paths; but, based, as it is, on a conscientious study of the chief secondary authorities, as interpreted by one for whom the last word rests with Marx, it is to be welcomed as revealing both the uses and the limitations of a treatment of its subject more often, in this country, commended in terms of resounding generality than applied in practice. Its plan can be simply stated. After an interesting introductory chapter, in which different interpretations of the word 'capitalism' are discussed and the author's usage of the term explained, he turns to his main theme. Five chapters (151 pp.) are devoted to the period between the later middle ages and the mid-eighteenth century, and one (55 pp.) to the Industrial Revolution and the nineteenth century. A concluding chapter (67 pp.) deals with the interlude between the two World Wars and its sequel. As, however, was to be expected, the problems arising proved too intricate for the discussion of them to be confined within a strictly chronological framework. The combination of history with theory is one of the merits of the book.

Space forbids an attempt to do more than indicate the direction of the argument. The essence of feudalism was serfdom; and the decline of serfdom was due less to the commercial forces often emphasized than to the inherent instability of the edifice based upon it. Of its nature a feeble economic engine, it involved an increasing pressure, at once intolerable and self-defeating, of the upper on the lower storey of the hierarchy. Either the leasing of the lord's demesne, or the substitution of hired labour for villein services as the means employed to work it, provided an escape from the *impasse*. In the meantime the profits of trade created in the towns a prosperous middle class. Monopoly or quasi-monopoly was the foundation on which it rested; and, as commerce expanded, a similar apparatus of corporate privilege was applied, with the support of governments, to foreign trade. Industrial capitalism developed partly through the investments of merchants in production, partly through the initiative of producers, who themselves organized industry on a capitalist basis. The collision of the interests thus created both with the London exporting syndicates, which controlled the access to foreign markets, and with the monopolies conferred by the Crown on favoured patentees, was, it is suggested, among the issues which prepared the way for the Civil War and determined the alignment of the forces engaged in it. The capital required for industrial development had been accumulated by a process involving two distinct stages. In the first, properties whose value was depressed by the embarrassments of aristocratic fortunes or the helplessness of peasants were acquired on attractive terms by the ascending *bourgeoisie*. In the second, the new owners disposed of them, when a favourable combination of economic circumstances had enhanced their value, in order to invest the proceeds in commercial and industrial ventures. Mercantilism, with its preoccupation with the export market, its conviction that demand is inelastic, and its obsession with the terms, as distinct from the volume, of trade, supplied the interests dominant in the latter phase with the appropriate rationalizations. A proletariat emerged on the scale required, not primarily as the natural consequence of a growing population, but as a work of political art, manufactured with the aid of peasant evictions, the corporate egotism of exclusive gilds, and the control of indispensable financial and marketing facilities by commercial middlemen. In the treatment of the Industrial Revolution and its sequel, the points underlined are the unique combination of circumstances which, for close on a century, floated the new economy from triumph to triumph; the part played, in particular, by a continuous enlargement of opportunities for investment; the significance of the depressions of the 1870's and 1880's as marking the close of an astonishing chapter; and the rush into combinations or clamour for protected markets occasioned by the change in the economic temperature. The two decades preceding 1914 are regarded as an Indian summer, in which the revival of capital exports and imperialistic politics combined temporarily to mask the demise of the great age of British capitalism, and the first World War as an incident which interrupted, but did not substantially alter, the operation of tendencies visible before it. An intensified restrictionism in the world of business; neo-mercantilist policies on the part of governments; the growth of an industrial salariate; and rigidities inseparable from modern mass-production methods—such were the characteristic features of the twenty years' interlude. It is with some 'form of state capitalism, democratically controlled and operated in the interests of Labour' that, Mr. Dobb suggests, the immediate future is likely to lie.

A summary, unaccompanied by the illustrations and arguments by which an author supports his conclusions, necessarily conveys an inadequate impression of his work. There is abundant room for *œuvres de synthèse* which, without pretending to mine unworked seams, kindle fresh light from materials already known. Within the limits fixed by his premises, the book of Mr. Dobb is a good example of them. It suffers, at times, in the opinion of the reviewer, from an excess of caution; but if, in its treatment of its materials, it hugs conventional shores, instead of using them to construct new charts, the instances which it assembles to exemplify and confirm the pattern followed are aptly selected, and the interpretation put on them not unfairly forced. There are occasions when, like most of us, it ignores or treats too lightly evidence which, if allowed due weight, might have modified its conclusions; but it handles with candour such evidence as it employs. It was inevitable that some of its citations from an author who wrote in the infancy of economic history should sound to-day slightly platitudinous and that others should date; but it does not proliferate to excess in invocations and doxologies. It drives useful paths through the jungle of gild and municipal regulations in which most students must at times have lost their way. In its determination 'to make sense of the notion of a primitive accumulation (in Marx's sense of the term), prior in time to the full flowering of capitalist production', it appears to an untheoretical layman to make needlessly heavy weather of topics which, with the audacity of ignorance, he once supposed to be not beyond his depth; but it alleviates his humiliation with a cluster of suggestions, some of them instructive, thrown out in the process of inflicting it. At the end of its long journey from Adam Smith to Schmoller, and Schmoller to Heckscher, the word 'mercantilism' sometimes seems to resemble the stamp on a parcel the contents of which have been changed in the post. Mr. Dobb has contrived, in a few pages, to say something new and to the point on a much-bedevilled subject. The student of works on the last century of economic history is apt to find himself buried beneath a mountain of inert facts. In his attempt to use analysis to enable the wood, as well as the trees, to be grasped by the reader, Mr. Dobb offers an example which deserves imitation.

Naturally, there are points of fact and interpretation where the author seems less sure-footed than elsewhere. The description of medieval Manchester by the treacherous term borough is supported by a reference to Miss Bateson's *Medieval England*; but, in view of the evidence from different quarters summarized by Professor Redford (*History of Local Government in Manchester*, I, 22–3), it ought to be reconsidered. Instances can, doubtless, be quoted to support the view that the leasing of the demesne was most likely to occur when land, relatively to labour, was scarce; but the converse situation was equally or more common. It was one in which land, valueless unless worked, was leased to enterprising peasants, till a change in market conditions caused lords to take it in hand or to let it in block to a substantial farmer. The remarks on the last days of serfdom and on copyholders appear to betray some confusion between status and tenure. The statement that 'many bondmen' survived under the Tudors seems to come, *via* Mr. Lipson, from a well-known article by Savine. It may well be true for the first half of the sixteenth century; but bondage, though it existed under Elizabeth, had become by her middle years something of a curiosity. The tenurial obligations mentioned by Mr. Dobb do not prove his point, since they are not a clue to the personal condition of the owners of the holdings owing them, who included, not only peasants, but well-to-do gentry. Custom continued to be a factor in copyhold not only, as stated by him, in the seventeenth century, but in our own. To cite the abolition in 1646 of the cumbrous and antiquated system of land-taxation, known as the feudal incidents, as a proof that 'the final disintegration of the feudal mode of production' did not occur till the Civil War, will hardly do. It is a solecism similar in kind, though smaller in degree, to that which would be involved in a reference to the long survival of descendants of the land-tax of 1692 as evidence that England has only recently ceased to be a predominantly agricultural country. In reality, the fiscal arrangements in question were not an indication of the continuance of any particular 'mode of production'; nor is there evidence that productive methods were affected by their abolition. A history of the growth of a proletariat still remains to be written; but the explanation of its absence by the existence among historians of a regrettable disposition to regard 'the stratagems of Lombard money-lenders and Amsterdam stock-jobbers as a more resplendent tale to tell than that of paupers branded and hanged and cottagers harried and dispossessed' ascribes to the *crétins* in question more elevated tastes than most of them can boast. Studies in English of either of the first two groups of paladins are conspicuously few; while not many of the now considerable number of works on agrarian history omit to refer to the additions to the ranks of the wage-earners made by evicted peasants. In his needlessly supercilious dismissal of the views expressed by Mr. Durbin on a later phase of the same topic, Mr. Dobb hardly maintains his usual standard of fairness. Mr. Durbin did not deny, but underlined, the increase in the proportion of the population employed under a contract of service. His point was the simple one that the area of life marked by features considered two generations ago to be characteristically proletarian has greatly contracted. If it is invalid, it should be disproved, not swept aside. *Brûler n'est pas répondre.*

Of these matters some, perhaps, deserve a second thought, before the appearance of a further edition of the book. The more interesting and important questions are those which concern the author's approach to his subject. Everyone knows the difficulties which arise when a particular topic, whether capitalism, enclosures or commercial policy, is pursued over a period of several centuries. Between starting-point and conclusion the economic and political context has changed, and with it the range and content of the subject discussed. Mr. Dobb's limitation of the term capitalism to a particular system of production, under which labour is employed on the basis of a wage-contract to produce surplus-value for the owner of capital, might seem, at first sight, to escape some of the ambiguities inherent in less restricted interpretations; but it raises problems of its own. It is not merely that, as he would agree, financial and commercial capitalism have been highly developed in circumstances when the institution, as interpreted by him, has been a feeble plant, and that to exclude these varieties on the ground that they do not fall within the four corners of a nineteenth-century definition is to beg the question. It is that, as his work shows, the origins and growth of the industrial species require for their elucidation to be considered in relation to the history of other members of the family, some of which have been among its progenitors. Obviously the capitalism of our day rests predominantly on a wage-system, and the latter is so familiar that it is tempting to treat it as historically a constant. The reality was less simple. Wages, like rents, remain for long an elusive category. The truth is that, during the earlier periods dealt with by Mr. Dobb, wages in something like the modern sense; prices paid for wares made to the order of commercial *entrepreneur*; intermittent fees for special jobs; other more eccentric methods of remuneration, and a variety of hybrids between all of them, are not easily distinguished; that permanent wage-workers were, in most districts, a minority; and that, while exploitation by the owner of capital was frequently rampant, it as often took the form of cut prices, usurious interest, or exactions by an extortionate middleman, as of sweated wages. To hit the mean between too wide and too narrow an interpretation is always difficult. Mr. Dobb is entitled to prefer the latter; and he partially atones for the resulting difficulties by an instructive account of the arrangements characteristic of 'the early and still immature stage where the pre-capitalist mode of production had been penetrated by the influence of capital ... but not completely transformed' by it. But, in the light of the facts set out in his book, has not the restricted sense which he favours, however natural two generations ago, ceased to be the usage most convenient for the purposes of history?

The question is more than a mere matter of words. The doubts suggested by it have a bearing on the treatment of some of the larger issues touched on by the author. His definition of capitalism leads at times to a misconception of the significance of the part played by capitalist interests in periods when an industrial wage-system was, in this country, in its infancy. The development of an institution, whether economic or political, must be explained partly in terms of the opportunities offered and strains imposed by the environment in which it functions. In his chapter on the Industrial Revolution, Mr. Dobb rightly calls attention to the favourable *conjunktur* created by the removal of impediments previously obstructing the growth of the great industry. Considerations of a similar order are relevant at other periods, when he seems less conscious of them. A population sparse in relation to land resources continued, as late as the first half of the seventeenth century, to give both the economy and the society of parts, not only of England, but of continental Europe, a semi-colonial stamp. The tardiness of the recourse to more intensive methods of production, of which capitalism is one, was partly the result of it. At a time when the natural resources of Europe were still but little depleted, and new worlds outside it had been opened to enterprise by an advance in geographical knowledge and nautical skill unaccompanied by a corresponding progress in the productive arts, output in most industries was inelastic, while commercial frontiers were in ceaseless motion. In such circumstances, it was natural that the most important standard-bearer of economic progress, who mobilizes productive energies, keeps the front advancing, and calls the tune to which other interests dance, should be, not the manufacturer or mineowner, but 'the master of the mystery of trade, the steward of the nation's wealth, the prudent merchant'. It was equally inevitable that such a situation should not last, and that, as the partial exhaustion of easily accessible supplies brought rising costs, the direction of interest to technological improvement, of which the highest landmark is the foundation of the Royal Society, but which, as patents show, had been under way for half a century or more before it, should announce that the age in which the trader ruled the roost, though it still had a long life before it, would one day pass. With the advance, during the last century, towards economic unification, the connexion, visible in these earlier cases, between different forms of capitalism and the external forces playing on it, became, of course, immensely more important. Both the depressions of the 1870's and 1880's and inter-war restrictionism—to mention nothing else—provide illustrations of it. One obvious factor in the latter, to which the present work devotes some pungent pages, was the scuttle to shelter on the part of a business economy organized for one kind of world, and thrown into helpless disarray when confronted by another.

It would not be reasonable to criticize Mr. Dobb for omitting to deal at length with aspects of economic life which are, after all, no more than the background of his subject; but it is permissible to think that his treatment of the latter would have gained in effectiveness could he have contrived to say somewhat more about the changes in the economic setting in which, in order to be intelligible, the development of capitalism must be seen. In the industrial sphere, which chiefly interests him, the most striking development of the sixteenth and seventeenth centuries was not, it may be suggested, the conquest by capitalism of the older crafts, which, though doubtless accelerated, was in principle an old story. It was the expansion outside them, under the pressure of environmental changes, of new or previously unimportant industries organized from the start on a capitalist basis. Mr. Dobb does not ignore that phenomenon, but he gives it a less prominent place than its importance deserves. Not only so, but his absorption in capitalism as 'a mode of production' leads at times to a single-track presentation of its history, under which the demon appears to unfold his criminal propensities, less in response to stimuli evoking them, than from the inner logic of his own infernal, though 'progressive', nature. It is possible to make too much of the dissolving effects of trade on early forms of agrarian organization; or of that most unrevolutionary of price-revolutions which, in England, extended over three to four lifetimes and half a dozen reigns; or of the effect of failing timber supplies in stimulating the transition from a wooden to an iron age; or of the economic consequences of international breakdowns. But, in order to avoid such errors, it ought not to be necessary to fly to the opposite extreme. There are moments when, in his preoccupation with the industrial engine, the author seems to assign to productive interests a preponderance of influence which, however valid for the nineteenth century, rarely in earlier periods belonged to them. Some of his interesting, though necessarily somewhat sketchy, observations on the economic background of the political conflicts of the seventeenth century are, perhaps, a case in point.

Contemporary usage, unlike our own, applied the term monopoly not only to grants of an exclusive right to conduct certain economic enterprises, but also to those conferring lucrative privileges of searching, sealing, measuring, weighing, registering, licensing, and fining, of the kind satirized by Jonson in Meercraft's project for the establishment of a national office for the Control of Toothpicks, to be reinforced by an official circular 'which every child that can read shall learn to pick his teeth by'. The former, salt, soap, glass and the rest may have numbered under Charles something over a dozen and under twenty; the latter ran into several scores. Mr. Dobb, in his anxiety to underline the collision between the Crown and the interests of 'parvenu industrialists', bent on establishing 'a condition of affairs ... where the possession of capital alone determined who should occupy the field', lays his whole emphasis on the first. In reality, popular exasperation with the second, which outraged, among other sentiments, the national enthusiasm for cheap beer and tobacco—both bedevilled by patentees—was probably as important, and certainly wider spread. There were parts, again, of provincial England, especially in the north and west, whose attitude to London Big Business was that of the Middle-West of 1890 to Wall Street; and the author is right in noting its significance. A detestation of the ways of metropolitan export rings was not confined, however, to the clothiers whose prices they cut, but, as he shows, was equally strong, or stronger, among country exporters, who found themselves excluded from continental markets or harried in their colonial fishing stations. The dispute, in fact, was primarily one between different groups of commercial capitalists; and when, as in 1621, a crisis came, it was not the industrialists, but the provincial merchants, who, because they carried the heavier political guns, played the leading part in prosecuting the quarrel. Mr. Dobb's remark that the textile districts tended to be strongly Parliamentarian is true enough; and certainly, since, at least, 1614, the economic imbecilities of the government in handling the cloth trade, which were almost on the same majestic scale as those of some of its twentieth-century successors in dealing with coal, had given them no cause to love it. But Clarendon and Baxter, who are quoted on the point, were not less emphatic as to the prevalence of the same temper among the yeomanry. The latter—in Gloucestershire, for example, 'most forward and seditious, being very wealthy'—may well have added to a general objection to taxation a feeling of resentment at the pretensions of the gentry to social superiority; but it is not easy to specify economic grievances peculiar to them of a kind to account for their political militancy. There is nothing to cause surprise in a situation in which some groups cursed their rulers because of memories of poverty caused by unemployment, and others because, like Jeshurun, they had waxed fat and kicked. The combination should warn us, however, against facile over-rationalizations of political attitudes. The treatment of motives by some economic theorists is apt to strike a mere child of nature as *simpliste* to excess. It would be unfortunate if similar *naïvetés* were to infect economic history.

To discuss at length the familiar thesis that 'political events in seventeenth-century England ... bear all the marks of the classic bourgeois revolution' would take us too far afield; but it is permissible to inquire whether the time has not arrived when this venerable acquaintance deserves the compliment of a more discriminating welcome than is here accorded him. The problem of the part played by economic interests in causing the political breakdown is not quite so simple as Mr. Dobb supposes; but, granted the primacy which, in a work on economic history, may pardonably be assigned them, the question of the categories to be employed in stating their character still remains to be considered. There were countries in which the lines of social stratification continued for another century and a half to be drawn by differences of legal status, and in which, therefore, the word bourgeois, which distinguished the unprivileged *roturiers* from the *noblesse* and clergy, possessed a definite connotation. In such circumstances, the question whether an individual was a bourgeois or not, was one, not of opinion, but of fact, and movements initiated by persons of the class so designated might properly be described as bourgeois movements. The application to this country by continental thinkers of a term of art long familiar in their own is not at all surprising; but, for reasons of the kind long ago suggested by de Tocqueville, English social development had followed a different course. In the England of Charles I, distinctions of juristic status were not wholly absent; but, except for the political privileges of peers, they were few and faint. Violent inequalities of wealth were, of course, the rule, but they did not coincide with them; and, apart from the life-long wage-earners, probably in most regions a minority, and a more numerous, though too often neglected, body of impoverished peasants, it is not easy to point to a class devoid of large elements which, judged by the sources of their incomes, might properly be described as bourgeois. Given such conditions, the term is too blunt an instrument to dissect the resulting complexities of social organization. Employed with discrimination, it may still be useful; but, clearly, its meaning is not that which belonged to it in, for example, France or Prussia. To ignore, in using it, the distinctive peculiarities of the English species of the genus is to beg not a few of the questions which to-day most require attention. The truth is that much water has flowed under historical bridges since the expression 'a bourgeois revolution' was coined, and that serious discussion has passed the point at which the mid-Victorian formula could continue to be invoked, without definition or qualification, as an illuminating contribution to it. Respect for a thinker is shown, not by repeating what, two generations ago, he said, but by considering what, in the light of knowledge acquired since he wrote, he might now have been disposed to say.

Apart from its introductory observations, more than half of *Studies in the Development of Capitalism* is devoted to periods before the great divide where an economic history distinctively modern is commonly held to begin. It has seemed proper, therefore, that a review should examine at some length the treatment accorded them. The crowded canvas of the last century and a half demanded, as Mr. Dobb remarks, a somewhat different approach. The two chapters which deal with it are, inevitably and properly, more selective. They are in the nature of an interpretation reinforced by illustrations and discussions, but they are also packed with matter; and, though the reader must not turn to them for a continuous narrative or for comprehensive surveys, they are not to be regarded as merely an epilogue. They state explicitly lessons conveyed by implication in the preceding pages. It is possible, indeed, that the earlier passages of the story owe part of their attraction for the author to the hints to be gleaned from them of morals written in larger letters in its latest phases.

The dominant conception, which determines the choice of materials and the construction put on them, can be simply stated. It is the transitional character of an economic system once regarded as the natural order of civilized societies, but convicted by events, if not of suicidal tendencies, of ineradicable infirmities. The two acts in the drama—offensive and defensive, Capitalism triumphant and Capitalism in decline—have provided opportunities for more than one tragedian; but an old tale may be so handled as to reveal new truths, and the familiarity of the plot does not diminish the interest of observing the stages by which, in the present work, the theme is carried to its *dénouement*. The passage on the Industrial Revolution, which forms the opening scene, says much in small compass. Had the antecedents of the movement been under consideration, more, in the opinion of the reviewer, should have been said of the scientific developments of the preceding century; nor, it seems to him, can an adequate verdict be passed on its concomitant social dislocation unless a larger place than Mr. Dobb allows is given to the Napoleonic wars and their domestic sequel. The essentials of the matter, however—the combination in England of factors one or more of which was present in other countries, but which in this were associated to a unique degree; the synchronization of changes affecting all sides of life which, far more than the speed of any one of them, makes appropriate the use of the word 'revolution'; the tardy social adaptation which, if technical innovation was less rapid than formerly was suggested, failed disastrously to keep pace with it—these and other points are well brought out and given the right emphasis.

If, as appears to be the view of Mr. Dobb, a wave which took its start in the last quarter of the eighteenth century, be regarded as advancing, in spite of periodical recessions, with heightened momentum for the best part of a hundred years and then as having spent its force, the causes of its long continuance and subsequent decline are obviously an intriguing question. The answer given by him, though complicated in detail, is, in essence, simple. It is that a succession of enlarged opportunities for investment—first the mechanization of textiles, iron and mining; then the extension of similar changes to other trades; then the growth of the machine-making industries; finally, the modernization of transport—sustained the upward movement. The process, however, could not of its nature be other than transitory. To ensure that the growing capital equipment should be fully employed, it was necessary that consumption should expand in a like degree. 'In a class society, where the consumption of the mass of the population is restricted by their poverty, while increases of surplus income above wages go predominantly into the hands of the rich ... it is obvious that ... a lag of consumption behind the growth of equipment will operate as a powerful tendency.' It is not clear from the author's dicussion of the depressions of the 1870's and 1880's, when other 'buoyancy-factors', such as foreign investment and railway construction orders, had temporarily flagged, whether he thinks that that tendency played a significant part in causing them. It is evident, however, that he regards it as an influence of the first importance in the period between the wars.

Particular aspects of Mr. Dobb's interpretation of the last half-century of economic history will naturally be challenged. The view which sees in the eighteen years from 1896 to 1914 a St. Martin's summer which, apart from the international collapse, was doomed to flicker out, may be correct; but it requires to be supported by fuller argumentation than the author offers. The summary dismissal of the economic consequences of the first World War appears to the reviewer neither plausible on *a priori* grounds, nor confirmed by such evidence as has come his way, nor supported by the additional experience provided by the second. It would have been useful if a book by a writer with the wide economic knowledge and strong social sympathies of Mr. Dobb could have told us somewhat more of his conclusions as to the practical effects of capitalism on its victims, as indicated by changes in their standard of life. The picture, taken from the Report of the La Follette Committee, of the outrageous industrial tyranny practised in the United States before 1935 is not overdrawn; but it is misleading unless accompanied by a recognition that, since that date, the tyrants, doubtless with some exceptions, have been brought to heel. On matters of this kind more than one opinion may reasonably be held. Those expressed by Mr. Dobb will rightly carry weight. The reader who finds himself dissenting from some of them will do so with the reflection that, had it been possible for them to be developed at greater length, he also might have ended on the side of the angels.

In certain of its main contentions, the book appears to push, with needless, if agreeable, vigour, doors already open. To labour the truism that capitalism, not less than the other works of man, is the creature of time or place, is surely to-day a task of supererogation. Twenty years have elapsed since Mr. Hobson's heresy, one variety of which is implicit in the present volume, left its mark on the blameless pages of an official report. It may be regarded, with verbal modifications, as invested by now with a halo of orthodox respectability which would have both pleased and alarmed its non-conforming inventor. If a more general criticism may be permitted, it is that the author, for all his insistence that capitalism is a historical category, appears in his concluding chapters not always to live up to the full logic of that premise. The familiar contrast between the individualistic, competitive phase of sanguine expansion and the later relapse on to a cautious defensive behind prepared positions is effectively stated. But the capitalism, in Mr. Dobb's words, 'of the golden age' was more than a particular type of economic organization. It owed its existence and character, not merely to the operations of profit-making *entrepreneurs*, but to a complex of social habits, political institutions and psychological attitudes in the society about them. Causation, as usual, has worked more than one way. The latter, which are influenced by economic factors, but which also at times move under their own steam, have reacted on the former, as well as the former on the latter. Thus the monster has proved more malleable than a century or so ago; when Socialist searchlights were first turned upon him, it seemed conceivable that he should. His designation remains that given him when he roared and ramped at will through cowering jungles; but, as in the case of feudalism, which also survived its first predatory phase, the identity of name masks a reluctant acquisition, under chastening strokes from above and below, of a slightly less unsocial nature. Such reflections, however, though prompted by the concluding pages of Mr. Dobb, are a primrose path which must end in a precipice of right-wing deviations. It would be both inhuman and futile to incite him to pursue them.

Notes

* *Economic History Review*, 2nd ser., II (1950), pp. 307–16.

1 M. H. Dobb, *Studies in the Development of Capitalism* (Routledge, 1946, pp.v + 396. 18*s*).

8
Devon and Dr Hoskins (1954)*

As I read Dr Hoskins' admirable book on Devon,[1] I found my thoughts travelling back three hundred years to the first great age of English regional history. The principal influences inspiring the twenty to thirty county histories and surveys published between the appearance in the 1570s of Lambard's *Perambulation of Kent* and the meeting of the Long Parliament were, I suppose, two. The first was the Elizabethan historical renaissance which, in most cases without design, forged, in the tranquillity of libraries and country houses, weapons later to be brandished by more truculent hands in the tumult and glare of political war. The second was the vivid regional patriotism natural in a loosely-knit, decentralised society in which the capital and its nasty ways had not yet over-shadowed the provinces; where local concerns, interests and obligations were the common stuff of life, and where, when a man spoke of 'my country', he commonly meant, not England, but what today *mon pays* means in France, my neighbourhood, district or county.

Of the works in question which have come my way, most are informative, many entertaining, some radiant with the delight in the scenes and personalities amid which the author's lot is cast that shine—to cite only one example—from the pages of that humanest of antiquaries, John Smythe of North Nibley, who valued his seat in the House, principally, I fear, because it gave him opportunities for rummaging for records in the Tower, and to whom the surroundings of his home on a hill in the western Cotswolds known to Shakespeare were the most enchanting corner of the most enchanting county of the land most blessed by Heaven on which the sun had ever shone. Dr Hoskins is all in that tradition. A scholar with a line of yeomen ancestors behind him, he not only possesses an easy mastery of the literature of his theme, but combines it with a personal intimacy with every by-way, bridge and building in his vast county—which only a life-time of patient exploration can confer. If Wordsworth's well-known words on poetry as emotion remembered in tranquillity are ever relevant to the historian's humbler art, then it is to books in which, as in Dr Hoskins', learning and affection are fused that they may with least profanity be applied.

Compared with the limestone and chalk regions to the north and east, the neolithic legacy of Devon is apparently small; but, as a treasury of bronze age culture, Dartmoor, with its intriguing hints of a cross-channel connection with Brittany and later of a climatic deterioration which made the moor too wet for even the roughest of rough graziers to stand—it must be almost unique. There are many English regions, again, where the hand of Rome has left a deeper mark; but the imperial naval base, if such it was, at Topsham; Exeter, the Empire's furthest out-post in the west; the great frontier road of the Fosse Way, at once barrier and highway, built in the early years of the occupation to shelter the civilised province from the turbulent tribes beyond the Severn and the Trent, and linking, across two hundred odd miles of moorland, hill and forest, the southern terminus on the Devon coast with the northern at Lincoln—these and other bold and simple features have an austere grandeur of their own. Most persons—to refer to a third point—must at times have wondered whether the diversity of physical characteristics among the inhabitants of different regions may not have its source in differences in the racial elements of which they are composed. Observing in Devon the pronounced inter-mixture of contrasted types and the recurrent patches of apparently pre-Saxon stock, Dr Hoskins interprets them in the light of the comparatively peaceful process by which, in most of the county, the English settlement seems to have taken place. Sharp conflicts, dignified by the name of battles, did, of course, occur; but the Celtic population was so thin, and the vacant area so vast, that the invaders, he suggests, could trickle in without necessarily submerging the natives. In this corner of the country, in short, Saxon infiltration and colonisation may be less misleading terms than Saxon conquest.

Those, therefore, to whom the twilights of history appeal as strongly as the sharper outlines of its more familiar noons, will find in Dr Hoskins' earlier chapters an abundant source of instruction and charm. But it is in treating of the economic foundations of Devon life and the changes in the social structure resting on them that he moves with greatest ease. I should have wished to refer to his account of the thirteenth-century rush in founding towns, which left the county with some seventy little privileged communities known at one time or another as boroughs; to the textiles which found their chief market in southern France, so that the fortunes of a score of ports were based on the exchange of native fabrics against wine and wheat from Bordeaux and Bayonne; to tin, lead and copper mining; to lace-making and other industries; but on these topics time forbids me to dwell.

Devon has been throughout its history overwhelmingly an agricultural country. Let me say something of Dr Hoskins' interpretation of its rural life. In all European countries, colonial expansion overseas has been preceded by a longer period of colonisation at home. Devon, whose Domesday population of, perhaps, 60,000 to 80,000, confronted some 1,600,000 acres of which probably not far short of half was waste, is a classical case in point. Dr Hoskins reveals the alternating sequence of advance, stagnation, and occasional retreat by which over many centuries the moving agricultural frontier was pushed forward and the wilderness tamed. Reclamation and settlement took place, it appears, not continuously, but by a succession of intermittent waves, of which the first, the great colonising effort of 1150 or so to 1300, was followed by a long recession, and that again by another movement of expansion from about the mid-sixteenth century to the Civil War. Each of these great waves left behind it a deposit of new, or sometimes merely extended, farms, carved by individual settlers from the moors. The multitude of isolated homesteads remote from villages, which cause the landscape of much of Devon to contrast so sharply with the Midlands and East Anglia, is the result. They register, and sometimes date, the successive stages in the long campaign by which nature was conquered.

The predominant role played in Devon by the struggle to subdue the waste has been accompanied by two other features whose cause is partly the same. Struck by the paucity of records revealing in that county the changes commonly epitomised by the ambiguous word 'enclosure', an earlier generation of scholars held that the famous open-field village, with its scattered arable strips and common use of grass, was never acclimatised in the south-west. The truth, it now appears, is less simple and more instructive. Recent work on other regions has shown that open-field farming was not the perverse miracle of squalid petrification formerly depicted, but was compatible with numerous improvements affected from below by the peasants themselves. Dr Hoskins has proved that, in medieval Devon, such farming was widely carried on, and that the reason why in his county enclosure was once more precocious and more painless than elsewhere was that the existence side by side of two different agricultural types caused its spontaneous introduction at an early date. Farmers made on their own initiative such re-arrangements of the agricultural lay-out of their villages as were needed in order to enable holdings in them to be worked by the more highly individualised methods in use of land reclaimed from the moor.

A third trait emphasised by Dr Hoskins is equally significant. As was to be expected in a region where land resources in relation to population were abundant, Devon has been throughout its history an area where the ownership of real property was widely distributed. The economic consequences of the Reformation tilted the scales in favour of the richer, more influential or more enterprising gentry; but, between the great redistribution of monastic landed wealth, and the so-called new Domesday of 1873, the striking feature of his county's social configuration was its stability. His account of the 'new agrarian revolution', as he calls it, of our day, is not the least impressive part of his book. Its effects are seen in an estimated increase in the occupying owners to not far short of two-thirds of the farming population, in the closing of all but a handful of the great houses of the past, and in the emergence of the Ecclesiastical Commissioners, National Trust, Colleges, and Co-operative Societies as the largest landowners in the county.

Without numberless preceding contributions, Dr Hoskins' full-length portrait could not, as he would be first to admit, have been painted. But why, it may be asked, should such local studies be pursued? An author whom I have mentioned, John Smythe, reflecting in old age on the twenty-eight books produced by him, apologised for his self-indulgence with the remark that he couldn't help it: 'a continuous delight of forty years haled me along'. My first, though not my only, answer to the question would be much the same. There are countries so unfortunate that one may travel in them for several days on end with no companion but nature, who is delightful but not by herself sufficient. England is at the opposite extreme. Something tragic or amusing has happened around every corner. There is, in the famous phrase, sweat and tears over all of it. To see one's surroundings with some knowledge of these human associations is to heighten the charm of those which are beautiful, and to feel a sympathetic zest in those which, at first sight, seem dull. It is a pleasure, for example—to mention a few of such irrelevant trivialities first—to recall, when fishing a Border burn, that this was 'the Wan Water' of the ballad, at which the eloping daughter of the Douglases and Lord William dismounted to drink and Lady Margery knew by the blood in her stream that her lover was near his end; or to talk, as twenty years ago one could, with old men who remembered the enclosure of their village under an Act of the 1860s, and to hear what was said to the local MP, who was lord of the manor, at the next election meeting after that event; or to follow a precipitous lane locally known as King Charles' Hill, because, on an early day in August of 1643, some enterprising staff officer contrived—how, Heaven knows—to get the royal army down it on the way to its fruitless siege of the most Puritan of cities; or to learn that a tranquil valley is known as Woeful Bottom because it was there, some time in the ninth century, that a band of marauding Danes is supposed to have got its deserts; or on inquiring why nine out of ten of the cottages in a certain village vote Labour while in another, a couple of miles off, much the same proportion vote the other way, to be answered 'Oh, well, you see, it was always like that: we were for the Parliament and they were for the King', and to reflect that the mentality of the former at both dates possibly had its source in the same fact. It was that the village in question was an early colony on the edge of an extensive common, originally inhabited, if not by lawless, at least by not aggressively law-abiding, persons, who snapped their fingers at squire and parson, and did what seemed in their own eyes good.

Such memories, associations and stories, some fictitious and some true, most between the two, are infinite in number. If one knows nothing of them, one might as well go to Hell at once, with the goggle-faced motorists who have eyes but see not, and ears but hear not, and who return from their excursions, drugged by speed, in the same state of mental vacuity as they started. But, of course, I am far from suggesting that such incidental oddities and felicities are more than happy interludes in the local historian's more serious tasks. His primary concern is to understand the origin, growth, and vicissitudes of local communities; and, speaking only for myself, I should say that the reasons which make that object seem worth the effort are three. A local community of one kind or another, is in the first place the normal environment of man, and the quality of his life depends in no small degree on what he makes of it, and what it makes of him. In the second place, the local units are the primary cells of a larger organism, in Europe usually the nation-state. As the vitality of the former is, so will the health of the latter be. And, finally, many issues often described as of national importance are of their nature such that, unless grasped in terms of their local setting, they cannot effectively be grasped at all.

A score of problems, which only the local historian can solve, leap to one's mind. How, to give only a handful of examples, has the geographical distribution of human settlements in a given county become what it is? Some sites on the light soils of the chalk and limestone regions seem to have been occupied continually from a remote past. Others, at first sight equally eligible, have never apparently been occupied at all. Others again, today vacant, at one time maintained large and prosperous villages of which, as Dr Hoskins has shown in other works, many hundreds have since disappeared. How are these vicissitudes to be explained? A vital problem of social history is the size of the population at different dates. Parish registers of marriages, births and deaths begin in the sixteenth century and are abundant in the seventeenth. An early census official attempted, with indifferent success, to use them as a means of estimating the population of pre-Census days. Ought not a more systematic effort on similar lines to be resumed?

Agrarian history seems today to be undergoing a slight boom. And here the principal snares have been two. The first has been the temptations sometimes besetting those of us who are interested in the history of manors to ignore their most important features in order to lavish labour on the genealogies of the often insignificant proprietors by whom manorial rights have, from time to time, been owned. The second consists of a disposition, instead of combining the use of documents with observation, to rely on documents alone. The truth is that the history of the agriculture of a region cannot be intelligently studied without a sufficient personal knowledge of its environment to grasp at least the elements of the practical problems to be solved, and that works which ignore that platitude are liable to commit every error short of making water flow up a hill. Or—to turn to topics of an institutional kind—when one passes the boundary of a county, what exactly does one cross? Is it a division between the territories of tribes? Or between small kingdoms? Or an administrative convenience established in our own day? Parishes vary greatly in size, and the complexities of their interlacing outlines sometimes pass belief. How are such contrasts and intricacies to be explained? A church, with a Roman villa underneath it and not a house in sight, stands in the middle of a field, while another, unusually imposing, church is to hand two miles off. If the former was erected before the latter, why did it survive? Not far distant from each other are two large villages, of which one established its right to the status of a borough, while the other, after prolonged struggles, failed to do the same. What was the cause of their different fortunes, and what the effect?

But it would be presumptuous for me to multiply examples of the local historian's tasks; nor must I pause to elaborate the truism that local history is itself national history seen from an angle which enables realities too often overlooked to be most easily discerned. I confine myself to expressing my gratitude to Dr Hoskins for his book and my hope that it will encourage other students to follow in his steps.

Notes

* BBC Radio (Third Programme) first broadcast on 6 June 1954.

1 W. G. Hoskins, *Devon* (1954).

9

The Church and the Stuarts (1957)*

Few chapters of English history seem, at first sight, more familiar than the forty years' slide towards catastrophe of the monarchy of the early Stuarts; nor can it be said that the ecclesiastical, as distinct from the political, landmarks on the downward path have suffered from neglect. It is of the nature of historical studies, however, that each of their successive achievements in reducing to order a tract of experience previously obscure discloses a further horizon of still uncharted territory waiting to be won. The two generations treated by Mr. Christopher Hill, from the accession to the primacy of Whitgift in 1583 to the meeting of the Long Parliament in November, 1640, are not an exception. The inquirer invited to explore in his company 'the part played by religion in preparing the seventeenth-century revolution' will err if, misled by the apparent triteness of the quest, he supposes that he is destined to re-traverse well worn ground. On the contrary, he will find himself introduced to a world at once novel and important, whose very terminology needs an effort to master, and through which, in the absence of Mr. Hill's skilled guidance, he would with difficulty pick his way.

The subject of *Economic Problems of the Church* can be simply stated. The majority of works on English religious life in the period covered by it have been primarily concerned to elucidate the origins, growth, and dissemination of the diversities of doctrine and creed distinguishing different religious bodies, and have interpreted in the light of those transcendent topics the dissensions on practical matters of Church government and ecclesiastical policy, long fermenting beneath the surface, which burst, with the collapse of authority, into vivid and contentious life. Mr. Hill is not of those who reduce all categories to one, nor does he underestimate the importance of these traditional aspects of his theme; but he approaches it by a road which, since the appearance nearly half a century ago of Usher's *The Reconstruction of the English Church*, few historians have attempted to pursue. In a world where form and matter, spirit and flesh, soul and body are inextricably intertwined, is it not, he seems to ask, the course of prudence to keep both members of the partnership in view at once, and when, for whatever reason, one or other has been neglected, to endeavour to redress the balance by directing attention to the significance of the role played by it and the obstacles by which its activities were beset?

Whatever else the English Church of the early seventeenth century may have been, it was, as it always had been, an institution, and, in the words of the author, 'not only a religious,' but also a 'political and economic institution of the greatest power and importance.' In considering its position and prospects on the eve of the political breakdown, ought not, in accordance with that truism, a larger space than is customary to be given to the everyday, mundane matters of organization, finance and the ownership of property, staffing and remuneration, legal rights and duties, determining for good or evil the manner in which the institution worked? The evidence on such subjects is abundant. Mr. Hill has explored it with admirable thoroughness and skill. The result is a valuable contribution to the economic history of the Church of England at a critical period, but it is also much more. Based on a wide acquaintance with the contemporary literature, scrupulous in reserving judgment on uncertain points, and not forgetting the Continental parallels and contrasts against which the English developments must be seen, his book not only throws fresh light on the financial maladies of the Church but helps the reader to acquire a sympathetic insight into the varying mentalities which prompted the contrasted remedies prescribed for them by different social and religious groups.

One feature of the story at once arrests the eye. It is that deplored by Hooker when he wrote that, 'it hath fared with the wealth of the Church as with a tower, which, being built at first with the highest, overthroweth itself after by its own greatness; neither doth the ruin thereof cease with the only fall of that which hath exceeded mediocrity, but one part beareth down another, till the whole be laid prostrate.' The redistribution of property, power and prestige resulting from the Dissolution is a familiar tale; but the partial disendowment of the Church was less an episode than a process, and the assault on ecclesiastical wealth which began with the monasteries did not end with them. Of the sequel under Elizabeth which, when still in its first youth, prompted Whitgift's acid comment that 'the temporalty seek to make the clergy beggars, that we may depend on them,' an exhaustive study is still, it seems, to seek.

Mr. Hill's treatment of that subject adds much to our knowledge and provides an invaluable starting point for further work. The most significant fact emerging from this part of his book is the scale on which, as a result of grants of Church lands by the Crown to favoured courtiers; of similar concessions wrung from intimidated or easy-going deans and chapters by influential magnates; and, not least, of irresponsibility and nepotism on the part of some of the episcopal children of light, the progressive impoverishment of the Church continued almost unabated to the death of the Queen. It was not till the self-denying ordinance enacted in the first year of her successor that the engines were reversed. Partly, Mr. Hill thinks, because the Crown, conscious of its need for friends, had come to see in the Church a dependable ally, the alienation, even in favour of the King, by bishops and archbishops of lands belonging to their sees was at last forbidden by the Act of 1604.

The practical significance of abuses of the kind which that belated measure was passed to prevent must not be overstressed. The economic embarrassment of certain sees was compatible with an opulence in others which, down to the Civil War, made indictments of the hierarchy's ungodly pomp a commonplace of Puritan critics, and proposals to lay the axe to the root of the offensively luxuriant tree by secularizing 'the lordly revenues of prelates' a recurrent text. Naturally, however, the most distressing forms and gravest consequences of ecclesiastical poverty were found in humbler spheres. Even after the author's rigorous and lucid analysis of the intricacies of patronage, tithes and impropriations, the methods of remunerating the rank and file of the clergy remain, it must be confessed, something of a mystery. Their basic element was normally the tithes, the great tithes—to mention only one of several different classifications—on corn, hay and wood, and the small tithes on other produce. The important factor was the *modus*—the customary standard of payment in different districts—and several factors tended in the later sixteenth century and early years of its successor to make the *modi* of convention out of date. The increase of grass at the expense of corn; a more intensive specialization in particular lines, such as dairy-farming and market-gardening; the difficulty of tapping the output of rural industries carried on in conjunction with farming; the progress of enclosure, and the decline of population which often followed it if the land concerned was turned to grass, are cases in point. The fall in the value of money cut both ways. It meant a loss to those who had commuted and a gain to those who continued to pay in kind. The last condition was more common, it seems, in the case of the great or rectorial tithes than in that of the small, personal or mixed tithes; but even when the rising price-level yielded an unearned increment, a crucial question remained. To whom did the windfall go?

The number of impropriated livings was estimated in 1603 as 3,800, and in the following year a committee of bishops stated that five-sixths of the benefices of the country were controlled by laymen, including the Crown, whose share, however, diminished with the progressive sale of its estates. Such figures need, perhaps, a grain of salt; but the massive weight in ecclesiastical matters conferred on lay opinion by conditions similar in kind to those depicted by them appears, in the light of contemporary utterances, a reality hardly open to dispute. The obvious course for the impropriator bent on making the most of his investment—if he did not, as sometimes he did, allow the fabric of the church concerned to fall into decay—was to draw his income as rector, while relying on a vicar or stipendiary curate, engaged on the cheapest terms that the market allowed, to do the work. In such circumstances any surplus accruing from the increase in the yield of glebe or tithe was unlikely to remain with the labourers in the vineyard. It tended to be absorbed by their superiors, 'the church robbers,' in the words of William Harrison, 'whom we falsely call patrons of the Church.'

The agents of demoralization did not act alone. Mr. Hill is within his rights in referring to the contemporary expansion of capitalist enterprise as a force whose intermittent reactions few sides of life escaped. It is less clear, however, that the specific evils, for example spoliation, on which he lays his heaviest stress, were characteristic of a capitalist rather than a feudal society; nor, in so far as they were, is it easy to discover from his pages the particular processes by which the invading demon made his malignant influence felt in the sphere with which the present work is specially concerned. Mr. Hill's contribution is so outstanding that any ambiguity in his interpretation is occasion for regret. For that reason it may be hoped that, when a second edition of his book is called for, he will take the opportunity to enlighten us further on such points.

In considering, again, the picture as a whole, account requires also to be taken, as in the present work it is, of forces of a different order—of encroachments on, and on occasion enclosures of, the glebe, of the difficulty of collecting that part of the parson's income which consisted of a multitude of irregularly recurring and increasingly unpopular dues, of the fiscal anomalies which, to judge by a comparison of the sums contributed in subsidies by laity and clergy, caused the latter to be over-taxed. It is true, of course, that the clerical profession, like others, had prizes to bestow; but, so far as the rank and file of the lesser clergy were concerned, Mr. Hill's portrait of a depressed proletariat does not seem to be overdrawn. The minute value of many benefices revealed by official returns, the shifts to which their holders found themselves reduced, the multitude of vacant livings at which no candidate would look—such evidence lends colour to the indignation voiced in the 1630s by Laud at the number of ministers in receipt of incomes 'scarce able to feed and clothe them.'

Contemporaries deepened the shadows by dwelling on the existence among the clergy of a minority of former servants and boon-companions—'bakers, butlers, cooks, good archers, falconers and horse-keepers'—to whom unscrupulous patrons had thrown ecclesiastical bones to gnaw; on the considerable—though, by the end of the century, substantially diminished—body of semi-illiterates, to whom the Lord's Prayer and the Ten Commandments were known rather by repute than at first hand; and, as the natural fruit of both deficiencies, on 'the general ignominy' which, in Herbert's words, 'is cast upon the profession'; but the fundamental evil was economic. It is against that background that the abuse of which most is heard, the form of clerical absenteeism known as pluralities, should be seen. For pluralists in high places, a venerable scandal, there was little to be said; but among the lesser clergy they were as inevitable in the England of the century following the Reformation as—to cite a modern analogy—were the so-called 'rickshaw professors' earning at several institutions at once the livelihood which work at one could not provide in the poverty-stricken Chinese universities of the early 1930s. In such conditions Bacon's dismissal as a contradiction in terms of the demand both for a learned ministry and for the abolition of pluralism hit the nail on the head.

Long before the turn of the century, therefore, the financial dilemma confronting the Church was plain for all to see. The four concluding chapters, grouped under the unexpectedly sardonic rubric, *The Church Triumphant*, in which the author examines the attempts made to loose or cut the knot, are among the most instructive of the book. The annual loss to the Church resulting from impropriations had been estimated by Hooker as £126,000, and the other items on the debit side of the account were not a trifle. How, and at whose expense, could a financial reorganization be effected which would restore to the service of religion resources diverted from it to more immediately remunerative ends? The answers given to that question differed, not only in detail but in principle, and the extremes lay far apart. At one end of the scale, the audacious programme brought by Bancroft in 1610 before the House of Lords proposed, in effect, a policy of re-endowment, to be achieved—to mention only a handful of points—partly by the revival of lapsed fees and charges; partly by a tithe system extended to new commodities and purged of the exemptions through which income leaked away; partly by the restoration to the Church of glebe lands absorbed by laymen, combined with the creation, by means of parliamentary taxation, of a fund to buy in impropriations. At the other, projects for providing funds for a preaching ministry by taxing lay impropriations or amalgamating small parishes shaded off into grandiose programmes for secularizing the estates of bishops and of deans and chapters, and substituting a stipendiary clergy for one supported mainly from the yield of land. Until the political breakdown forces were too equally balanced for drastic policies of either colour to be more than paper plans, and down to 1640 the characteristic development advanced on different lines. It took, in the main, the form less of a frontal collision between champions of innovation and enthusiasts for the *status quo* than of antithetic interpretations of the ambiguous word reform, and of a soberly conducted struggle to capture or defend particular key-positions, the command of which would enable the group concerned to exercise in future a measure of control over ecclesiastical policy and religion.

Of efforts launched on the left with that aim in view, one of the most celebrated is discussed at length by Mr. Hill. As always, he has something new and to the point to say; but the striking feature of his treatment of the so-called Feoffees for Impropriations is less perhaps the novel information added by him than the success with which he sets that ostensibly innocuous departure in perspective as, not an isolated episode, but a leading specimen of a movement by which voluntary enterprise seeks to turn the flank of official policy and, in grappling piecemeal with the problem of clerical poverty, initiates a silent revolution in the relations between Church and State. The financial provision made by groups of provincial business men in London to subsidize clerical stipends, increase the number of ministers, and endow lectureships in their native counties is another case in point. A third and more significant is illustrated by examples cited by the author of parishes which undertake to pay or to augment the stipend of a minister on condition that they are accorded a voice in his appointment. The resulting development before 1640 of arrangements under some of which ministers were, in effect, selected by a congregation or a town was obviously important. Mr. Hill's suggestion that it was in this '*de facto* voluntaryism' rather than in Continental influences that the origins of Independency are to be sought is an illuminating contribution to a long-debated problem.

An even more dramatic revelation of the shift in the balance of power was given by the struggle of the 1630s on the tithe question between the

City of London and the authorities of the Church. The figure of 2s. 4d. in the pound on rent, at which in the later years of Henry VIII tithes on London property had been settled, had been during the following three-quarters of a century, with the connivance of the Lord Mayor's Court, systematically ignored. At last, in 1618, a judgment in the Court of Exchequer confirmed the figure fixed; and Laud as Primate, with Juxon, the Bishop of London and Lord Treasurer, at his elbow, decided in the 1630s to fight the battle through. After a long delaying action by the City, followed by inevitably inconclusive negotiations between parishes and incumbents, the issue remained undecided when, three years later, the financial emergency of the Scottish war rolled the ball irrevocably to the City's feet.

The defeat, as in effect it was, of ecclesiastical authority in the metropolitan tithe case was an episode of some moment. It not only meant that henceforward the jurisdiction in such matters of the Lord Mayor's Court would remain unchallenged, and that no subsequent increase in the income concerned could in London be expected to take place. It also set a precedent which nipped in the bud provincial movements to bring tithes up to date. The tithes question, however, important though it was, was merely one position on an extended front at several other parts of which—for example, patronage, impropriations, the future of secularized Church estates—the ashes were still hot. It is one of the merits of Mr. Hill's book that it aids us to appreciate the passions of the day by depicting not merely in detail, but as an interdependent whole, the inflammable materials on which they fed.

In view of the mild and moderate authoritarianism of the English old regime, the odious reputation of Charles's government as the enemy of property has naturally occasioned some surprise. The economic policies sometimes cited, such as anti-depopulation measures, forest claims, price and wage controls, and fiscal innovations seem a somewhat slender basis to sustain so grave a charge. A further justification for it may, perhaps, be found by turning to a different sphere and considering the programmes at the same period in the air for setting a poverty-stricken Church on its financial feet. Their principal architect, Laud, emerges from Mr. Hill's pages as an altogether larger-minded and more formidable figure than the conscientious, but irritable and intolerant, pedant of tradition. Many besides he realized that economic and political changes—the price revolution, the rise of new forms of business enterprise, the policy of plunder—had condemned to partial obsolescence methods of Church finance inherited from the past; nor was he alone in discerning the remedies partly in a modernized tithe system, partly in the restoration to the Church of property whose transference to lay hands he regarded, in view of the methods by which that transference had often been effected, as indefensible by arguments compatible with the Christian faith. His salient characteristics, as revealed by Mr. Hill, were two.

The first was the synoptic outlook to which the author refers when he writes that

> Laud's policy was to get back behind the Reformation in everything but the papal supremacy—recovering impropriations; restoring tithes, if not to a true ten per cent., at least to what they had been before the rise in prices; restoring the coercive power of the Church courts . . . ; restoring the privileged social position of the priests.

The second trait was a persistent drive towards action, which left little room for the appeasing gulf between the rigours of principle and the necessities of practice, by which suppler and more prudent statesmen avert disaster. Given these convictions and qualities in the Archbishop, given also the royal attitude revealed by the Act of Revocation applied in 1625 to ecclesiastical estates secularized in Scotland since 1542, it is not surprising that doubts as to the soundness of their views on the sanctity of property should have caused alarm.

Mr. Hill's account of the content and methods of the different steps attempted by Laud towards his goal of a prosperous and respected Church; of their author's frustration at the hands, not only of opponents, but of colleagues and subordinates wedded to abuses which officially they denounced; and finally of the nemesis of reform too long delayed, forms a moving conclusion to an original, thorough and illuminating book.

Note

* Review of C. Hill, *Economic Problems of the Church* (Oxford, 1957), in *Times Literary Supplement*, 1 February 1957.

10

J. L. Hammond, 1872–1949 (1960)*

The death on 17 April 1949, of John Lawrence le Breton Hammond deprived the Academy of a fellow distinguished by his combination of a gift for original work in history with unusual literary power. Born on 18 July 1872 in the Yorkshire village of Drighlington, where his father, the radical scion of a Jersey family, was vicar, Lawrence attended Bradford Grammar School from 1886 to 1891; entered in the latter year St. John's College, Oxford, as a classical scholar; and ended his academic career with a Second in Greats in 1895. Later, as an author, he found his chief field of work in the early phases of the social problems inherited by his generation from the age of the first Reform Act; but the Clio of his devotion, for all her preoccupation with the vicissitudes of English rural and industrial life, did not on that account cease to be a Muse. His humanity, imaginative insight, and unobtrusive wisdom, even more than his impressive range of knowledge, are the traits which those privileged to know him will first recall.

I

Hammond's undergraduate friends included Hilaire Belloc; J. S. Phillimore, later Professor of Greek at Glasgow; the well-known economist, F. W. Hirst; and the future Lord Chancellor, J. A. Simon; but the Oxford personalities whose mark on him was deepest belonged to an older generation. They were a fellow and tutor of his college, Sidney Ball, and Professor Gilbert Murray. It was partly to the former, a member of the Fabian Society in the days when academic Socialists were few, that the Liberalism of the Hammonds owed its strong social bent. Their life-long friendship with the latter strengthened the devotion to the literature and civilization of classical antiquity which remained to the end a vital element in their outlook both on the past and on contemporary affairs. An historian, Lawrence once remarked to a younger colleague, requires an intellectual and moral base outside the prevalent assumptions of his day and his special sphere of work. No reader of the Hammonds' books can remain long in doubt as to the influences by which, in their case, that independent standpoint was principally supplied. Whether reflecting on the horrors of the pre-Chadwickian age of English urban life; or on Nationalism as a constructive and destructive force; or on the debt owed by civilization to France, it is to lessons learned from the sages of the Graeco-Roman world that the authors constantly recur.

It was natural that a young man with Lawrence's tastes and powers should see his future in some form of literary work. He entered adult life at a moment when the mentality and policies conventionally epitomized by the word Imperialism laid a spell on the imagination of ardent youth. Five years were to elapse before, in 1902, Mr. J. A. Hobson's analysis of the movement's economic aspects saw the light; but, apart from such exposures of its seamy side, a doctrine which idealized as a mission the extension of British rule over subject peoples, seemed to Hammond, the spiritual father of whose Liberalism was Gladstone, a lie in the soul. Confirmed by the shock of the South African War, that attitude found expression in *Liberalism and the Empire* (1900), in which, in conjunction with Murray and Hirst, he examined the assumptions and tendencies of the fashionable creed. The views then advanced continued to be proclaimed by him after an unforeseen change of circumstances had given him a pulpit of his own from which to preach. On leaving the university, he had combined journalism with the position of secretary to Sir John Brunner, whose multifarious interests included the ownership of a weekly journal, the *Speaker*. It is not surprising that, on the acquisition of that paper some years later by a group of Liberals of the Left, and the resignation of its first editor, Wemyss Reid, Hammond, as a leading figure among the younger intellectuals of that persuasion, should have been invited to take his place.

Judged by the distinction of the contributors whom he gathered round him, as well as by the commendations of such pillars of Liberal orthodoxy as Morley, Courtney, and Bryce, Hammond's six years editorship more than fulfilled the hope raised by his appointment. He crusaded for unpopular causes; challenged the policies which had led to war; gave publicity to the facts of disease and mortality in South African concentration camps which Miss Emily Hobhouse, the sister of his friend, Professor Leonard Hobhouse, had been among the first to expose, and welcomed with modest elation the odium which his refusal to suppress unpleasant truths entailed. His heart, however, was in scholarship. He had contrived, amid his other preoccupations, to produce a study of Charles James Fox; but he was increasingly conscious that systematic historical work could not easily be reconciled with the duties of an editor. It was partly, therefore, as a step towards a future promising ampler leisure for historical research and writing that, on the conversion of the *Speaker* into the *Nation*, he accepted in 1907 the post of secretary to the Civil Service Commission, which he held till 1913. His marriage in 1901 with Miss Lucy Barbara Bradby had given him a partner who not only shared his interests and sympathies, but co-operated on equal terms in the production of their books. Of the results of their labours something is said below. Here it is sufficient to note that the first of their joint works, *The Village Labourer 1760–1832*, appeared in 1911, and that three years later, by the summer of 1914, a sequel to it was virtually complete. But for the outbreak of war, it would have been published in that year.

Hammond, a hater of violence, worked to the last with those who strove, as the crisis deepened, for the maintenance of peace; but he was not a pacifist in the conventional sense of that ambiguous word. 'The right of a nation', he had written, in describing the political creed of Fox, 'to choose and develop its own civilisation was a fundamental article of his political faith.' His hero's views on that point were his own, and his conviction of the duty to defend the right in question, if all else failed, by arms was stronger than his loathing of war. His gentle and unassuming manner, unfailing courtesy, and frail physique concealed, as in the case of Falkland, of whom at times he reminded one, a chivalrous, ardent, and, where principles were concerned, uncompromising spirit. Convinced by the invasion of Belgium that a cause deemed by him sacred was at stake, he insisted, at the age of forty, on obtaining a commission in the R.F.A., only, after several months of training, to be pronounced, much to his chagrin, unfit on grounds of health for service abroad. Later, he used to express his gratitude to the Army for having taught him how to ride and groom a horse; but his momentary disappointment was keen. It is to the credit of the authorities that, having bestowed those accomplishments on him, they smoothed the way for his return from non-combatant duties to civil life.

Hammond's release from the forces enabled him to discuss with historically minded friends the proofs of *The Town Labourer*, and to see that work, together with, two years later, its companion volume, *The Skilled Labourer*, through the press; but his concern for the international and social issues looming ever more insistent as the war dragged towards its close would not let him rest. They carried him first into a post in the recently established Ministry of Reconstruction; then, as special correspondent of the *Manchester Guardian* from December 1918 to April 1919, to the Peace Conference at Paris; and finally, into participation in the struggle for freedom, as he thought it, of a nation nearer home. His letters from Paris struck from the start a sombre note. The greatest peril, he insisted, to a constructive peace had its source not, as often thought in England, in French frontier policy, but in the refusal of Britain and the United States, who alone possessed the means, to come promptly to the rescue of a Europe in danger of relapsing from 'a family of nations' into 'a cockpit of maddened tribes fighting for food'. If disaster was to be avoided, the economically viable states, he wrote in April 1919, 'must put their credit behind the victims of the war ..., must be ready to renounce debts ..., must feed the countries where want and hunger are raging ..., must lend money and raw materials so that industry may revive'. A year or two later these truths were widely held. Stated by Hammond within barely six months of the Armistice, they fell on stony ground.

Returning to England in the early summer, he quickly found himself involved in a second crisis. Sharing the views of those who held that the government's Irish policy sowed the wind to reap the whirlwind, he thought it his duty to throw himself into the campaign launched in England for the adoption of a more generous and far-sighted course. The result was a visit to Ireland, his attendance, on behalf of the *Manchester Guardian*, at the Conference of October to December 1921, and between the two a series of articles, principally in that paper, which made it the leading advocate of a negotiated peace. In a moving pamphlet published in the spring of 1921 he had pleaded for reconciliation before it was too late. The principles and methods expounded in it did not differ greatly from those by which in December a settlement was at last achieved.

II

Hammond's connexion with the *Manchester Guardian* continued throughout his life. Except, however, at moments of unusual stress, his principal preoccupation during the twenties and thirties consisted in the execution, in collaboration with Barbara Hammond, of their programme of historical work. Of the ten volumes, exclusive of their minor writings, produced by them between 1911 and 1938, the last and longest, Lawrence's *Gladstone and the Irish Nation*, stands in a class by itself. The remainder include, in addition to the biographies of Lord Stansfield and C. P. Scott, the seven studies of the consequences for English society of the economic transition under way between the accession of George III and the Great Exhibition. It was these books, and in particular the opening trilogy on the three generations before the first Reform Act, which made their authors' influence most widely felt.

On the forces accelerating the growth of an economy of a novel type they do not, save in one work, dwell at length. They were concerned less with causes than effects, and the principal aims inspiring their treatment of the latter were two. The first was to reveal the characteristic features of the social order emerging from the Great Divide; the second to aid their readers to approach that order with criteria in mind more discriminating and humane than it had been easy, in the first flush of its economic triumphs, for the classes floated to fortune by them to apply. Regarding the modernization of the land system and the rise of the Great Industry, not as decorative fringes on more majestic themes, but as fraught with issues as momentous as any which even the England of the long war had been called upon to meet, they thought that, with all their virtues, historical treatments of those aspects of the age had suffered from one disastrous, though remediable, fault.

That defect—a weakness as conspicuous then as it is unusual now—could, it seemed to them, be simply stated. It consisted in the inability or reluctance of most previous writers to give their proper prominence to the sufferings and achievements of the much-enduring British people. 'Many histories', they remark, 'have been written of the governing classes which ruled England with such absolute power in the last century of the old régime. These histories have shown us how that class conducted war, how it governed the colonies, how it behaved to continental powers, how it managed the first critical chapters of our relations with India, how it treated Ireland, how it developed the parliamentary system, how it saved Europe from Napoleon. One history has only been sketched in outline. It is the history of the way in which this class governed England.' Toynbee's well-known lectures (1884), Mantoux's *La Révolution Industrielle au XVIIIe siècle* (1906), the Webbs' two books on Trade Unionism (1894–7) and the successive volumes of their great history of English Local Government (1906–13)—to mention nothing else—had, in their different ways, contributed to redress the balance. The social histories of the Hammonds, though much else as well, were partly an attempt to serve the same neglected cause. They would do something, their authors hoped, to bridge the gulf between history and common life, by revealing 'what was happening to the working classes under a government in which they had no share'.

Few writers could have been freer than the Hammonds from the controversial spirit. But their work made some cherished legends look dim, and their first three volumes, in particular, touched on occasion sensitive nerves. The discussion caused by their books—it is not the least of their services to have started it—has been fruitful, and, a few exceptions apart, has been conducted with politeness and good sense. If it is easier today than a generation ago, not only to appreciate the importance of the Hammonds' contribution, but to grasp the points at which their picture needs amendment, it is chiefly they themselves to whom gratitude is due. In addition to possessing a knowledge of the voluminous printed sources unrivalled in their day save by Sir John Clapham and the Webbs, they were among the first to use the Home Office papers to throw light on aspects of social history previously little known. They were not, of course, infallible, but no one who has travelled even a few steps in their wake will speak lightly of the conscientious labour on which their generalizations rest. Whatever the verdict on their conclusions, their courage in grappling with the jungle of official and private papers, and their candour in interpreting the data brought to light, earned, as they deserved, respect.

The Hammonds' choice of the rural problem as the point from which to start should not cause surprise. Not only did the treatment between 1760 and 1832 of the issues composing it impress them as peculiarly characteristic of the closing decades of the old régime, but an almost topical interest belonged to it at the moment when the authors wrote. In the early years of the present century, when the long depression of cereal farming seemed to have run its course, questions relating to the country's agricultural future were much in debate. Lord Ernle has described in a striking passage the crop of competing specifics in which it was suggested that salvation should be sought. It was natural that the discussion of these and kindred topics should stimulate an interest in agrarian history, and, in particular, in the last great reconstruction which, over an extensive area, had fixed the framework of farming and rural life. Thus *The Village Labourer, 1760–1832* was not a lonely landmark. In reality, it was one of a group of not far short of a dozen works published on allied themes in the decade and a half following 1905, and pointing to the need for a reassessment of verdicts and policies long accepted as beyond dispute.

Apart from the book's literary power, its distinctive characteristics were two. It was designed, in the first place, not as a history of agriculture, but, in the words of its sub-title, as '*A Study in the Government of England before the Reform Bill*'. Dealing, as it does, not with one sphere of life alone, but with the tangled frontier-region where political, economic, and religious interests meet, it omits much that a more strictly economic history would include, and includes more for which such a history ought, perhaps, to find a place, but commonly does not. A second feature is partly a corollary of the first. The thread of continuity which holds the book together consists in its account of the changing level of popular well-being during the three generations preceding 1832; of the diverse forms which those vicissitudes assumed; and of the activity or inertia on the part of the powers of the day with which the social situation produced by them was met. Thus—to give a summary illustration—the subject of the first chapter is the virtual monopoly of political and social power wielded by a minute ruling class of substantial landowners, and that of the two last the employment of that power by the same class, when its day was drawing to a close, to crush in 1830 the agitation of despairing labourers in parts of southern England. The intervening links are supplied by four chapters on different aspects of inclosure and other causes of distress. They include, in addition to an account of the procedure involved in passing and applying the required Private Acts, two on the wage-earner's loss of subsidiary income, the food-riots of 1795, and the rejection by Parliament of one of the few constructive social policies brought before it—Whitbread's minimum wage bills of 1795 and 1800—and these passages, again, are followed by the description, among other morbid symptoms, of the expansion of poaching, in spite of savage game laws, from a local custom, half-sport, half-expedient to eke out short supplies, into a business enterprise financed at times from London. Comedy and tragedy mingle in the prescriptions for poverty commended by the rich, from cheap soups and other substitutes for wheaten bread as the labourers' staff of life, to the by no means novel, but rapidly expanding, administrative opiate known after 1795 as the Speenhamland system. Finally, it should be noted that the authors are concerned, not only with changes in popular well-being in terms of money, food, and clothes, but with the attitude of the masters of wealth and power, at a period of unusual stress, towards matters of vital moment to their poorer fellow countrymen. Cobbett once remarked that the former 'Commons of England' were spoken of in his later years 'by everyone possessing the power to oppress them ... in just the same manner in which we speak of the animals which compose the stock upon a farm'. It was necessary, in short, for the Hammonds, in addition to depicting the conditions in which the lower orders lived, to interpret also the assumptions and aims of their more philosophically minded betters. Taine's *La Révolution* has been called a study in the psychology of Jacobinism. Parts of the Hammonds' work might be described with equal propriety as an essay on the social philosophy of the English ruling classes.

The Village Labourer, therefore, is not of the books from which a reader rises with the conviction that, in spite of tragic episodes, all was for the best. In view of its range, of the diversity of conditions in the regions covered by it, and of the intricacy of certain of the topics treated, it was to be expected that differences of opinion should arise as to the validity of some of the conclusions reached. On the minor points of controversy it would be unprofitable, even if space allowed, to dwell. The more formidable criticisms have had as their targets less particular errors or omissions than the impression left by the volume as a whole. To judge, for example, by the expansion of the cultivated area, the advance of more intensive farming, and the rise of rents and profits, agricultural progress during much of the period covered by the Hammonds, though not in the post-war years, was more than ordinarily pronounced. It is true, no doubt, that their attention, like that of Cobbett, was fixed, not on improving landlords and capitalist farmers, but on the mass of small landholders and, still more, of labourers dependent on weekly earnings; but, even so it might be asked, was not the scene of deepening gloom depicted by them the product less of harsh realities than of jaundiced eyes? It is a commonplace, again, that a growing and increasingly urbanized population, together with the blow to imports dealt by war, made a larger cereal output an urgent need, and equally a platitude that, in meeting that emergency, the accelerated speed of the changes epitomized as inclosure—over 1,900 Acts in the war years alone—played an important part. Yet on that point *The Village Labourer* spoke, it was thought, not merely in indifferent, but in hostile, tones. What could be more irresponsible than for historians sensitive to popular distress to frown on improvements which, by augmenting the food supply, might do something to blunt its edge? Were not the Hammonds Balaams in reverse, who cursed when they should have blessed?

At the time when *The Village Labourer* was on the stocks, the first of these questions—that of agricultural wages—remained, for lack of evidence, in suspense. Relying on a return prepared by the Poor Law authorities for a Select Committee of 1825 on Labourers' Wages, Sir John Clapham estimated that a not negligible increase had taken place between 1795 and that date. Lord Ernle, while printing the figures, had described them as 'very defective and unreliable', and the Hammonds also had put them on one side.[1] A courteously conducted discussion between Sir John and Lawrence Hammond ended in each making a slight concession to the other, but left the central issue much as before. Controversy on the second problem has enjoyed a more continuous and, at times, exciting life. Less than a quarter of the book was occupied with inclosure; but it was largely, nevertheless, on its treatment of that topic that verdicts on it turned. Its analysis of the legal and administrative procedure involved in carrying through the changes in question was generally recognized to be the most thorough yet produced; but there agreement ceased. At one extreme were those who deplored the distorted vision which minimized the benefits of the new order and maximized its incidental ills. At the other, so eminent an authority on European, and particularly English, agrarian history as Professor—later Sir Paul—Vinogradoff, was not alone in praising *The Village Labourer* as an outstanding work, which stated with courage and cogency truths too long ignored. The questions at issue had behind them centuries of argument, as well as of contentions not confined to words; and much water has flowed under bridges since the Hammonds and their critics added a further chapter to the great debate. How do their conclusions look today?

The most obvious tendency of recent work can be simply stated. It has been to lengthen the perspective in which innovations formerly assigned to the later eighteenth and early nineteenth centuries must be seen. The evidence of land-tax assessments, the pioneers of whose use were Mr. A. H. Johnson and Dr. E. Davies, has pushed the crisis in the history of the small occupying owner farther back, from the period when parliamentary inclosure was at its height, into an age in which inclosure by Private Act had hardly yet begun. The progress of Local History has yielded somewhat similar results on a broader front. The open-field village of mid-eighteenth-century England was rarely, it seems, either the Sweet Auburn of the poets or the perverse miracle of squalid petrifaction denounced by duller pens. More often it was an institution behind whose traditional façade of command, organization and control changes profoundly affecting, not only its economy and structure, but its vitality and capacity for collective action—changes in the distribution and size of holdings, in the management of commons, and in the growth and dimensions of a wage-working proletariat—had long been under way. Not a few, in short, of these rural communities have the air of crumbling from within, under the pressure of heightened economic strains, before dismembered by the parliamentary hatchet from without. In such cases a Private Inclosure Act remained, of course, of great importance, but it was less the precipitate supersession of an old order by a new than the climax of a process of piecemeal modifications, readjustments, and decay already far advanced.

Verdicts on the social consequences of inclosure, with which the Hammonds were primarily concerned, must depend in part on the view taken of the conditions obtaining before that decisive and irreversible event took place. The disposition of the authors to touch lightly, if at all, on those crucial antecedents, and to write at times as though the fall of man occurred in the reign of George III, is among the weaker features of their book. In their treatment of another aspect of their subject, and one of greater practical moment, they stand on firmer ground. To reopen ancient controversies would be pointless, but one neglected commonplace, which continues to be relevant to a judgement on their work, may not be out of place. It is that the beginning of wisdom is to distinguish between two issues still too frequently confused. The first is the merits of inclosure as a system of land utilization; the second, the verdict to be passed on the procedure by which, in the regions where open-field farming had been the rule, an economy based on inclosure was established in its place.

With the former of these questions the Hammonds do not deal at length. The technical advantages of inclosure were a thrice-told tale, which they thought it useless to challenge and needless to repeat. It was the latter point—the particular methods employed in England to effect the transition—on which their attention was principally fixed and to which the strictures voiced by them referred. The critics, on their side, have not always been careful to distinguish between ends and means. The statement, for example, still sometimes heard that the choice was between inclosure and starvation is a case in point. Its air of hard-boiled realism takes the unwary reader off his guard; but what precisely does it mean? If it merely asserts that, other things being equal, a larger yield per acre could be obtained from a compact holding than from neglected or overstocked commons and strips in open fields, it is a platitude which few, and certainly not the authors of *The Village Labourer*, would dispute. If, on the other hand, it is advanced in justification of the English procedure of inclosure by Private Act, it begs the question. Its suggestion that only by that method could the required changes have been effected is, in fact, an insular solecism which assumes conclusions requiring to be proved.

In judging the Hammonds' treatment of a contentious theme two obvious considerations may, with advantage, be borne in mind. It should be remembered, in the first place, that their condemnation of the methods of inclosure commonly employed was not an emotional eccentricity peculiar to them, but had behind it contemporary opinion of unquestioned weight. Sir John Sinclair, the President of the Board of Agriculture; Arthur Young, its secretary and probably the most influential writer of the day on agricultural questions; Marshall and Kent, both experienced land-agents; Eden and David Davies, whose books on social conditions are still not out of date, were neither sentimentalists nor ignoramuses. All of them advocated inclosure carried out with due regard to the interests of all concerned. All of them condemned a procedure which deprived cottagers of the measure of independence conferred on them by rights of grazing, cutting turf, and gathering wood, or which, in Lord Ernle's words, caused 'previous occupiers to be ... reduced to landless labourers'. Nor, in weighing that conclusion, should a second point be overlooked. England was not, of course, unique in inheriting from a distant past a landed lay-out which, if rarely so static as it was formerly the fashion to suggest, required, as conditions changed, a controlled reconstruction in order to keep in step with novel facts. It is significant, however, that, though applauded by foreign agriculturalists for her precocity in initiating and her resolution in carrying through a reorganization elsewhere long delayed, she was none the less a pioneer whose methods of effecting the transition most of her continental admirers, when they modernized their land systems, were careful to avoid. A comparative study of the procedure of inclosure in different countries is still to seek; but foreign examples of the English policy of throwing the reins on the neck of powerful local interests, with the minimum of central control, appear to be few.

In some, perhaps many, of the States concerned, inclosure was accompanied by measures designed to break the shock to the smaller men. In England the experts of the Board of Agriculture, mindful of the future and with no private axe to grind, had endeavoured for a time to achieve by less imperious methods a similar result. The Hammonds rightly, therefore, devote some instructive pages to the provisions inserted by them in the General Inclosure Bill of 1796 in order to ensure that, when inclosure took place, part of the waste should be vested in perpetuity in a corporate body acting for the village as a whole, to be used by it for the grant of rent-free allotments for terms of up to fifty years to labourers who could point to cottages built and fenced by them in substantiation of their claims for land. Unfortunately, while some of the continental peasant-protection policies were destined to bear fruit, their solitary English analogue, mild though it was, sent a shudder through the House of Commons and was deleted from the Bill. Toynbee long ago remarked that the distribution of landed property in the England of his day was to be explained less in economic than in political terms, and later authorities, such as Mantoux, Hasbach, Slater, and most emphatically Sir William Ashley,[2] have said in different words the same. In endorsing that conclusion the Hammonds did not propound a novel heresy, but confirmed with further and more detailed evidence a well-established, if at times reluctantly admitted, truth.

III

The Village Labourer remained its authors' last word on rural questions till the time, a quarter of a century later, when Lawrence's study of Gladstone's Irish policy compelled him to face the problems of peasant poverty in a harsher and more tragic form. During the intervening years, the social transformation under way in pre-Reform Bill England continues to be the Hammonds' central theme; but the particular aspect of the movement which claims the lion's share of their attention undergoes a change. Henceforward, it is not the dissolution of an old régime, but the emergence of a new, on which their eyes are fixed.

The immediate successors, therefore, of the Hammonds' opening volume consisted of two further works, resembling it in spirit but primarily concerned to make intelligible the social consequences of the rise of the Great Industry, by stating them in human terms. And these books, in their turn, required a sequel to drive their lesson home. Whatever view may be taken of the industrial leviathan's crude and sanguine youth, the speckled record of that early phase of his career—beneficent achievements, needlessly inflicted casualties, here and there atrocities too long condoned—is not open to dispute. Hence the authors, after disposing of that chapter, found a further task awaiting them. It consisted in an analysis of the efforts of pioneer reformers to domesticate the serviceable, but undisciplined, monster by forcing a bit and bridle, in the shape of Factory, Mines, and Public Health Acts, between his reluctant jaws. Finally, when only the first of those later studies, that on Shaftesbury, had seen the light, a background was provided for the series as a whole by an essay in a different vein. A combination of imaginative insight with breadth of culture was not the least among the Hammonds' gifts. The long perspectives, rich in illuminating comparisons and contrasts, of *The Rise of Modern Industry* exemplify that power. A work of synthesis in which the industrial capitalism of the opening decades of the nineteenth century is displayed against the background of earlier economic civilizations, it remains at once the most instructive and the most original introduction to the social and economic aspects of history available in English. Successive generations of students have been captivated by its spell; but the influence wielded by the authors has had its principal source in their graver, more original, and more intensive works. Its secret has been the conviction inspired in their readers that, in the struggle of conflicting policies depicted by them, issues, not only of material well-being, but of profound, and not yet exhausted, moral significance, were at stake.

The Town Labourer and *The Skilled Labourer* illustrate in different ways that quality of the Hammonds' work. Originally planned as parts of a single volume, they supplement each other, and the reader noticing in the former an apparent error or omission will be prudent, before voicing his criticism, to make sure that the latter does not make the seeming defect good. The subject and period treated are the same in both. Both take the economic aspects of the Industrial Revolution for granted, as topics sufficiently expounded by other pens. Both, therefore, turn their search-lights primarily, not on the mobilization of productive power on a scale previously unknown, but on the reactions to it of the increasing proletariat of hired employees by whom its pressure was most continuously felt. While, however, the theme of these books is, at first sight, the same, their methods of treating it are far apart. *The Town Labourer* is concerned, in the words of its preface, with 'the general features of the new civilisation', and offers the reader a synoptic view. Opening with an account of the dehumanizing rigours of factory discipline in the days when employers, uncontrolled by trade unions or the law, were responsible to themselves alone, it continues with a description of the antiquated local machinery for the maintenance of order, and then, having analysed the policies on which, at moments of agitation, apprehensive ministers relied to keep rebellious workers in their place, climbs to a loftier plane of principles, aspirations, and ideas. It concludes with half a dozen chapters depicting the intellectual and moral chasm dividing, in the phrase shortly to be famous, the two nations of the rich and the poor. *The Skilled Labourer* makes no similar attempt to scale the heights, but examines the chequered fates of particular groups of workers struggling for a foothold in, as it seemed to the authors, an increasingly unfriendly world. The series of miniature industrial histories contained in it has a double value for the reader. It at once illustrates in detail the vicissitudes of different trades and reveals the nature of the evidence on which the generalizations of the preceding volume, as well as its own more intensive analysis, are based. Of the four concluding chapters three tell the tragic story of the Luddite Movement of 1811–14; the fourth is in a lighter vein. Its subject is the instructive, scandalous, and entertaining career of Oliver the Spy.

The Town Labourer was probably that of all the Hammonds' works on social history which made the most immediate, if not the most enduring, mark. Published at a moment when dreams of post-war reconstruction were in the air, it moved a reviewer in *The Times Literary Supplement*[3] to pay tribute to the prophetic gifts of historians who had 'helped towards a better understanding, not only of the early nineteenth century, but of the problems of today'. In the cooler atmosphere of peace the spirit animating the book, the premisses from which it started, and the conclusions to which it appeared to point, were scrutinized with less indulgent eyes. Granted the accuracy of the authors' facts, did not, it was asked, their deductions and interpretations require to be buttressed by statistical data of a kind for which their eloquent pages had failed to find a place? Had not their humanitarian indignation at the incidental miseries of the new order closed their eyes to the blessings which, however questionable its principles, in practice it conferred, and caused them at moments of emotion to write

> *as when a painter dips*
> *His pencil in the gloom of earthquake and eclipse?*

Was not, in short, the Hammonds' magic mirror too often a distorting glass?

It may readily be conceded that wage statistics are rarely cited in the Hammonds' works. It must be remembered, however, that, in spite of the pioneering labours of Sir Arthur Bowley and Mr. G. H. Wood, data on wage-history were still scanty at the time when *The Town Labourer* and *The Skilled Labourer* were on the stocks, and that Bowley himself had uttered an emphatic caution on the unreliability of wage figures for the period with which those works were principally concerned. Since that time knowledge has increased, and a recent book by a scholar of unquestioned weight[4] gives grounds for thinking that, from 1780 or so onwards, the wages of skilled workers showed an upward trend. He again, however, is careful to point out that, in the absence of evidence as to the growth or decline of fines, overtime, unemployment, allowances in kind and—a not less crucial deficiency—reliable indexes of alterations in the cost of living, mere figures of wage-rates or earnings leave us not much wiser than before. Attempts to derive from them conclusions as to changes in standards of life are not, in Professor Ashton's judgement, a hopeful task.

An author might be pardoned for hesitating to build on so precarious a foundation; but, even had the data been more convincing, to base their work on figures was not the Hammonds' line. 'On what men enjoy and what they suffer through their imagination', wrote Lawrence in a characteristic passage, 'statistics do not throw a great deal of light'; and the truth is that the Hammonds and their critics were concerned with different aspects of life. The primary interest of the latter was in movements of pecuniary income. The former did not forget the importance of rising and falling wages; but they regarded as of equal or greater significance the physical environment and moral atmosphere in which men passed their lives. It was the effect of that environment on human sensibilities and emotions, rather than its economic aspects, which haunted the Hammonds' minds. They thought that, in the case both of individuals and peoples, additions to money income could be bought too dear.

The first question asked by them, therefore, in considering the effects of industrialization, is always the same. It is in what surroundings, and with what opportunities for the enjoyment of nature and art, does the population in question live and work? They were far from disparaging the improvements which, on certain sides of life, had taken place; but, comparing the lot of children employed in cottage industries with that of their fellows in mills and mines; or the make-shift hovels of squatters on commons with the urban slums which were apt to take their place; or the hearty turbulence—violent work and violent play—of the Middleton of Bamford's youth with the factory-town of his later years, they felt some doubts whether the argument was quite so much one way as the Babbages and Ures proclaimed. It was true that, thanks to the modernization of productive methods and communications, the age-old spectre of famine was in most parts of Europe in retreat; but could not, the authors asked themselves, that economic triumph have been won at a lower and more equitably apportioned human cost? The evidence of official inquiries proving the injury done to children by—to mention nothing else—excessive hours of labour in factories and mines could hardly, save on points of detail, be contested, nor could the ravages of disease among both young and old resulting from conditions resembling, in Chadwick's words, those of an 'encamped horde or undisciplined soldiery' be simply waved aside. Was it a convincing apologia to retort that in unindustrialized regions mortality from hunger reached, when crops failed, an even more appalling height?

It was natural, in pondering such problems, to turn for light to a figure whose achievements suggested the quarter in which solutions might most hopefully be sought. The Hammonds' *Lord Shaftesbury* sounds throughout a dual note. The portrait of a lonely, self-tormenting, ascetic is combined with salutes to the hero of a score of public causes, from Ragged Schools, Public Health, and the humanization of obsolete Lunacy Laws to the rescue of child chimney sweeps, and from that again to the defence of evangelical truth against Unitarian heresies and ritualist corruptions, on both of which the reforming fundamentalist waged unceasing war. But, if admiration and distaste find in turn their voice, the former takes the lead. The passages of Shaftesbury's career of most interest to the authors were the chapters concerned with his struggle for an effective mining and factory code, which produced in 1842 the first Coal Mines Regulation Act and later, in 1847, the unsatisfactory, but seminal, measure for textiles, miscalled down to 1874—when further legislation made the title apt—the Ten Hours Act. It was that long drawn-out campaign, together with his subsequent crusade to end the scandal of climbing boys, which caused Ashley, for all his extravagances and morbidities, to win the Hammonds' hearts.

The conflict was one in which passions have at times run high. In the first decade of the present century when the smoke at last had cleared, 'Sadler's Report'—the Report, that is to say, of August 1832 on the 'Bill for regulating the labour of children and young persons in the mills and factories of the United Kingdom'[5]—was commended by the authors of the standard *History of Factory Legislation*[6] 'as one of the most valuable collections of evidence on industrial conditions that we possess'. The Hammonds shared that view; and recent attempts to discredit, not only the document in question, but both the principle of legal restrictions on freedom of contract between employer and employed and the writers' account of the lions' den of hostile interests through which for long it had to fight its way, have not been happily conceived. It is true, no doubt, that Sadler, a religious humanitarian, regarded with horror the abuses accompanying the exploitation of children, and that, in his efforts to move Parliament to stamp such evils out, he showed less than would have been prudent of the cool detachment becoming in the chairman of a Select Committee. A detailed examination, however, of the charge of sharp practice brought against him is not here in place, since he dropped out of public life on the loss of his seat in the election of December 1832.[7] It is not with Sadler, but with the chapter that opened when, early in 1833, he was succeeded by Ashley as the spokesman of the cause, that the Hammonds' volume is principally concerned.

In reality, of course, the suggestion that its authors derived their opinions on child labour from one Report alone is a mare's nest. The melancholy truth is that evidence from other sources to much the same effect is only too abundant. The Commissioners of 1833, appointed at the instance of the employers and led by a hard-headed economist, Thomas Tooke, the unemotional Chadwick, and a physician with industrial experience, Southwood Smith, denounced 'hired agitators' and rejected allegations of cruelty as unproved; but on the larger issues they had little new to say. 'They too', in the words of Sir Llewellyn Woodward, 'realised the need for legislation, and their report confirmed the existence of the evils reported by the first inquiry.'[8] The limitations on juvenile employment recommended by them were in some respects, indeed, more stringent than those contained in Sadler's—later Shaftesbury's—Bill, while the government was sufficiently impressed to establish special machinery of enforcement in the form of an inspectorate appointed by the Crown. The analogous, though different, scandals of child labour in collieries and mines shown to exist, though not equally in all coal-fields, by the Commission appointed on Ashley's initiative in 1840, and depicted by the Hammonds in a moving chapter, are a further case in point. Finally, the extension during the twenty years following 1847 to other factory industries of the principles of the Act of that year reveals both the prevalence in unregulated trades of abuses needing treatment and the conversion by experience of public opinion to protective policies of a kind formerly opposed. If, in short, the authors were guilty of an error, it was one for which they may, perhaps, be pardoned. It consisted in an over-sanguine assumption that their critics would be as conscientious as themselves in mastering an official literature at once voluminous, painful, and dull.

The lesson deduced by the Hammonds from this chapter of history can be simply stated. It was that, in an industrial civilization, the welfare of the majority of its members depends on the existence of conditions, physical and moral, which only collective action can create. The validity of that truism, however, was not confined to relations between employer and employed, with which Ashley had been principally, though not exclusively, concerned. The warning voiced by it was equally relevant to the legacy left by the early years of the Industrial Revolution in the shape, not only of factories, but of towns. Hence their *Lord Shaftesbury* led to further works. The authors had begun by analysing the inevitable dehumanization of an industrial system dominated, as it seemed to them, by a single-minded concentration on pecuniary gain, and had pointed to the prophylactic by which the resulting evils could be held in check. Two later studies, *The Age of the Chartists, 1832–1854*, and a revised version of it entitled *The Bleak Age*, are concerned with a second aspect of the same general theme.

Few books, it is probable, on the domestic history of nineteenth-century England introduce that subject by a chapter of preliminary reflections on Graeco-Roman life. The reason which led the Hammonds to that agreeable innovation is characteristic of their thought. It is that they interpreted Chartism not, in the conventional manner, as a struggle of contending classes, with, as its distinctive feature, the first political appearance of the industrial proletariat as an independent force, but as an upheaval of a more fundamental kind. Its essence, in their view, was rather ethical than economic. It was, in short, a moral revolt against a conception of society which, while showering luxuries, and the leisure to enjoy them, on the few, relegated the mass of their fellow countrymen to the position—surprising phrase—of 'a necessary part of the social system'. The civic life of classical antiquity, the authors suggest, for all its servile taint, had been prodigal in its provision of the means of refreshment for body and mind—baths, theatres, temples and other noble buildings—with the result that a large proportion of the population could share in the enjoyment of the art and culture of the day; while medieval cities had rivalled each other in architectural magnificence and in the encouragement of festivals, pageants, and plays. The English town of the first half of the nineteenth century, with its lack of common amenities and its precipitate class divisions based on wealth, stood at the opposite extreme from both. Cut off by the growth of population, as well as by Inclosure Acts, from the contacts with nature which once they had enjoyed; too often devoid of the necessities of decency and health; without public parks, gardens, galleries, libraries, museums, or even an adequate supply of schools, what could the Manchester or Liverpool of the 1840s offer to its inhabitants but the hope, if victorious in the scramble for pecuniary success, of ultimately escaping from its grim and depressing self? The Churches might have played, and in some localities, the writers remark, did play, a unifying and humanizing role; but too often both Anglicans and Methodists continued to defend abuses, such as pew-rents, which kept rich and poor apart. In spite of notable examples to the contrary, it was rarely, it seems, that Christian teachers, whatever their denomination, challenged the prevalent idolatry of wealth.

Thus the Hammonds' study of Chartism avoids the beaten track. It is primarily concerned, not with the struggle for the famous Six Points, but with the more important question, as they thought it, of the environmental conditions which, for half a century, made working-class resentment, not merely an intermittent episode in the life of industrial England, but endemic. Challenged to explain the transition from the political fevers of the thirties and forties to the comparative tranquillity of the two ensuing decades, they did not, of course, ignore the growth of a more propitious economic climate; but they laid their main emphasis on developments in the sphere of policy resulting from the long-delayed emergence of a genuine, if rudimentary, social conscience. They saw as the crucial turning-points the Factory Act of 1847, the doctrineless collectivism of the Public Health Acts of 1848 and 1875, the gradual extension from the forties onwards of such sources of common enjoyment as public libraries, museums, galleries, gardens, and parks, and finally—the wizened seed of a mighty tree—the Elementary Education Act of 1870.

IV

Hammond did not write for choice on individuals, unless, like Shaftesbury, they were identified with a cause. It was with three such personalities that his subsequent biographical studies were concerned. Sir James, later Lord, Stansfield, a friend of Mazzini, had devoted the first part of his career to the struggle for Italian freedom, and then, after holding office during the years 1871–4 as President of the Poor Law Board in Gladstone's first cabinet, abandoned the broad highway of political success to throw himself into the agitation for the repeal of the Contagious Diseases Acts of 1864–9, which attained its goal in 1886.

Hammond's account of him was a tribute to one to whose sacrifice of personal ambitions to a crusade of mercy in an unpopular, and to some repellent, field, public life has not too many parallels to show. In the second, and more intimate, study of his former chief, the ethical appeal to which Lawrence responded was equally pronounced. C. P. Scott was not only a shrewd political observer, but a man of lofty principles, who viewed the *Guardian* not primarily as a means to money or power, but as an organ of education in the broadest sense, and whose character, together with the paper's influence, made him one whose opinions political leaders of varying views were glad at critical moments to ascertain. In the view of persons better qualified to judge than the present writer, Lawrence's success in doing justice to both these aspects of a noble personality was not the least of the achievements of his literary career.

Four years later, in 1938, appeared the last, and to some the most impressive, of Hammond's major works. Among the topics treated in *Gladstone and the Irish Nation*, two will not surprise the reader of his earlier books. The English industrial wage-earner had been the theme of all but one of his and Barbara Hammond's previous social studies. The Irish counterpart of that figure was the peasant. In the former case the edge of notorious evils had been, in the authors' view, blunted by legislation designed to improve conditions of employment and the health of towns. Might not, in the latter, different, but equally constructive, policies relating to the ownership and use of the land, of a kind made familiar since the Revolution by the experience of large parts of peasant Europe, have yielded in Ireland equally beneficent results? Intertwined with that economic problem was a second, and even graver, issue. The suppression of the individuality of a weaker by a stronger people was, in Hammond's eyes, an unpardonable wrong; nor could he persuade himself that foreign critics erred when to Poland and unemancipated Italy they added Ireland as a case in point. The relations between Ireland and England before and during the age of which he wrote seemed to him an example of the nemesis which that wrong entailed.

Since the publication in 1903 of Morley's *Life*, not only had the Gladstone papers been made more usable by students, but new material had become available in the shape of biographies, correspondence, and memoirs. That additional evidence was grist to Hammond's mill. His volume, however, is primarily a study, not of Anglo-Irish relations, but of a figure unique, as he thought, among English statesmen in its imaginative insight into Irish needs. Political strategy and tactics, therefore, are not its central theme. Gladstone more than once remarked that politics were not his true vocation. The words were those of one whose lightning speed in unravelling economic and legal complexities astonished his officials hardly less than did his eloquence the crowds that hung upon his lips; but in neither of those regions does his biographer find the secret of the magician's spell. It consisted less, he thinks, in Gladstone's mastery of means than in his vision of large and lofty ends, less in his acumen in grappling with financial technicalities and the mysteries of Irish land-law than in the long perspectives and distant horizons which, amid the dusty details of office, were rarely absent from his mind, and in whose significance, because he himself believed in it, he caused others to believe. The impression left by Hammond's pages is that, if at times Gladstone bestrode the political world like a Colossus, the reason was partly that politics were only half his life. He was, in short, for all his parliamentary ardour and ministerial zeal, less interested in the practice of the politician's art than in the moral principles by which, he held, men and states should live.

These principles, as expounded with sympathetic insight by Hammond, form the kernel of the book. They include, to mention nothing else, Gladstone's reliance on Greek civilization and Christianity as the compasses by which to steer his course; his conception of Europe as a family of nations united by an ethical code derived from both, whose member states should pursue 'objects which are European by means which are European, in concert with the mind of the rest of Europe and supported by its authority'; his reverence for Aristotle, St. Augustine, Dante, and Butler as oracles of political wisdom in preference to Locke, Bentham, and Mill; and the religious convictions which caused him to see Ireland as 'the minister of God's retribution upon cruel and inveterate and but half-atoned injustice'. The author does not directly comment on the contrast between Gladstone's indignation at the afflictions of the Irish peasant and his comparative unconsciousness—to judge by the paucity of his allusions to them—of poverty and economic oppression beneath his eyes at home; but he underlines a characteristic of which that apparent indifference might be held, perhaps, to have been the shadow side. 'Gladstone', he writes, 'became the greatest popular leader of his age, although he never mastered or seriously studied great social problems, because he offered the working classes something that satisfied their self-respect. ... He was a most sincere democrat because he believed that free discussion and self-government were essential to human dignity.'

V

Shortly before the First World War the Hammonds had abandoned London for a house near Hemel Hempstead. It was there, at Piccotts

End, amid the animals, tame and wild, whom they loved, but within reach of the Record Office and British Museum, that their books were written, and that the bulk of Lawrence's work as a journalist was done. To them, as to others, the events of 1939 brought a revolution in their way of life. To strengthen its hand for the crisis, the *Guardian* invited Lawrence to exchange his position as an occasional, though frequent, contributor for that of a full-time member of the staff. He responded to the appeal, and started work on the new conditions on 1 September. From that date till six years later, in 1945, he and Mrs. Hammond made Manchester their home. 'They lived', wrote a friend describing a visit to them shortly after their arrival, 'in a couple of rooms in a students' hostel, with four chairs and a table covered with press cuttings. ... Mrs. Hammond cut out for Lawrence anything that might deserve comment in the *M.G.*, and he carried off in the evening his selection. They were both very gay about the austerity. She made us tea on the floor.'

Hammond's war-time work on the *Guardian* was not confined to one department of affairs; but events, as well as his own inclinations, caused the greater part of it to be focused on themes which he had made in calmer times his own. French history and culture were near his heart, and, in his case, the saying *chacun a deux patries, la sienne et la France* was not mere sentimental rhetoric, but the voice of a conviction deeply felt and firmly held. With all his faith in France, he was haunted by the fear that, at a moment when sympathy, encouragement, and confidence in her future were among her most urgent needs, a cold or condescending attitude on the part of uncomprehending allies might prolong both the miseries of the occupation and the period during which she was unable to resume her proper place among the leaders of the common cause. If that disaster was partially avoided, it was largely, in the opinion of one equally at home in France and England, to the warmth and understanding of a section of the British press that the credit for averting it was due. 'Continuously, for more than four years', writes Professor Brogan, 'the leading articles on French themes in the *Manchester Guardian* were the sanest, best informed, most generous and so most wise lead given to British public opinion, which was in real danger of going wrong. ... To the human temptation to error they opposed reason, understanding and truth.'[9]

Professor Brogan's words are a fitting tribute to the Hammonds' services in time of war. On their achievements as historians the weightiest testimony is that of scholars who have worked on the period and problems of which they wrote. George Unwin had seen in youth too much of poverty and over-work to be accused of the exaggerated sensibility to the thought of these afflictions with which the Hammonds were sometimes charged. Individualism—good sense and absurdities at once—was in his bones, and he cherished an ineradicable conviction that, whenever governments start to improve the lot of man, they kill more patients than they cure. He was delighted, however, by the Hammonds' first three volumes of social history, which—since he died in 1924—were all that he had a chance to read, and was emphatic in his hope that *The Town Labourer* would be followed by a complementary study of the lives, thoughts, and achievements of contemporary entrepreneurs. The admiration of their work expressed by Mr. A. P. Wadsworth, joint-author with Miss J. de L. Mann of a book on Lancashire and the rise of its cotton industry described by Sir John Clapham as the best industrial history to be produced by English scholars, was equally warm. A native of Rochdale and a master of the story of his county's economic growth, he was an authority to whom Lawrence turned for counsel on aspects of the subject alive in local memories, but sometimes overlooked in books. The Hammonds, he remarked, were the humblest and least opinionated of people, and accepted corrections with an alacrity not always shown by authors; but the points requiring amendment were, he added, few, for the reason partly that the writers were 'thorough and honest scholars', partly that their view both of the agrarian innovations of the later eighteenth century and of the accelerated industrialization at the same time under way 'rested on evidence of a kind which later research had done little to rebut'. Professor T. S. Ashton has written of them more recently in different, but equally enthusiastic, terms. While welcoming the Hammonds' recognition that the Industrial Revolution increased the material welfare of the masses, he is careful to set that conclusion in the right perspective by emphasizing that an upward movement of money wages did not necessarily imply a corresponding advance in the quality of their recipients' lives. Their *Lord Shaftesbury*, with its illustrations of that truism, was ranked by him among 'the greatest of English biographies'. 'Few', he remarks, 'have done so much to make ordinary men and women understand that a study of the past may be the best preparation for an understanding of the present. ... Their place in English historiography is secure.'

The educative influence applauded by Professor Ashton was not the least of their gifts for which gratitude is due. Its most obvious aspect was the addition to historical knowledge which the authors made, but even more impressive was their genius for stimulating thought and disseminating ideas. It is not an exaggeration to say that during the early years of the present century economic and social history continued to be regarded as an unprofitable by-path, which might be of interest to specialists but did little to illumine the major issues of human life. If today it is seen in a less depressing light, as a study concerned with large, central, and permanent interests of mankind, the Hammonds' part in effecting that conversion has not been small. And that, again, if the most conspicuous of their contributions, is not the most profound. Important as has been their achievement in widening mental horizons, it is in the ethical rather than the intellectual sphere that the secret of their power must be sought. *Habemus publice egestatem privatim opulentiam* was a warning rarely absent from their minds. Like Morris and Ruskin, in their different ways, they regarded 'wealth' and 'riches', not as synonyms, but as terms denoting antithetic aims and styles of life, of which the second, when pampered and given its head, inevitably undermined and finally destroyed the first. Honours came their way, the honorary degrees of D.Litt. conferred on both by Oxford, the election of Lawrence as Hon. Fellow of his College of St. John's and as Fellow of the British Academy, the Hon. D.Litt. bestowed on him by the University of Manchester, and, in the year before his death, the compliment paid to him by France in making him *chevalier* of the *Légion d'Honneur*. His reason for declining a Companionship of Honour was characteristic. It was that, as a working journalist, he ought not, he thought, to compromise his independence by accepting a decoration from a British government of whose policies it was his duty to take an impartial view.

Dr. Gilbert Murray once described the political Liberalism of his day as blessed with two incorrigible deviationists, himself on the international, and Lawrence Hammond on the social, plane. In reality the latter's version of the faith was less the doctrine of a school or party than an ecumenical creed, to whose humanitarian sympathies some ideologies labelled liberal were hardly less repulsive than the cynical opportunism, as he was apt to think it, of his Fabian friends and the truculent hyper-intellectualism of Marx. It led him, in considering social policies and systems, to scrutinize assumptions as keenly as results, and to challenge, not only failures, but standards of success. These people, a shrewd observer of the peasant farmers in the Isle of Axholme had written long before, 'are very poor respecting money, but very happy respecting their mode of existence'. The imponderables of life were seen by the Hammonds with equally discerning eyes. Their first question, in the words of an appreciation of Lawrence published on his death, was always 'not what would pay, but what was true, what was right, what was human'. Their politics, in short, were based on moral premisses, not on economic expediency or on visions of future Elysiums to be purchased at the price of present wrong. In a world in retreat, not only from particular principles, but from the very idea that political principles exist, it is natural that such convictions should seem a remote and worn-out creed. It is, however, that quality in the Hammonds' works, even more than their learning and the mingled charm and power of their style, which causes them to live.

LIST OF WORKS

(1) J. L. and Barbara Hammond

The Village Labourer, 1760–1832. 1911

The Town Labourer, 1760–1832. 1917

The Skilled Labourer, 1760–1832. 1919

Lord Shaftesbury. 1923

The Rise of Modern Industry. 1925

The Age of the Chartists, 1832–1854. 1930

'Poverty, Crime and Philanthropy', in *Johnson's England*, ed. A. S. Turberville, vol. i, chap. 8, pp. 200–36. 1937

The Bleak Age. 1947

(2) J. L. Hammond

Charles James Fox: a political study. 1903

James Stansfield: a Victorian champion of sex equality. 1932

The Growth of Common Enjoyment: Hobhouse Memorial Trust Lecture. 1933

C. P. Scott, of the Manchester Guardian. 1934

'The Factory System', in *Encyclopaedia of the Social Sciences*, 1931–5, vol. vi, pp. 51–4.

Gladstone and the Irish Nation. 1938

Faith in France. 1946

(3) J. L. Hammond, joint works with other authors, and reprinted articles

'A Liberal View of Education', in *Essays on Liberalism by Six Oxford Men*. 1897

'Colonial and Foreign Policy', in *Liberalism and the Empire*, by Francis W. Hirst, Gilbert Murray, and J. L. Hammond, 1900

'The Case of South Africa', in *England a Nation*, being the Papers of the Patriots' Club, ed. by Lucian Oldershaw. 1904

Lord Hobhouse, a Memoir, by L. T. Hobhouse and J. L. Hammond. 1905

Preface to, and one or more chapters in *Towards a Social Policy*, suggestions for constructive reforms, representing the conclusions of a Committee of nine, including, in addition to J. L. Hammond, C. R. Buxton, F. W. Hirst, J. A. Hobson, C. F. G. Masterman, Vaughan Nash, and others. Undated, but between 1907 and 1909

'A Tragedy of Errors', reprinted from *Nation* of 8 Jan. 1921

'The Terror in Action', reprinted with App. from *Nation and Athenaeum* of 30 Apr. 1921

Introductory Essay to *Selections from the Writings of H. W. Massingham*, ed. by H. J. Massingham. 1925

'Gladstone and the League of Nations Mind', in *Essays in Honour of Gilbert Murray*, ed. by H. A. L. Fisher, 1936, pp. 95–118. (See also in same volume, pp. 119–40, 'The Battle for Open Spaces', by Barbara Hammond.)

Britain and the World Order, by A. J. Toynbee and J. L. Hammond. Undated

'Relief Measures for Agriculture', pp. 92–97, in *When Hostilities Cease*, ed. Sir Julian S. Huxley

Notes

* *Proceedings of the British Academy*, XLVI (1960), pp. 267–93.

1 See the following: J. H. Clapham, *Economic History of Modern Britain*, ed. of 1926, vol. i, pp. 123, 127–8, and ed. of 1930, reprinted with corrections 1939, Vol. I, second preface, pp. ix–x; J. L. Hammond, 'The Industrial Revolution and Discontent', in *Econ. Hist. Rev.*, Jan. 1930; Ernle, *English Farming Past and Present*, ed. of 1927, App. IX, n. 1.

2 Ashley's views will be found in his article, 'Comparative History and the English Landlord', in the *Economic Journal*, xxiii, no. 90, June 1913, pp. 165–88, and in the *Report of the Agric Tribunal*, 1924, App. For those of other authors of the same period, see P. Mantoux, *La Révolution industrielle au XVIIIe siècle*, 1959 ed., pp. 165–83; W. Hasbach, *History of the English Agricultural Labourer*, 1900, chaps. i–iii *passim*; G. Slater, *Growth of Modern England*, 2nd ed., pp. 126–7.

3 19 July 1927.

4 T. S. Ashton, *An Economic History of England: the Eighteenth Century*, pp. 233–4.

5 H. C., 1831–2, XV.

6 B. L. Hutchins and A. Harrison (Mrs. F. H. Spencer), *A History of Factory Legislation*, 1903, 3rd ed. 1926, p. 34.

7 As the Hammonds have been criticized for their appreciative references to Sadler, the reader may be assisted by a brief statement of the part played by him in connexion with the Bill and Committee of 1831–2:

(*a*) Sadler obtained permission to introduce his Bill on 15 Dec. 1831. He was opposed to the appointment of a Select Committee as involving needless delay, but agreed to that procedure on learning that otherwise the government would oppose the Bill. Hence on 16 Mar. 1832, after a lengthy speech (Hansard, 3rd ser., vol. xi, pp. 340 et seq.), in which he moved its second reading, he also moved that a Select Committee be appointed. Both resolutions were carried.

(*b*) The committee then appointed numbered 36. It appears to have been in close touch with employers, as well as—presumably—with employees. According to R. B. Seeley (*Memoirs of the Life and Writings of Michael Thomas Sadler*, 1842, p. 381) it was 'amply supplied by the Factory Interest with zealous and able advocates of their view', and 'eight at least [of its members] were the earnest guardians of the interests of the mill-owners'. It is possible that Seeley, who, after Sadler's death in 1835, published a volume containing selections from his works, was biased in his favour. It should also be noted, however, that R. H. Greg (*The Factory Question*, 1837) who disapproved of Sadler's Bill and strongly resented the Report of the Select Committee, does not suggest that the latter was unrepresentative or packed.

(*c*) The point most emphasized by Sadler in his second-reading speech had been the injury to juvenile workers caused by excessive hours of labour, over-pressure, and in some cases inhuman treatment. In the ensuing debate attention was directed by critics also to the economic dangers of his Bill; but it was on the charge of his alleged gross over-statement of the evils of child labour that the heaviest stress was laid (see, e.g., the first speaker, Lord Althorpe, 'Some of the Hon. Member's statements appear to be almost incredible', Hansard, loc. cit.). It was natural, therefore, that the greater part of the evidence called by Sadler should be such as to substantiate his assertions on that point. It is also not surprising that the witnesses summoned should have consisted largely of relatives, friends, fellow-workers, overlookers (i.e. foremen), together with some doctors, as the persons most likely to have first-hand knowledge of the conditions in which the children worked, and of the effect of those conditions on their physical and moral health.

(*d*) The committee is stated (Seeley, op. cit., p. 300) to have met on forty-three days between 12 Apr. and 7 Aug. On 8 Aug. it laid the result before the House (*C J.*, vol. 87, p. 566), in the shape of a brief statement that it had made progress with the matters referred to it, together with a mass of evidence taken by it, which composes the bulk of its Report. In considering the harvest of its labours, two points often over-looked should be borne in mind. *First*, 'as an arrangement for mutual convenience and to save money' (Greg, op. cit., p. 7), the committee had agreed at an early stage of its proceedings, that Sadler should take his witnesses first, and that 'the other side' (i.e. the opponents of the Bill) should then take theirs. *Second*, Parliament was prorogued on 16 Aug. to 16 Oct., and subsequently, after a further prorogation to 11 Dec., was dissolved by a Proclamation dated 3 Dec. 1832. A prorogation brings the life of Select Committees to an end. For the former of these decisions—the order in which witnesses were to be heard—Sadler presumably bears part of the responsibility; for the latter—the prorogations—he has, as far as is known, none. Given these conditions it was hardly possible for the Report on his Bill to be other than one-sided in the literal sense of deriving its *data* predominantly from supporters of the measure, though it should be remembered that, on the subject of child labour, several leading industrialists in the regions most affected held similar views. It may well have been the case that some of the witnesses heard by the committee exaggerated the prevalence of the evils to be overcome. For the charge of wholesale mendacity, as distinct from inaccuracies and over-statements, little convincing evidence appears to exist.

8 E. L. Woodward, *The Age of Reform* (*The Oxford History of England*, vol. xiii), 1939, p. 144.

9 A selection from the articles in question was subsequently published under the title *Faith in France*, with a preface by Professor D. W. Brogan (Manchester, John Sherratt & Son, 1946).

Index

For Product Safety Concerns and Information please contact our EU representative GPSR@taylorandfrancis.com
Taylor & Francis Verlag GmbH, Kaufingerstraße 24, 80331 München, Germany

www.ingramcontent.com/pod-product-compliance
Ingram Content Group UK Ltd.
Pitfield, Milton Keynes, MK11 3LW, UK
UKHW022110190926
475702UK00013B/1369

* 9 7 8 0 4 1 5 6 9 2 4 4 1 *